MIKE CAREY   MIKE PERKINS   ANDY TROY

ROWANS RUIN™

BOOM!
STUDIOS

**BOOM!
STUDIOS**

ROWANS RUIN, November 2016. Published by BOOM! Studios, a division of Boom Entertainment, Inc. Rowans Ruin is ™ & © 2016 Michael Carey & Michael Perkins. Originally published in single magazine form as ROWANS RUIN No. 1-4. ™ & © 2015, 2016 Michael Carey & Michael Perkins. All rights reserved. BOOM! Studios™ and the BOOM! Studios logo are trademarks of Boom Entertainment, Inc., registered in various countries and categories. All characters, events, and institutions depicted herein are fictional. Any similarity between any of the names, characters, persons, events, and/or institutions in this publication to actual names, characters, and persons, whether living or dead, events, and/or institutions is unintended and purely coincidental. BOOM! Studios does not read or accept unsolicited submissions of ideas, stories, or artwork.

A catalog record of this book is available from OCLC and from the BOOM! Studios website, www.boom-studios.com, on the Librarians page.

BOOM! Studios, 5670 Wilshire Boulevard, Suite 450, Los Angeles, CA 90036-5679. Printed in China. First Printing.

ISBN: 978-1-60886-902-2, eISBN: 978-1-61398-573-1

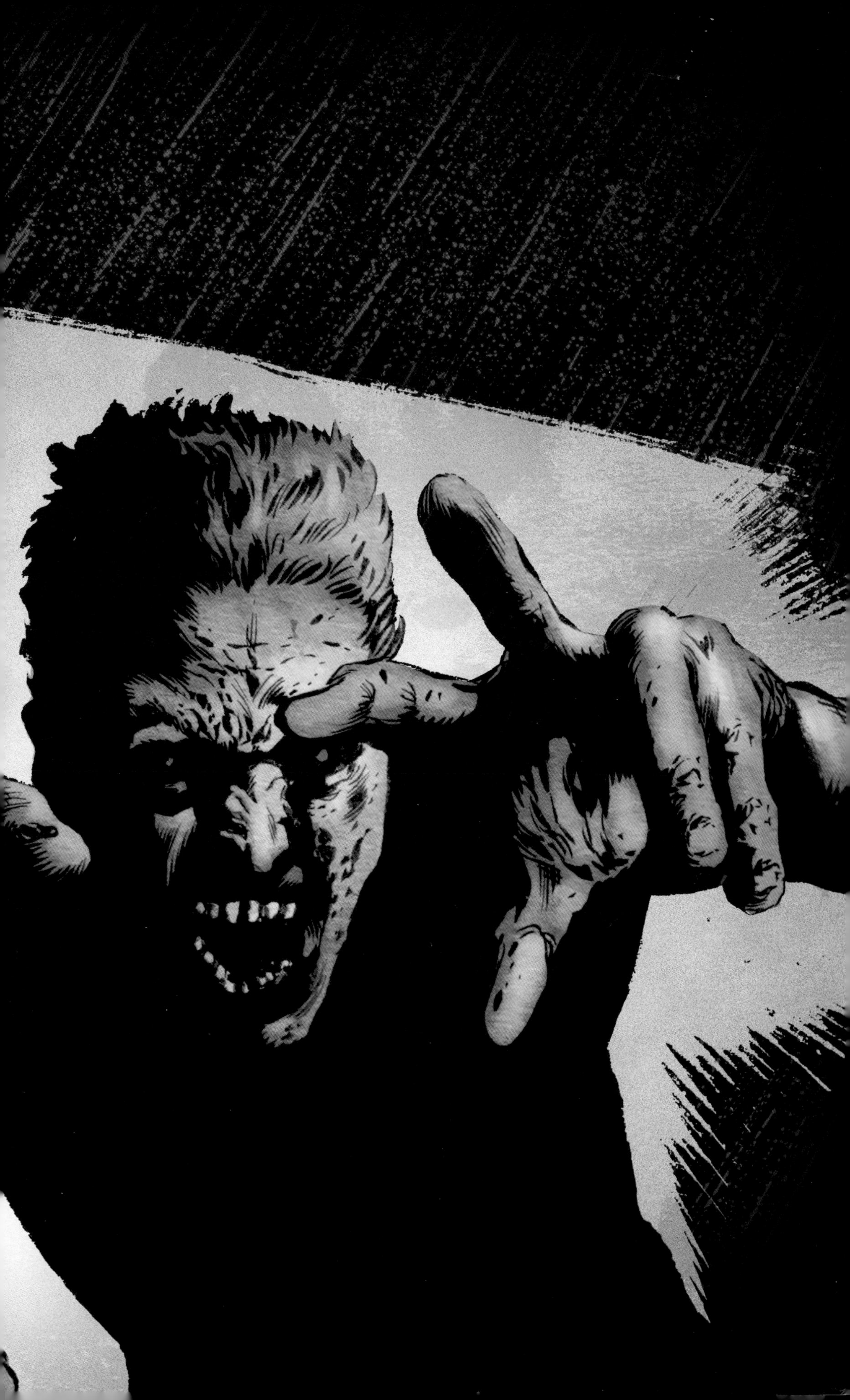

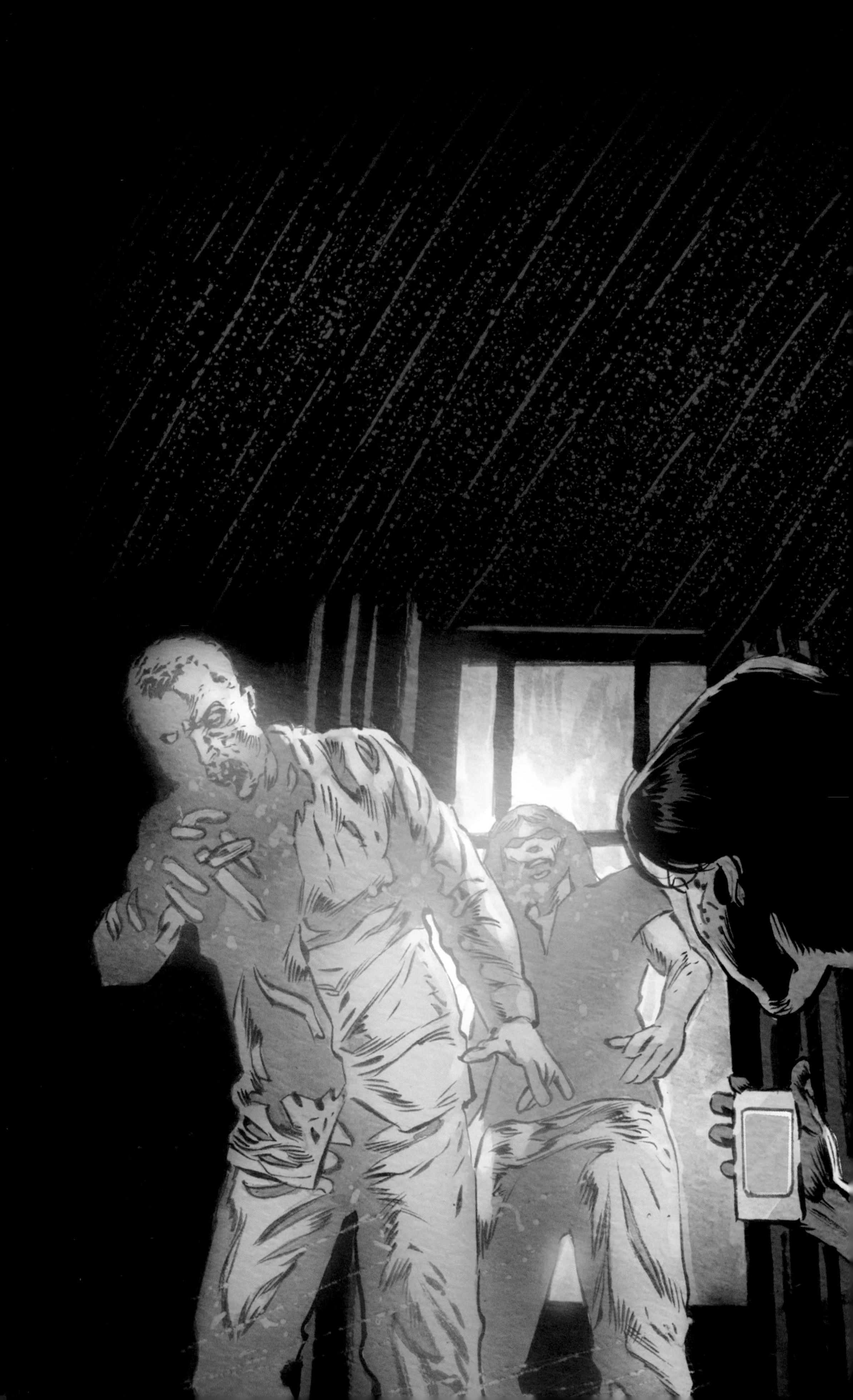

WRITTEN BY
MIKE CAREY

ILLUSTRATED BY
MIKE PERKINS

COLORED BY
ANDY TROY

LETTERED BY
JIM CAMPBELL

COVER DESIGN BY
KELSEY DIETERICH
WITH ART BY MIKE PERKINS

DESIGNER
KELSEY DIETERICH

ASSISTANT EDITOR
MARY GUMPORT

EDITOR
DAFNA PLEBAN

ROWANS RUIN™

CREATED BY
MICHAEL CAREY
& MICHAEL PERKINS

CHAPTER ONE

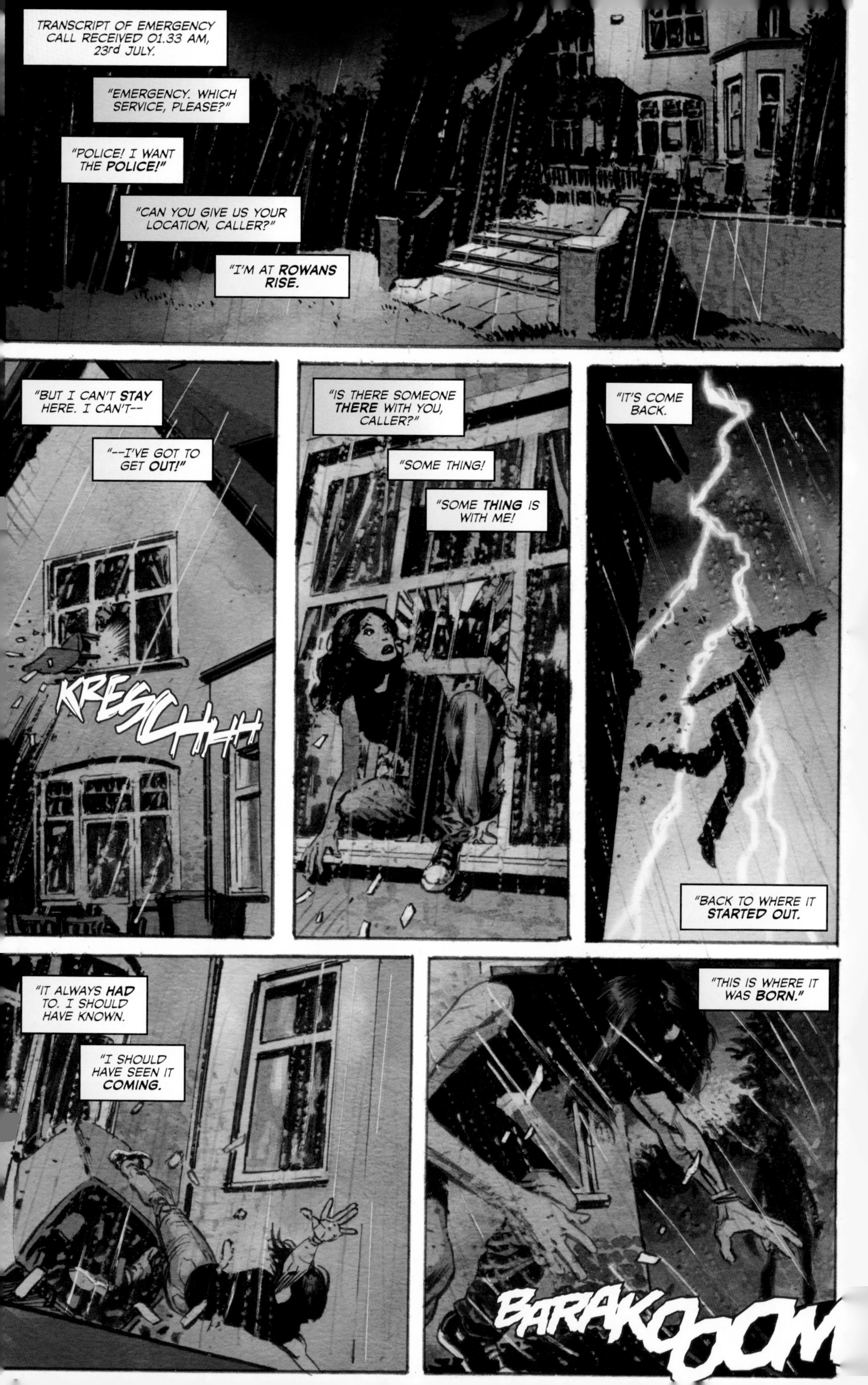
TRANSCRIPT OF EMERGENCY CALL RECEIVED 01.33 AM, 23rd JULY.
"EMERGENCY. WHICH SERVICE, PLEASE?"
"POLICE! I WANT THE POLICE!"
"CAN YOU GIVE US YOUR LOCATION, CALLER?"
"I'M AT ROWANS RISE.
"BUT I CAN'T STAY HERE. I CAN'T--
"--I'VE GOT TO GET OUT!"
KRESCHHH
"IS THERE SOMEONE THERE WITH YOU, CALLER?"
"SOME THING!
"SOME THING IS WITH ME!
"IT'S COME BACK.
"BACK TO WHERE IT STARTED OUT.
"IT ALWAYS HAD TO. I SHOULD HAVE KNOWN.
"I SHOULD HAVE SEEN IT COMING.
"THIS IS WHERE IT WAS BORN."
BARAKOOOM

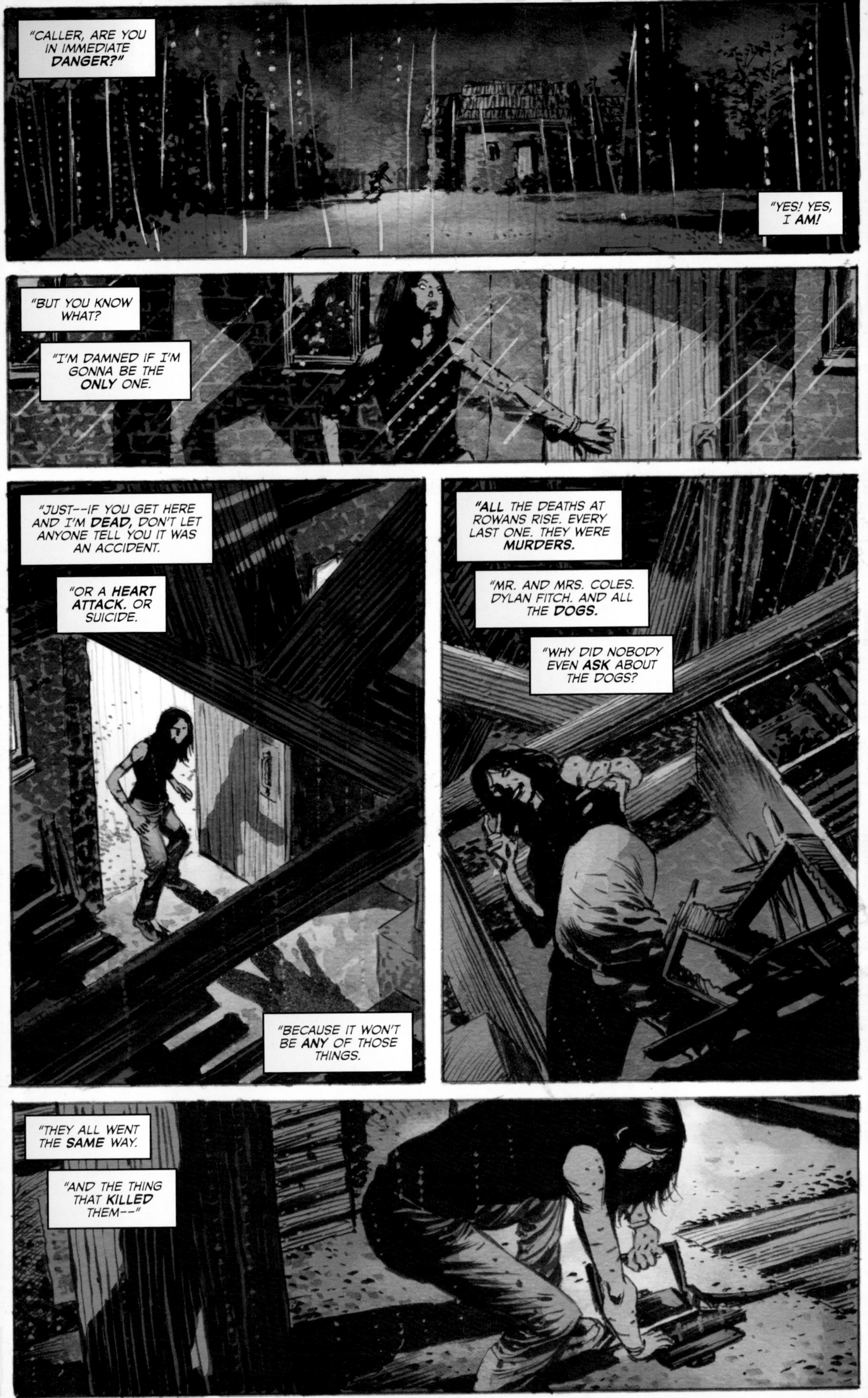
"CALLER, ARE YOU IN IMMEDIATE DANGER?"
"YES! YES, I AM!
"BUT YOU KNOW WHAT?
"I'M DAMNED IF I'M GONNA BE THE ONLY ONE.
"JUST--IF YOU GET HERE AND I'M DEAD, DON'T LET ANYONE TELL YOU IT WAS AN ACCIDENT.
"OR A HEART ATTACK. OR SUICIDE.
"BECAUSE IT WON'T BE ANY OF THOSE THINGS.
"ALL THE DEATHS AT ROWANS RISE. EVERY LAST ONE. THEY WERE MURDERS.
"MR. AND MRS. COLES. DYLAN FITCH. AND ALL THE DOGS.
"WHY DID NOBODY EVEN ASK ABOUT THE DOGS?
"THEY ALL WENT THE SAME WAY.
"AND THE THING THAT KILLED THEM--"

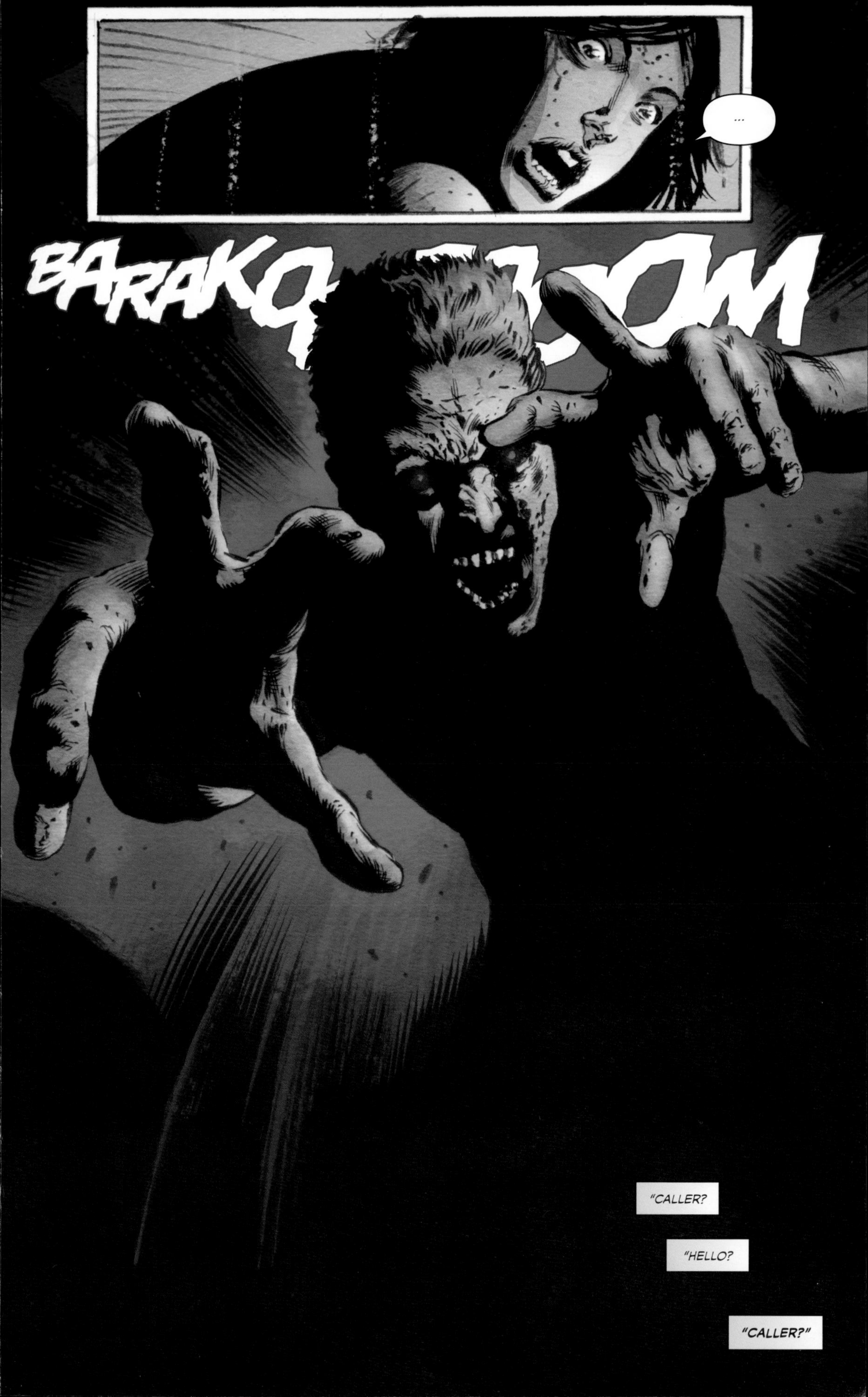
...
BARAKOOOM
"CALLER?
"HELLO?
"CALLER?"

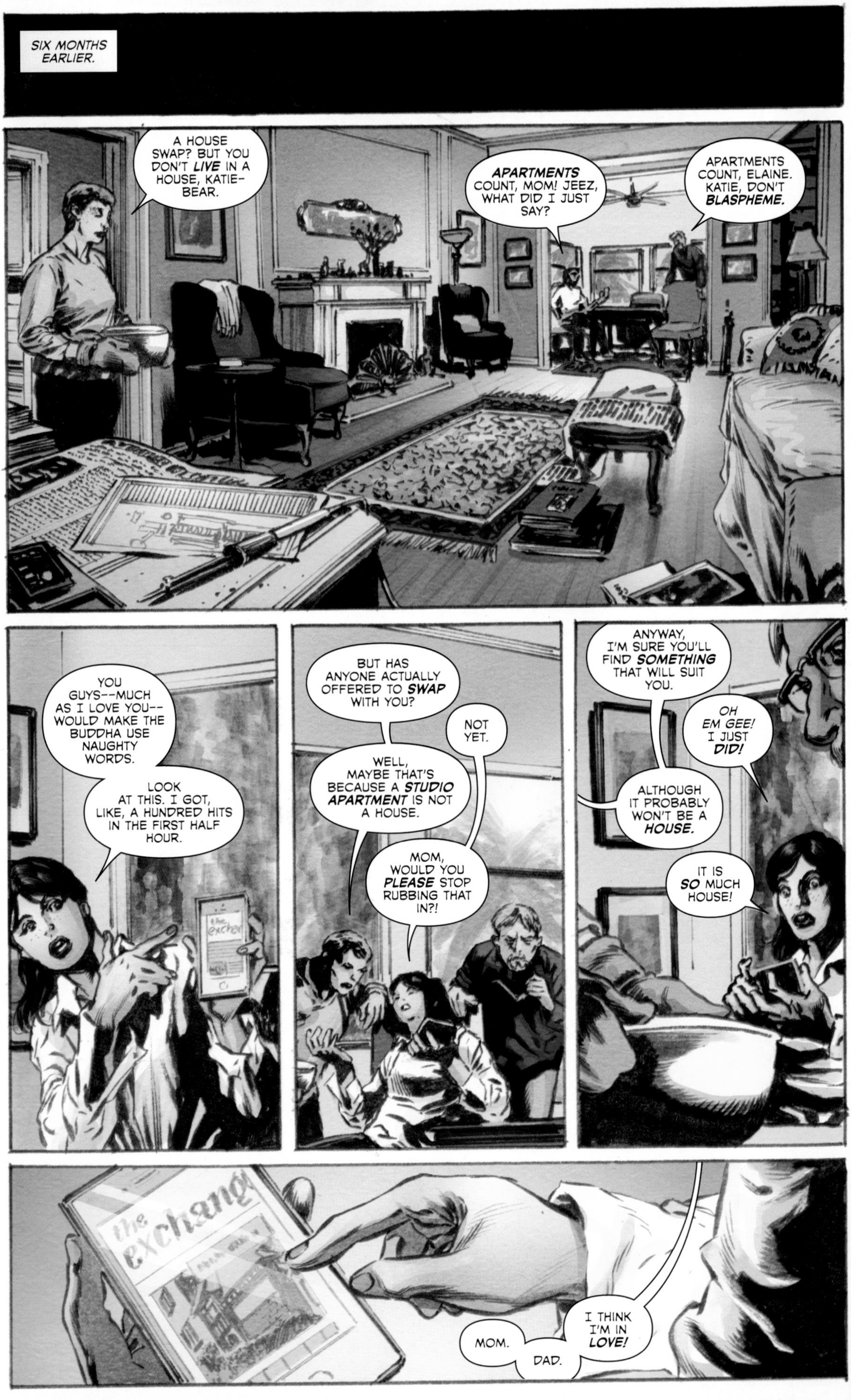
SIX MONTHS EARLIER.
A HOUSE SWAP? BUT YOU DON'T *LIVE* IN A HOUSE, KATIE-BEAR.
APARTMENTS COUNT, MOM! JEEZ, WHAT DID I JUST SAY?
APARTMENTS COUNT, ELAINE. KATIE, DON'T *BLASPHEME.*
YOU GUYS--MUCH AS I LOVE YOU--WOULD MAKE THE BUDDHA USE NAUGHTY WORDS.
LOOK AT THIS. I GOT, LIKE, A HUNDRED HITS IN THE FIRST HALF HOUR.
BUT HAS ANYONE ACTUALLY OFFERED TO *SWAP* WITH YOU?
NOT YET.
WELL, MAYBE THAT'S BECAUSE A *STUDIO APARTMENT* IS NOT A HOUSE.
MOM, WOULD YOU *PLEASE* STOP RUBBING THAT IN?!
ANYWAY, I'M SURE YOU'LL FIND *SOMETHING* THAT WILL SUIT YOU.
OH EM GEE! I JUST DID!
ALTHOUGH IT PROBABLY WON'T BE A *HOUSE.*
IT IS *SO* MUCH HOUSE!
MOM.
DAD.
I THINK I'M IN *LOVE!*

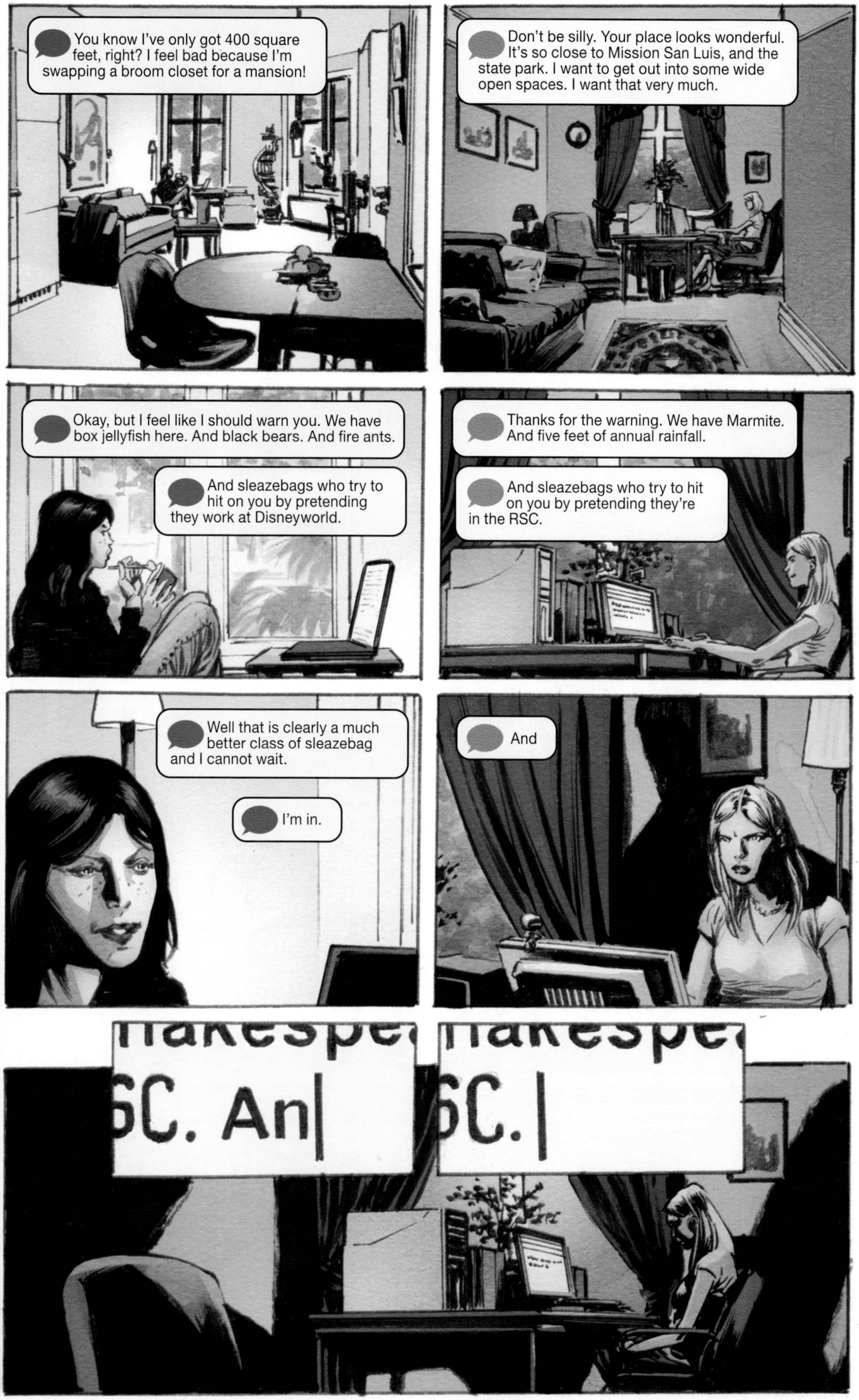
You know I've only got 400 square feet, right? I feel bad because I'm swapping a broom closet for a mansion!
Don't be silly. Your place looks wonderful. It's so close to Mission San Luis, and the state park. I want to get out into some wide open spaces. I want that very much.
Okay, but I feel like I should warn you. We have box jellyfish here. And black bears. And fire ants.
And sleazebags who try to hit on you by pretending they work at Disneyworld.
Thanks for the warning. We have Marmite. And five feet of annual rainfall.
And sleazebags who try to hit on you by pretending they're in the RSC.
Well that is clearly a much better class of sleazebag and I cannot wait.
I'm in.
And
hakespe
SC. An
hakespe
SC.

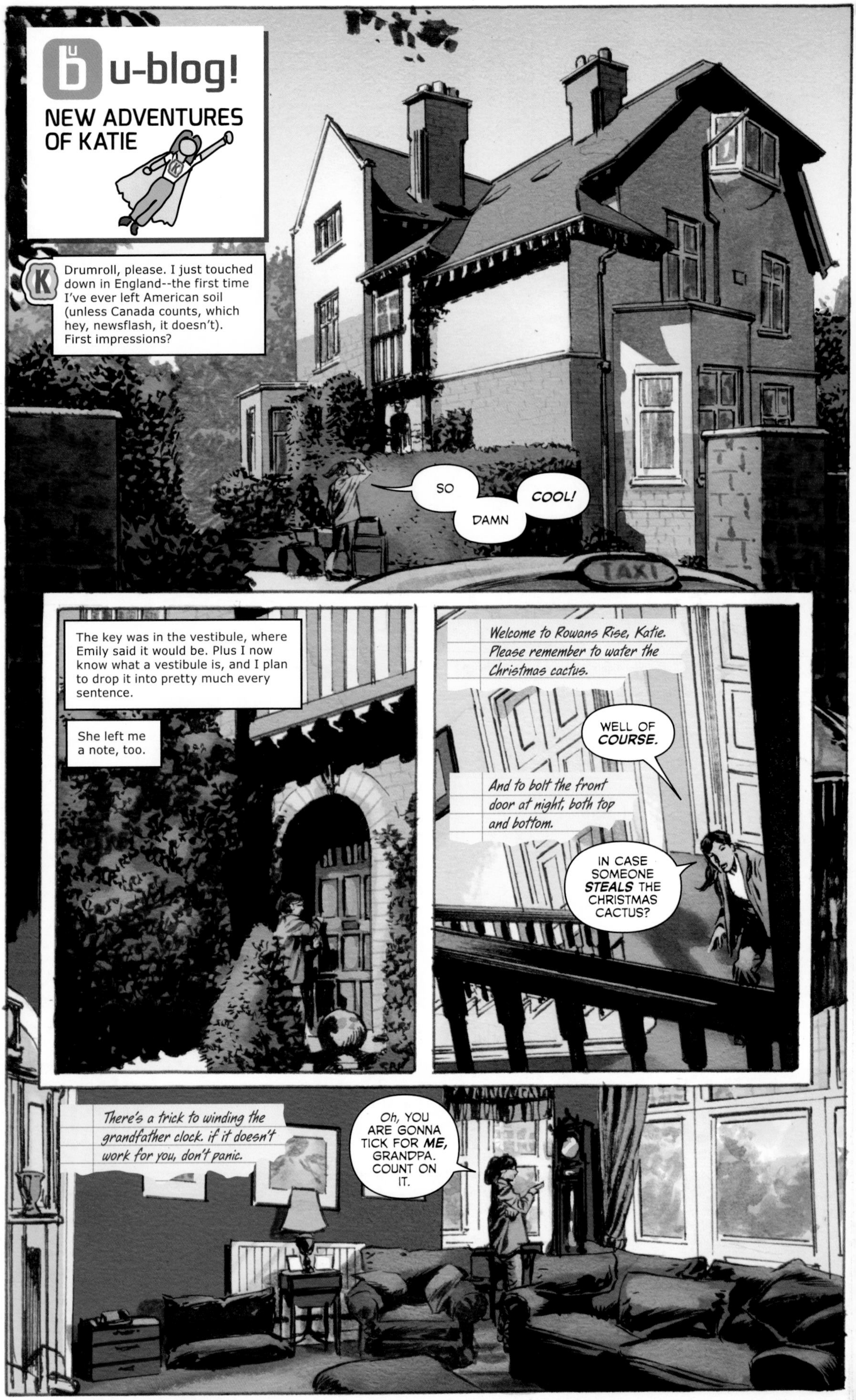
u-blog!
NEW ADVENTURES OF KATIE
Drumroll, please. I just touched down in England--the first time I've ever left American soil (unless Canada counts, which hey, newsflash, it doesn't). First impressions?
SO
DAMN
COOL!
TAXI
The key was in the vestibule, where Emily said it would be. Plus I now know what a vestibule is, and I plan to drop it into pretty much every sentence.
She left me a note, too.
Welcome to Rowans Rise, Katie. Please remember to water the Christmas cactus.
WELL OF COURSE.
And to bolt the front door at night, both top and bottom.
IN CASE SOMEONE STEALS THE CHRISTMAS CACTUS?
There's a trick to winding the grandfather clock. if it doesn't work for you, don't panic.
Oh, YOU ARE GONNA TICK FOR ME, GRANDPA. COUNT ON IT.

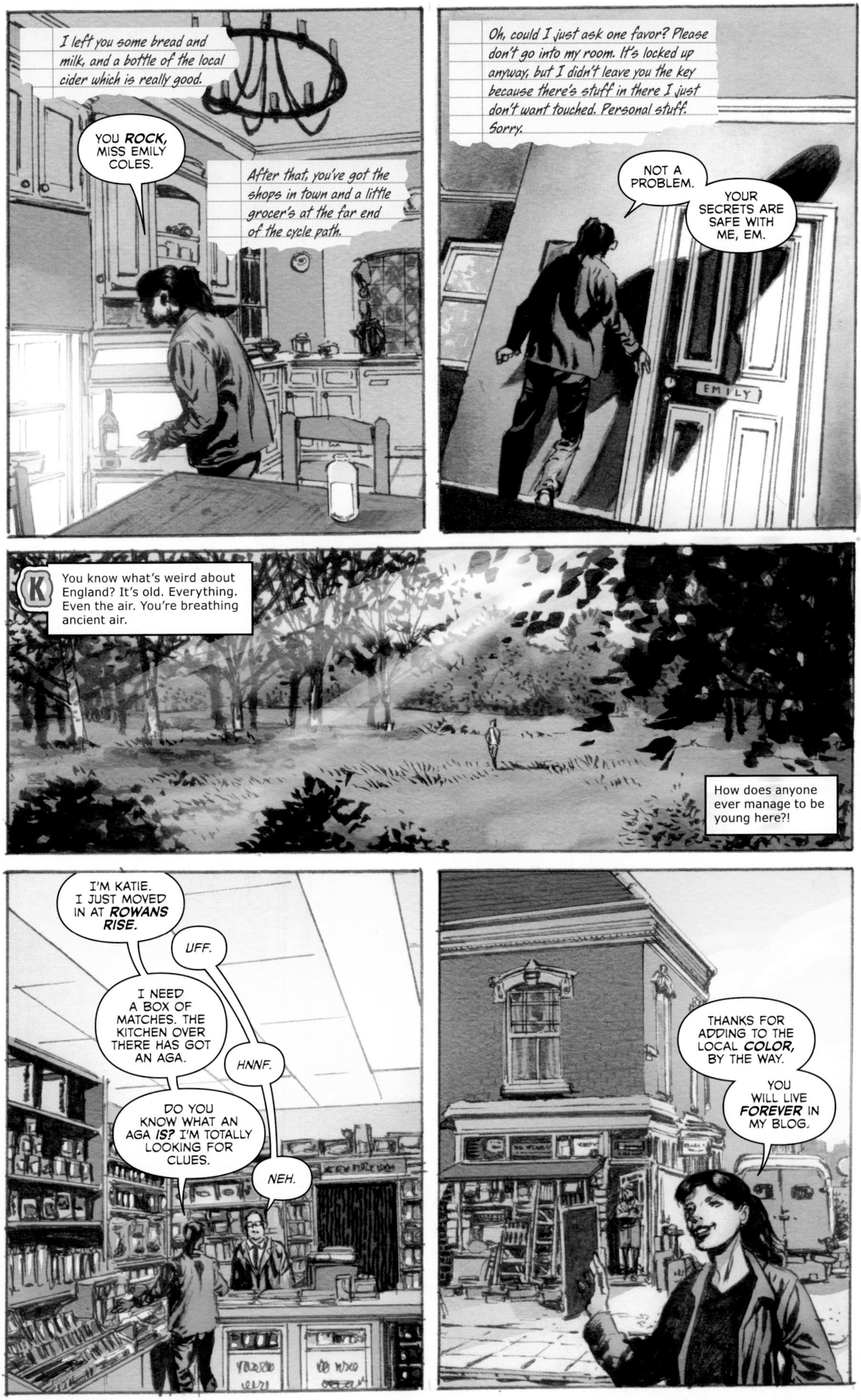
I left you some bread and milk, and a bottle of the local cider which is really good.
YOU ROCK, MISS EMILY COLES.
After that, you've got the shops in town and a little grocer's at the far end of the cycle path.
Oh, could I just ask one favor? Please don't go into my room. It's locked up anyway, but I didn't leave you the key because there's stuff in there I just don't want touched. Personal stuff. Sorry.
NOT A PROBLEM.
YOUR SECRETS ARE SAFE WITH ME, EM.
EMILY
You know what's weird about England? It's old. Everything. Even the air. You're breathing ancient air.
How does anyone ever manage to be young here?!
I'M KATIE. I JUST MOVED IN AT ROWANS RISE.
UFF.
I NEED A BOX OF MATCHES. THE KITCHEN OVER THERE HAS GOT AN AGA.
HNNF.
DO YOU KNOW WHAT AN AGA IS? I'M TOTALLY LOOKING FOR CLUES.
NEH.
THANKS FOR ADDING TO THE LOCAL COLOR, BY THE WAY.
YOU WILL LIVE FOREVER IN MY BLOG.

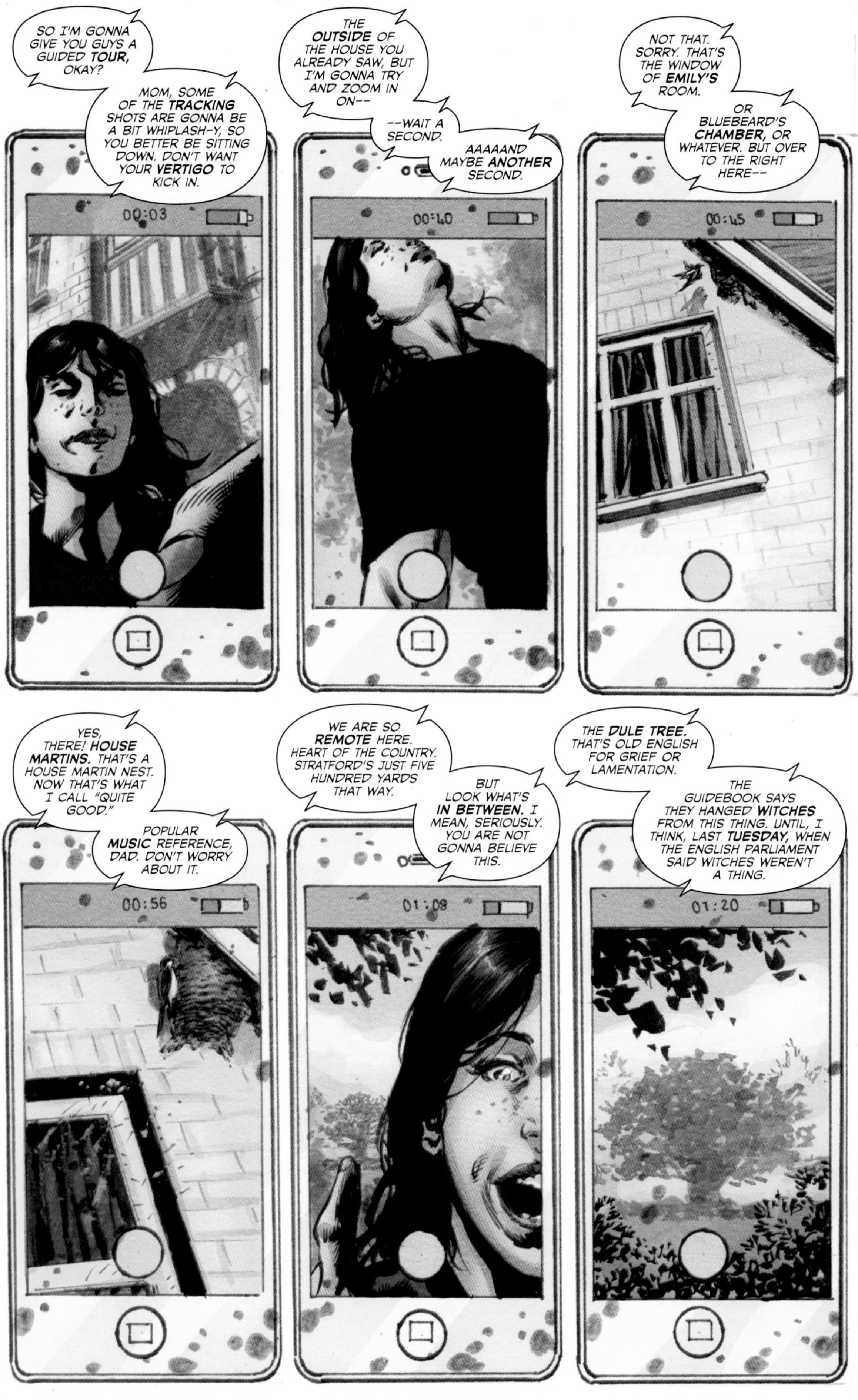
SO I'M GONNA GIVE YOU GUYS A GUIDED TOUR, OKAY?
MOM, SOME OF THE TRACKING SHOTS ARE GONNA BE A BIT WHIPLASH-Y, SO YOU BETTER BE SITTING DOWN. DON'T WANT YOUR VERTIGO TO KICK IN.
00:03
THE OUTSIDE OF THE HOUSE YOU ALREADY SAW, BUT I'M GONNA TRY AND ZOOM IN ON--
--WAIT A SECOND.
AAAAAND MAYBE ANOTHER SECOND.
00:40
NOT THAT. SORRY. THAT'S THE WINDOW OF EMILY'S ROOM.
OR BLUEBEARD'S CHAMBER, OR WHATEVER. BUT OVER TO THE RIGHT HERE--
00:45
YES, THERE! HOUSE MARTINS. THAT'S A HOUSE MARTIN NEST. NOW THAT'S WHAT I CALL "QUITE GOOD."
POPULAR MUSIC REFERENCE, DAD. DON'T WORRY ABOUT IT.
00:56
WE ARE SO REMOTE HERE. HEART OF THE COUNTRY. STRATFORD'S JUST FIVE HUNDRED YARDS THAT WAY.
BUT LOOK WHAT'S IN BETWEEN. I MEAN, SERIOUSLY. YOU ARE NOT GONNA BELIEVE THIS.
01:08
THE DULE TREE. THAT'S OLD ENGLISH FOR GRIEF OR LAMENTATION.
THE GUIDEBOOK SAYS THEY HANGED WITCHES FROM THIS THING. UNTIL, I THINK, LAST TUESDAY, WHEN THE ENGLISH PARLIAMENT SAID WITCHES WEREN'T A THING.
01:20

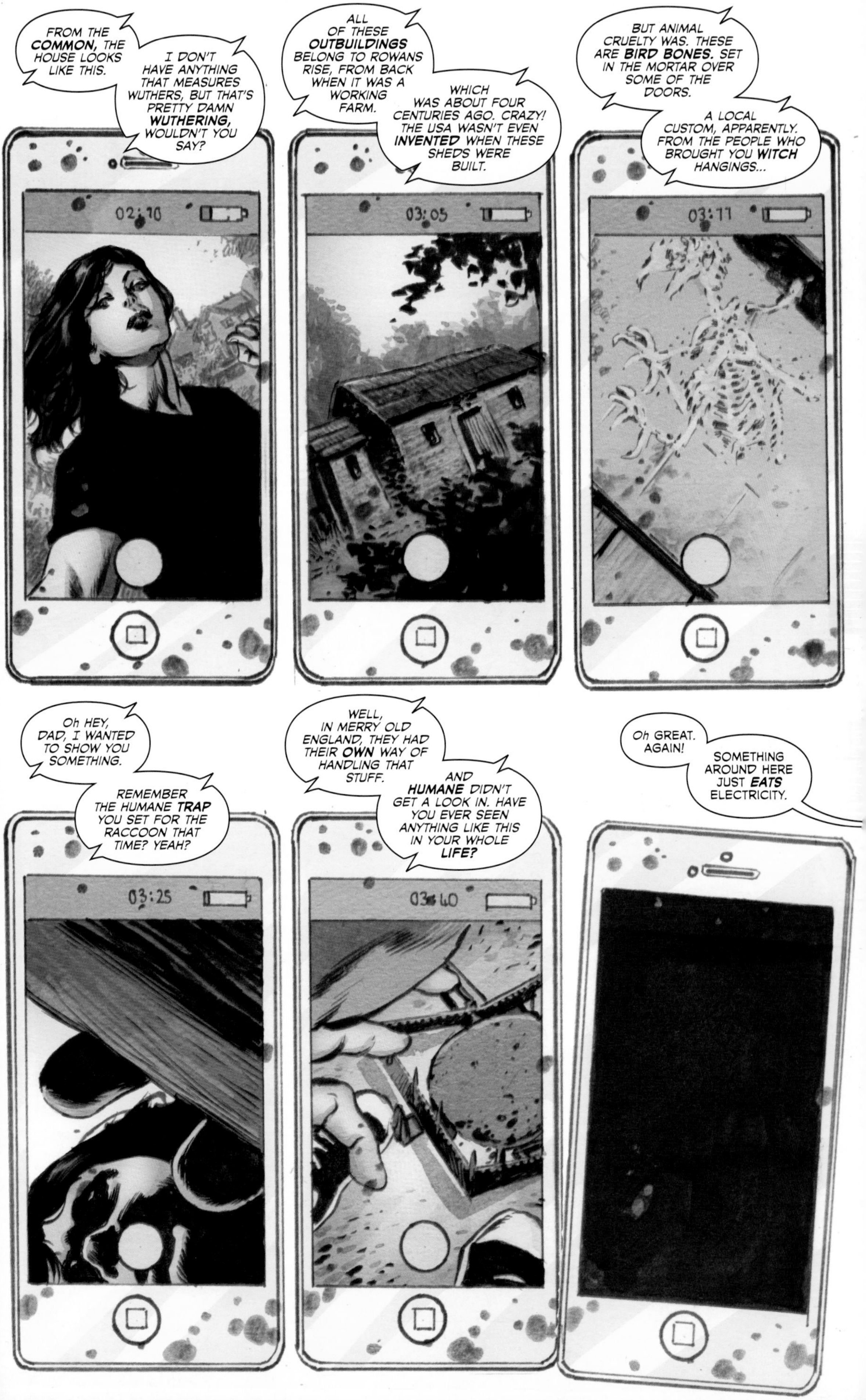

FROM THE COMMON, THE HOUSE LOOKS LIKE THIS.
I DON'T HAVE ANYTHING THAT MEASURES WUTHERS, BUT THAT'S PRETTY DAMN WUTHERING, WOULDN'T YOU SAY?
ALL OF THESE OUTBUILDINGS BELONG TO ROWANS RISE, FROM BACK WHEN IT WAS A WORKING FARM.
WHICH WAS ABOUT FOUR CENTURIES AGO. CRAZY! THE USA WASN'T EVEN INVENTED WHEN THESE SHEDS WERE BUILT.
BUT ANIMAL CRUELTY WAS. THESE ARE BIRD BONES. SET IN THE MORTAR OVER SOME OF THE DOORS.
A LOCAL CUSTOM, APPARENTLY. FROM THE PEOPLE WHO BROUGHT YOU WITCH HANGINGS...
Oh HEY, DAD, I WANTED TO SHOW YOU SOMETHING.
REMEMBER THE HUMANE TRAP YOU SET FOR THE RACCOON THAT TIME? YEAH?
WELL, IN MERRY OLD ENGLAND, THEY HAD THEIR OWN WAY OF HANDLING THAT STUFF.
AND HUMANE DIDN'T GET A LOOK IN. HAVE YOU EVER SEEN ANYTHING LIKE THIS IN YOUR WHOLE LIFE?
Oh GREAT. AGAIN!
SOMETHING AROUND HERE JUST EATS ELECTRICITY.

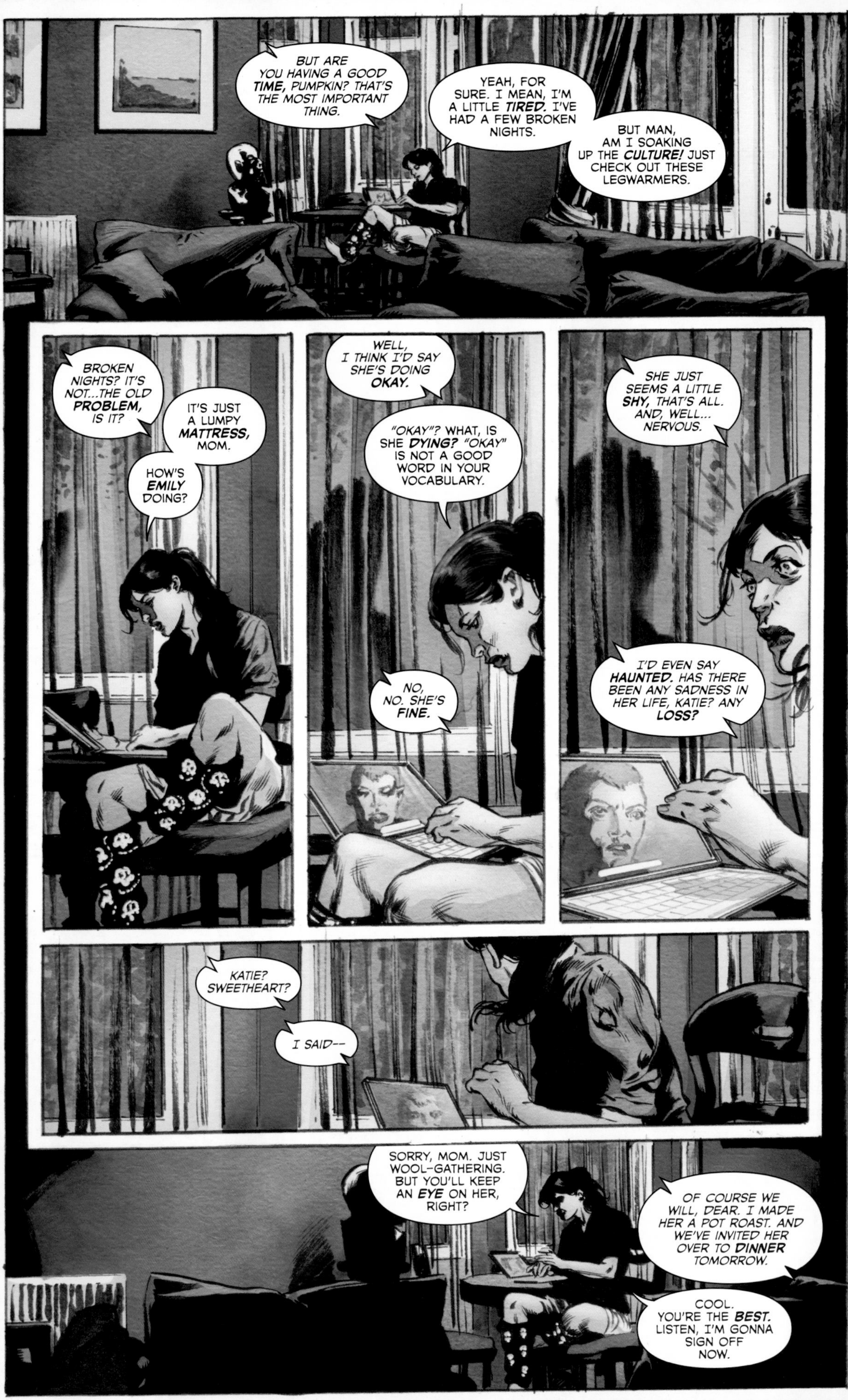

BUT ARE YOU HAVING A GOOD TIME, PUMPKIN? THAT'S THE MOST IMPORTANT THING.
YEAH, FOR SURE. I MEAN, I'M A LITTLE TIRED. I'VE HAD A FEW BROKEN NIGHTS.
BUT MAN, AM I SOAKING UP THE CULTURE! JUST CHECK OUT THESE LEGWARMERS.
BROKEN NIGHTS? IT'S NOT...THE OLD PROBLEM, IS IT?
IT'S JUST A LUMPY MATTRESS, MOM.
HOW'S EMILY DOING?
WELL, I THINK I'D SAY SHE'S DOING OKAY.
"OKAY"? WHAT, IS SHE DYING? "OKAY" IS NOT A GOOD WORD IN YOUR VOCABULARY.
NO, NO. SHE'S FINE.
SHE JUST SEEMS A LITTLE SHY, THAT'S ALL. AND, WELL... NERVOUS.
I'D EVEN SAY HAUNTED. HAS THERE BEEN ANY SADNESS IN HER LIFE, KATIE? ANY LOSS?
KATIE? SWEETHEART?
I SAID--
SORRY, MOM. JUST WOOL-GATHERING. BUT YOU'LL KEEP AN EYE ON HER, RIGHT?
OF COURSE WE WILL, DEAR. I MADE HER A POT ROAST. AND WE'VE INVITED HER OVER TO DINNER TOMORROW.
COOL. YOU'RE THE BEST. LISTEN, I'M GONNA SIGN OFF NOW.

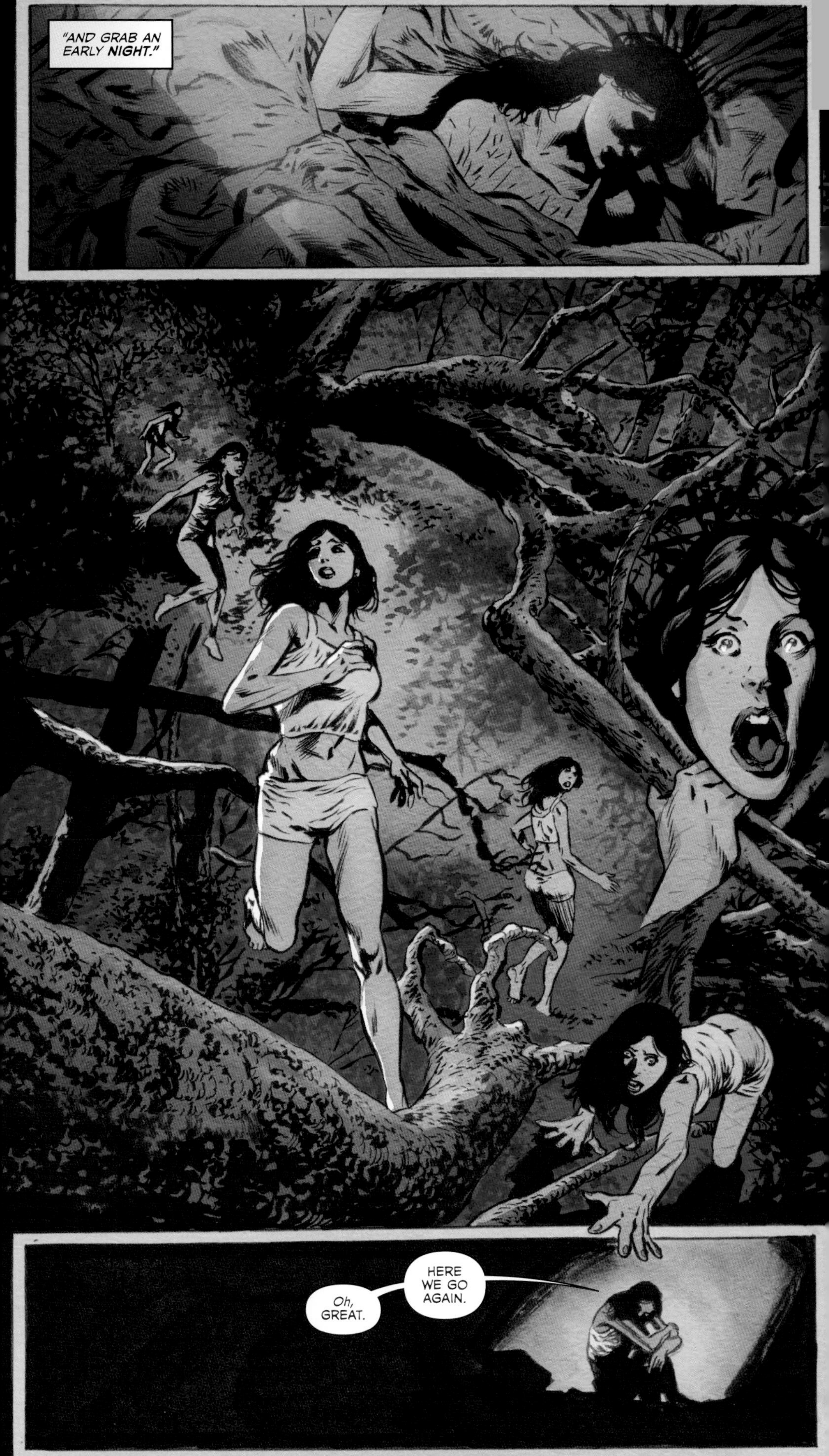
"AND GRAB AN EARLY NIGHT."
HERE WE GO AGAIN.
Oh, GREAT.

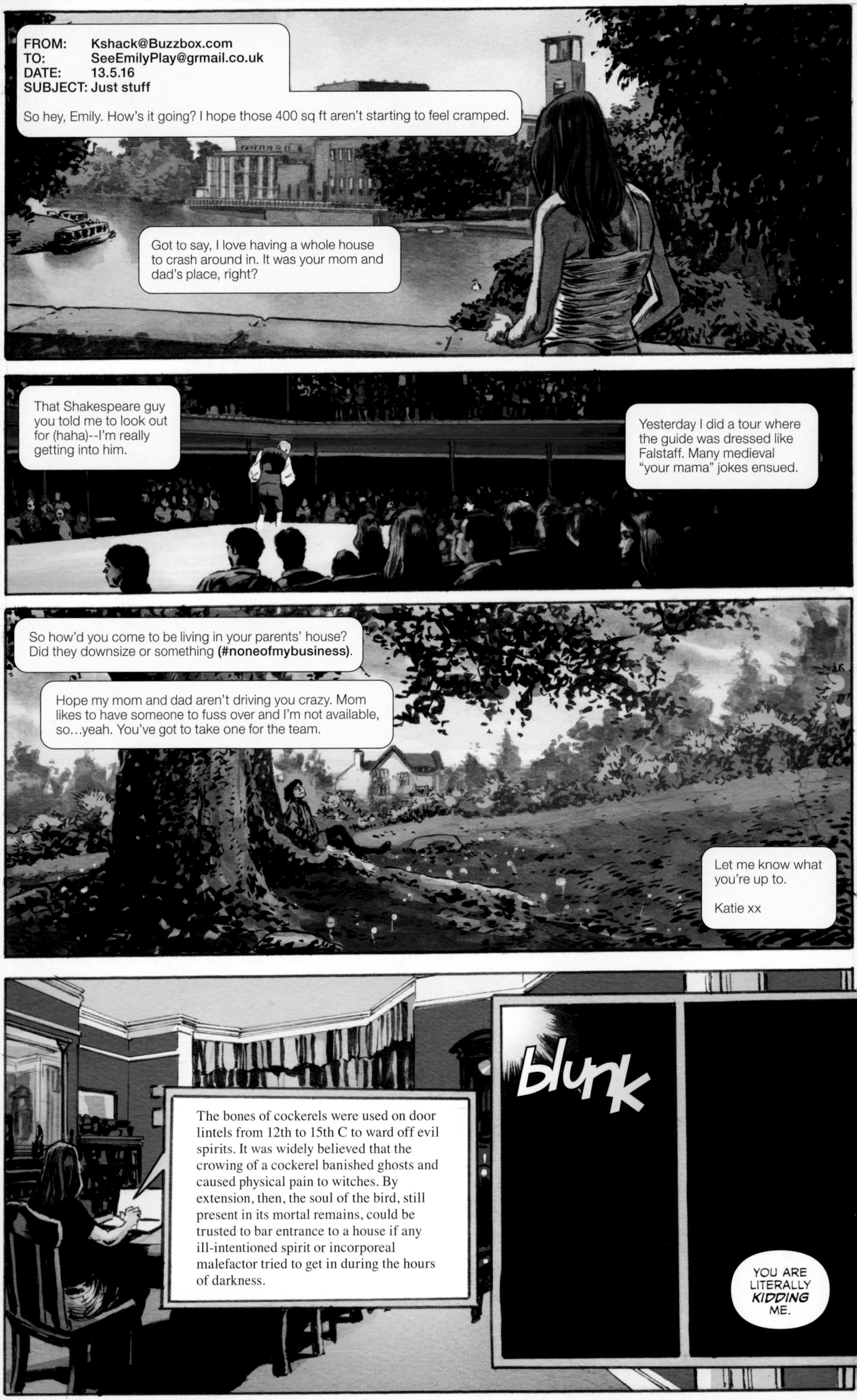
FROM: Kshack@Buzzbox.com
TO: SeeEmilyPlay@grmail.co.uk
DATE: 13.5.16
SUBJECT: Just stuff
So hey, Emily. How's it going? I hope those 400 sq ft aren't starting to feel cramped.
Got to say, I love having a whole house to crash around in. It was your mom and dad's place, right?
That Shakespeare guy you told me to look out for (haha)--I'm really getting into him.
Yesterday I did a tour where the guide was dressed like Falstaff. Many medieval "your mama" jokes ensued.
So how'd you come to be living in your parents' house? Did they downsize or something **(#noneofmybusiness)**.
Hope my mom and dad aren't driving you crazy. Mom likes to have someone to fuss over and I'm not available, so…yeah. You've got to take one for the team.
Let me know what you're up to.
Katie xx
The bones of cockerels were used on door lintels from 12th to 15th C to ward off evil spirits. It was widely believed that the crowing of a cockerel banished ghosts and caused physical pain to witches. By extension, then, the soul of the bird, still present in its mortal remains, could be trusted to bar entrance to a house if any ill-intentioned spirit or incorporeal malefactor tried to get in during the hours of darkness.
blunk
YOU ARE LITERALLY *KIDDING* ME.

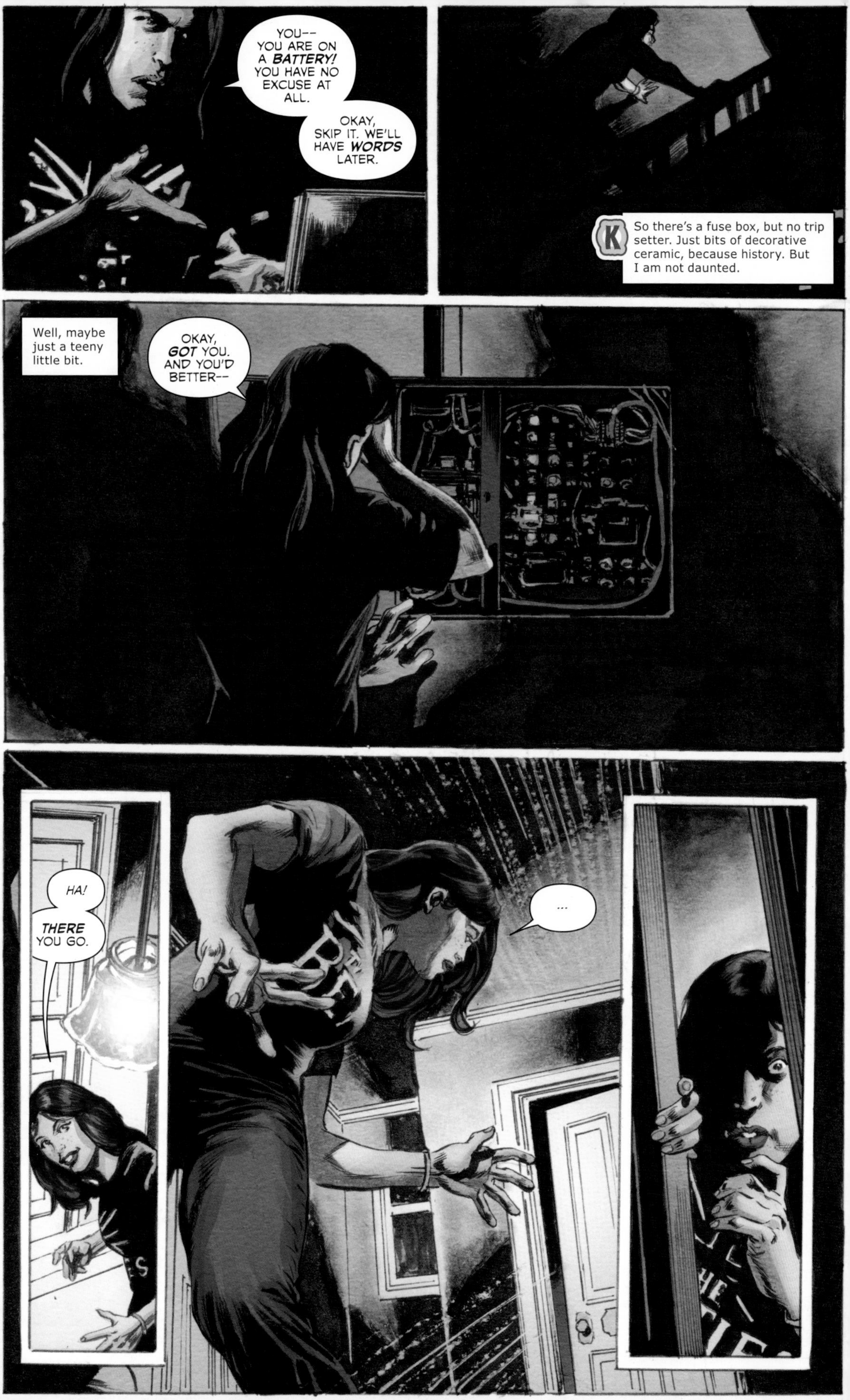
YOU-- YOU ARE ON A BATTERY! YOU HAVE NO EXCUSE AT ALL.
OKAY, SKIP IT. WE'LL HAVE WORDS LATER.
So there's a fuse box, but no trip setter. Just bits of decorative ceramic, because history. But I am not daunted.
Well, maybe just a teeny little bit.
OKAY, GOT YOU. AND YOU'D BETTER--
HA!
THERE YOU GO.
...

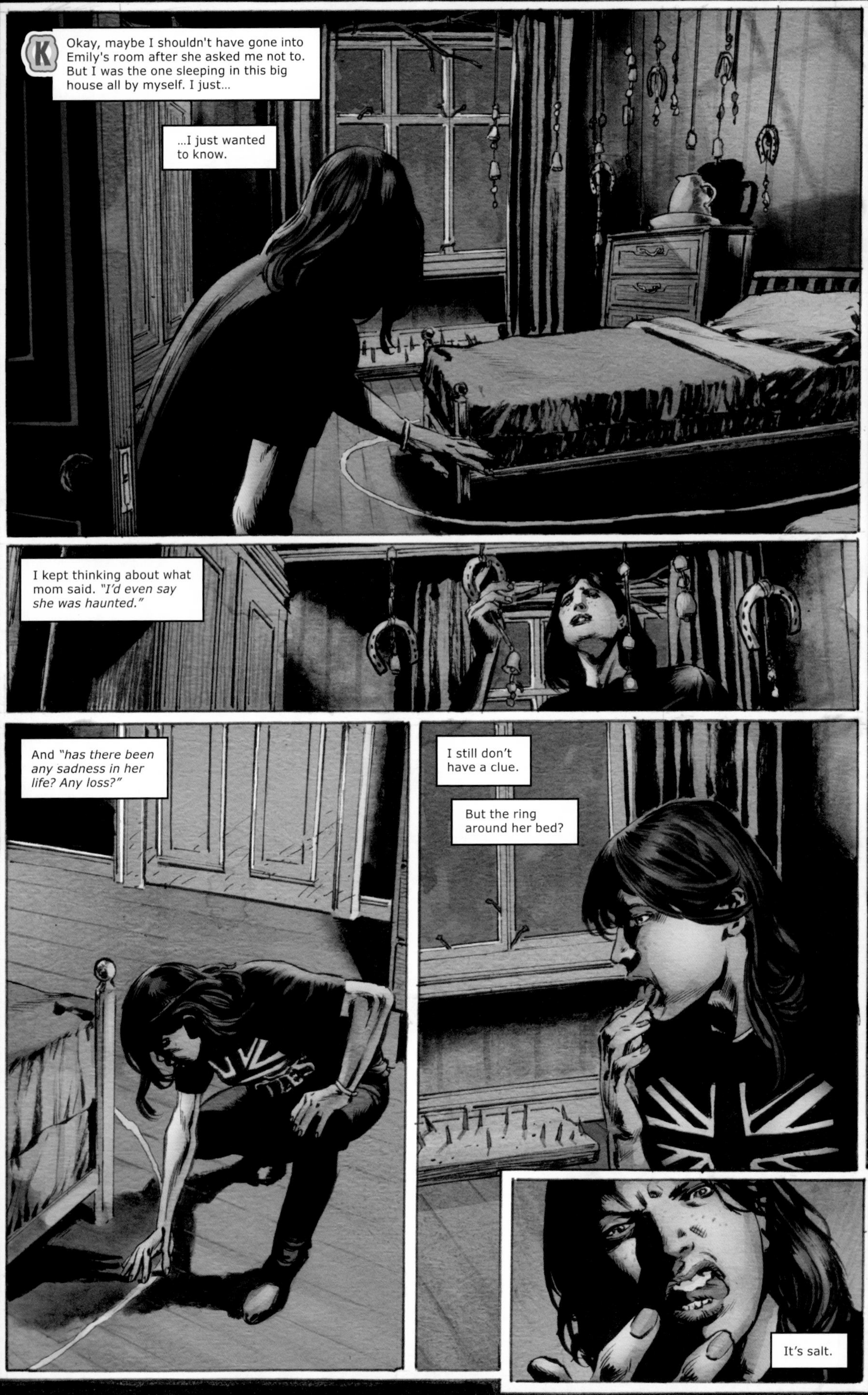
Okay, maybe I shouldn't have gone into Emily's room after she asked me not to. But I was the one sleeping in this big house all by myself. I just...
...I just wanted to know.
I kept thinking about what mom said. *"I'd even say she was haunted."*
And *"has there been any sadness in her life? Any loss?"*
I still don't have a clue.
But the ring around her bed?
It's salt.

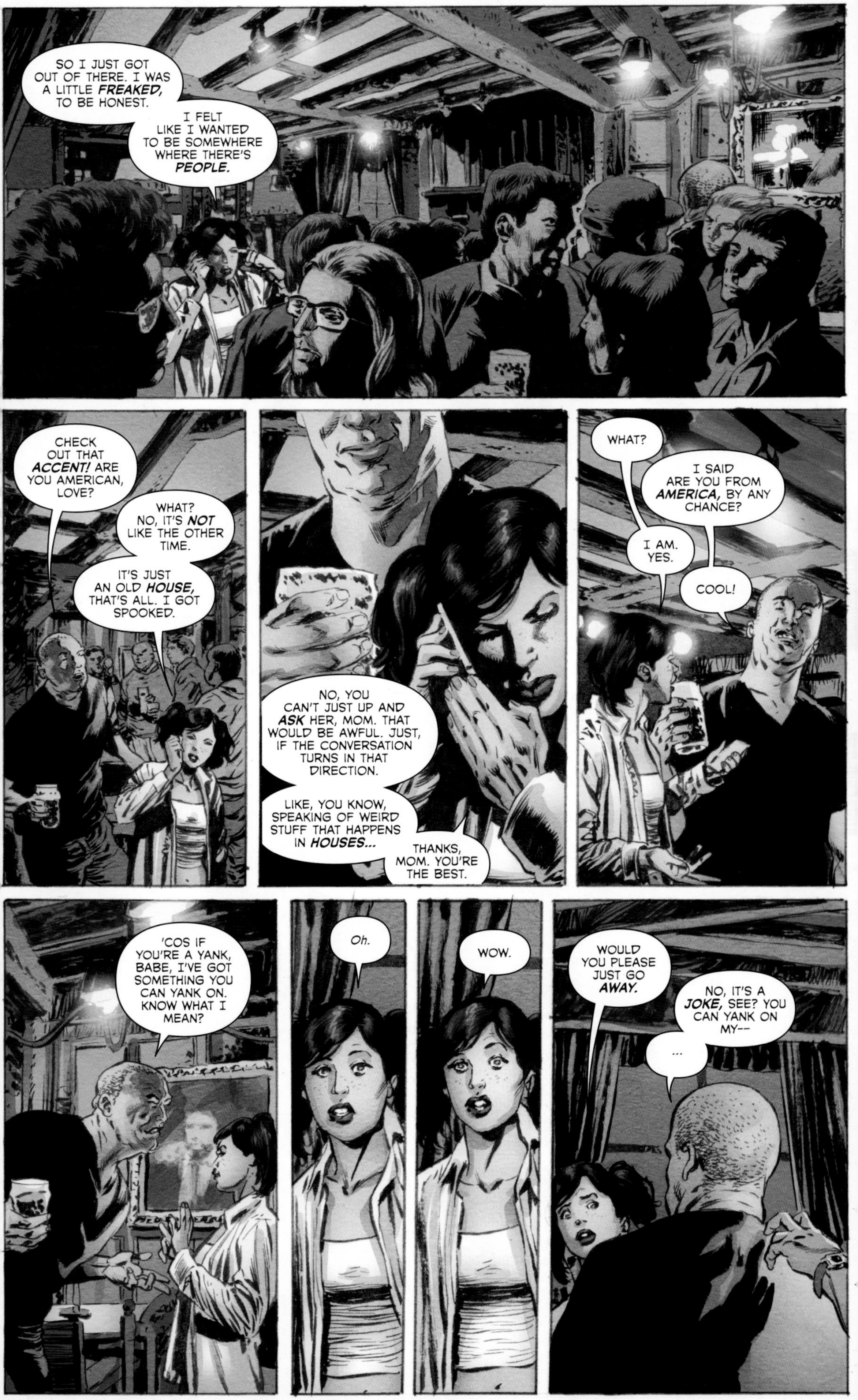
SO I JUST GOT OUT OF THERE. I WAS A LITTLE FREAKED, TO BE HONEST.
I FELT LIKE I WANTED TO BE SOMEWHERE WHERE THERE'S PEOPLE.
CHECK OUT THAT ACCENT! ARE YOU AMERICAN, LOVE?
WHAT? NO, IT'S NOT LIKE THE OTHER TIME.
IT'S JUST AN OLD HOUSE, THAT'S ALL. I GOT SPOOKED.
NO, YOU CAN'T JUST UP AND ASK HER, MOM. THAT WOULD BE AWFUL. JUST, IF THE CONVERSATION TURNS IN THAT DIRECTION.
LIKE, YOU KNOW, SPEAKING OF WEIRD STUFF THAT HAPPENS IN HOUSES...
THANKS, MOM. YOU'RE THE BEST.
WHAT?
I SAID ARE YOU FROM AMERICA, BY ANY CHANCE?
I AM. YES.
COOL!
'COS IF YOU'RE A YANK, BABE, I'VE GOT SOMETHING YOU CAN YANK ON. KNOW WHAT I MEAN?
Oh.
WOW.
WOULD YOU PLEASE JUST GO AWAY.
NO, IT'S A JOKE, SEE? YOU CAN YANK ON MY--
...

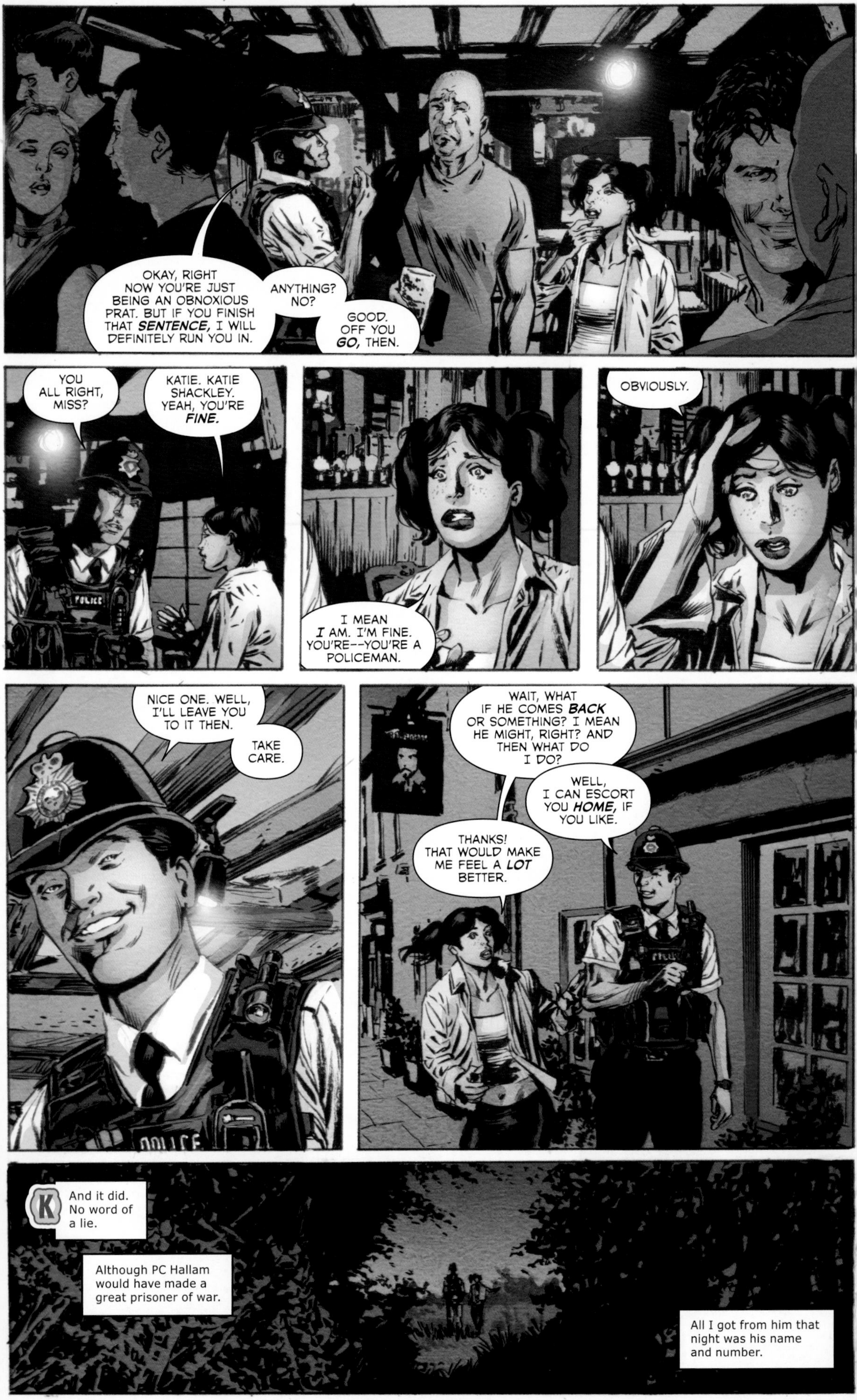
OKAY, RIGHT NOW YOU'RE JUST BEING AN OBNOXIOUS PRAT. BUT IF YOU FINISH THAT SENTENCE, I WILL DEFINITELY RUN YOU IN.
ANYTHING? NO?
GOOD. OFF YOU GO, THEN.
YOU ALL RIGHT, MISS?
KATIE. KATIE SHACKLEY. YEAH, YOU'RE FINE.
I MEAN I AM. I'M FINE. YOU'RE--YOU'RE A POLICEMAN.
OBVIOUSLY.
NICE ONE. WELL, I'LL LEAVE YOU TO IT THEN.
TAKE CARE.
WAIT, WHAT IF HE COMES BACK OR SOMETHING? I MEAN HE MIGHT, RIGHT? AND THEN WHAT DO I DO?
WELL, I CAN ESCORT YOU HOME, IF YOU LIKE.
THANKS! THAT WOULD MAKE ME FEEL A LOT BETTER.
And it did. No word of a lie.
Although PC Hallam would have made a great prisoner of war.
All I got from him that night was his name and number.

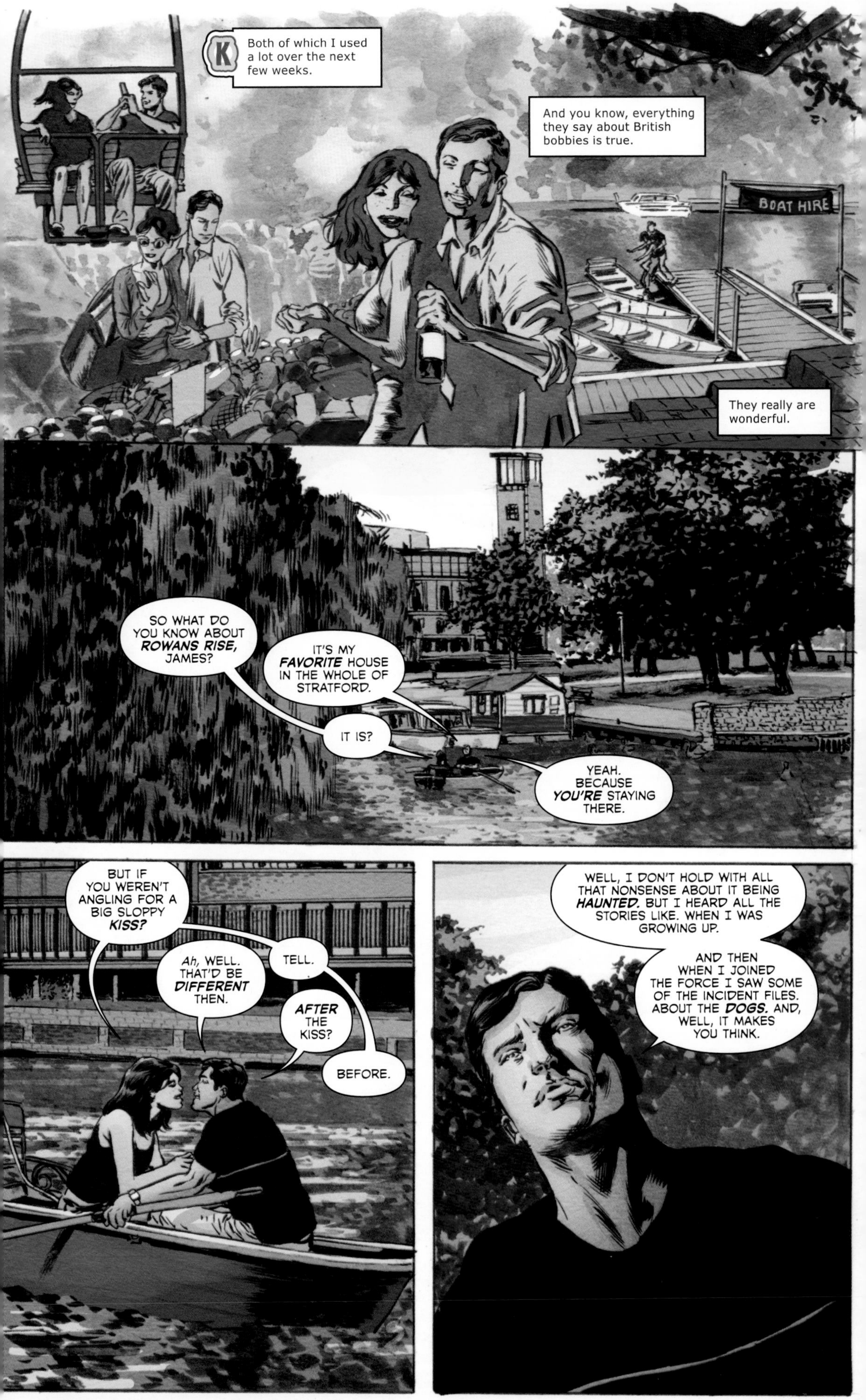

Both of which I used a lot over the next few weeks.
And you know, everything they say about British bobbies is true.
BOAT HIRE
They really are wonderful.
SO WHAT DO YOU KNOW ABOUT ROWANS RISE, JAMES?
IT'S MY FAVORITE HOUSE IN THE WHOLE OF STRATFORD.
IT IS?
YEAH. BECAUSE YOU'RE STAYING THERE.
BUT IF YOU WEREN'T ANGLING FOR A BIG SLOPPY KISS?
Ah, WELL. THAT'D BE DIFFERENT THEN.
TELL.
AFTER THE KISS?
BEFORE.
WELL, I DON'T HOLD WITH ALL THAT NONSENSE ABOUT IT BEING HAUNTED. BUT I HEARD ALL THE STORIES LIKE. WHEN I WAS GROWING UP.
AND THEN WHEN I JOINED THE FORCE I SAW SOME OF THE INCIDENT FILES. ABOUT THE DOGS. AND, WELL, IT MAKES YOU THINK.

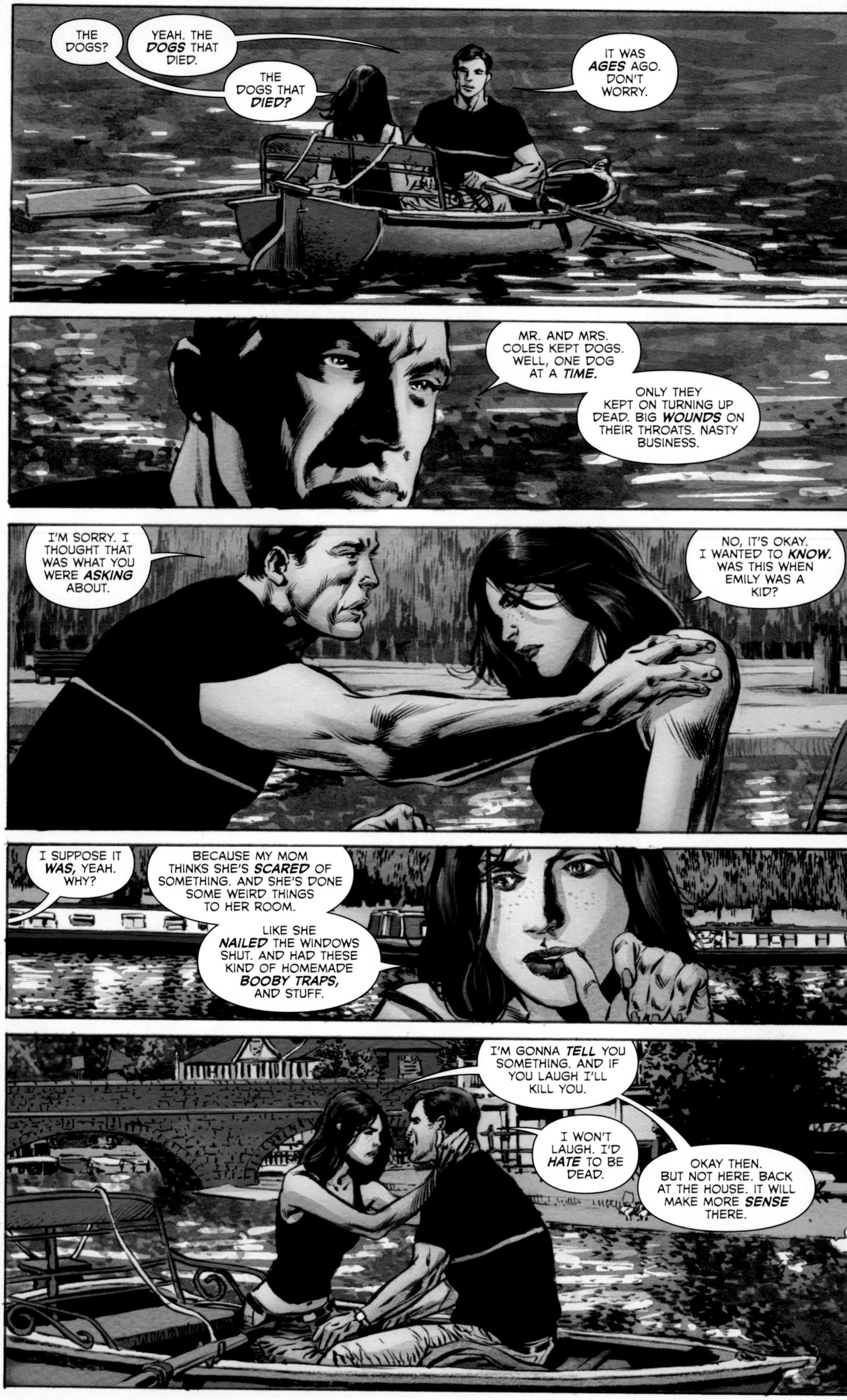
THE DOGS?
YEAH. THE DOGS THAT DIED.
THE DOGS THAT DIED?
IT WAS AGES AGO. DON'T WORRY.
MR. AND MRS. COLES KEPT DOGS. WELL, ONE DOG AT A TIME.
ONLY THEY KEPT ON TURNING UP DEAD. BIG WOUNDS ON THEIR THROATS. NASTY BUSINESS.
I'M SORRY. I THOUGHT THAT WAS WHAT YOU WERE ASKING ABOUT.
NO, IT'S OKAY. I WANTED TO KNOW. WAS THIS WHEN EMILY WAS A KID?
I SUPPOSE IT WAS, YEAH. WHY?
BECAUSE MY MOM THINKS SHE'S SCARED OF SOMETHING. AND SHE'S DONE SOME WEIRD THINGS TO HER ROOM.
LIKE SHE NAILED THE WINDOWS SHUT. AND HAD THESE KIND OF HOMEMADE BOOBY TRAPS, AND STUFF.
I'M GONNA TELL YOU SOMETHING. AND IF YOU LAUGH I'LL KILL YOU.
I WON'T LAUGH. I'D HATE TO BE DEAD.
OKAY THEN. BUT NOT HERE. BACK AT THE HOUSE. IT WILL MAKE MORE SENSE THERE.

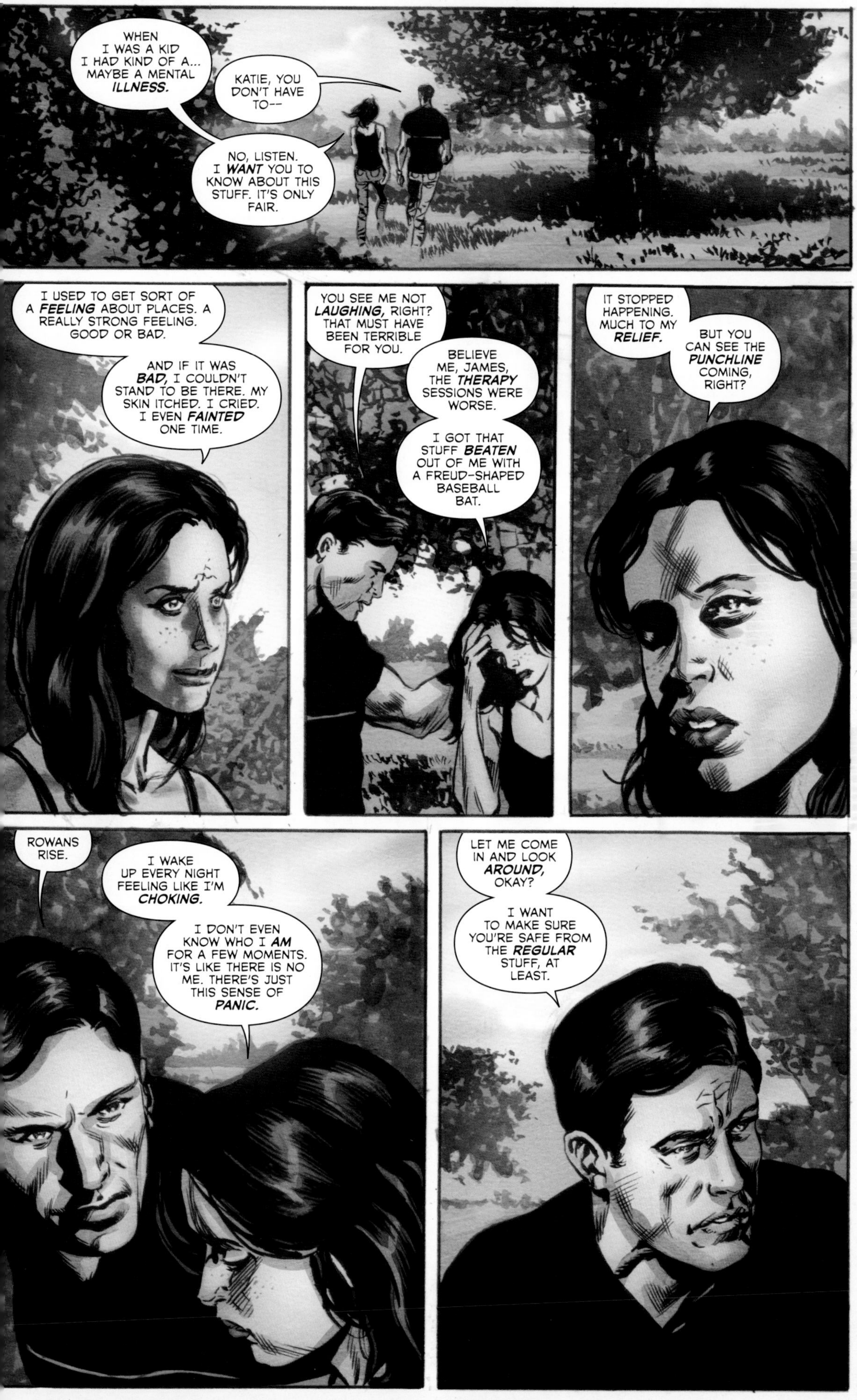
WHEN I WAS A KID I HAD KIND OF A... MAYBE A MENTAL ILLNESS.
KATIE, YOU DON'T HAVE TO--
NO, LISTEN. I WANT YOU TO KNOW ABOUT THIS STUFF. IT'S ONLY FAIR.
I USED TO GET SORT OF A FEELING ABOUT PLACES. A REALLY STRONG FEELING. GOOD OR BAD.
AND IF IT WAS BAD, I COULDN'T STAND TO BE THERE. MY SKIN ITCHED. I CRIED. I EVEN FAINTED ONE TIME.
YOU SEE ME NOT LAUGHING, RIGHT? THAT MUST HAVE BEEN TERRIBLE FOR YOU.
BELIEVE ME, JAMES, THE THERAPY SESSIONS WERE WORSE.
I GOT THAT STUFF BEATEN OUT OF ME WITH A FREUD-SHAPED BASEBALL BAT.
IT STOPPED HAPPENING. MUCH TO MY RELIEF.
BUT YOU CAN SEE THE PUNCHLINE COMING, RIGHT?
ROWANS RISE.
I WAKE UP EVERY NIGHT FEELING LIKE I'M CHOKING.
I DON'T EVEN KNOW WHO I AM FOR A FEW MOMENTS. IT'S LIKE THERE IS NO ME. THERE'S JUST THIS SENSE OF PANIC.
LET ME COME IN AND LOOK AROUND, OKAY?
I WANT TO MAKE SURE YOU'RE SAFE FROM THE REGULAR STUFF, AT LEAST.

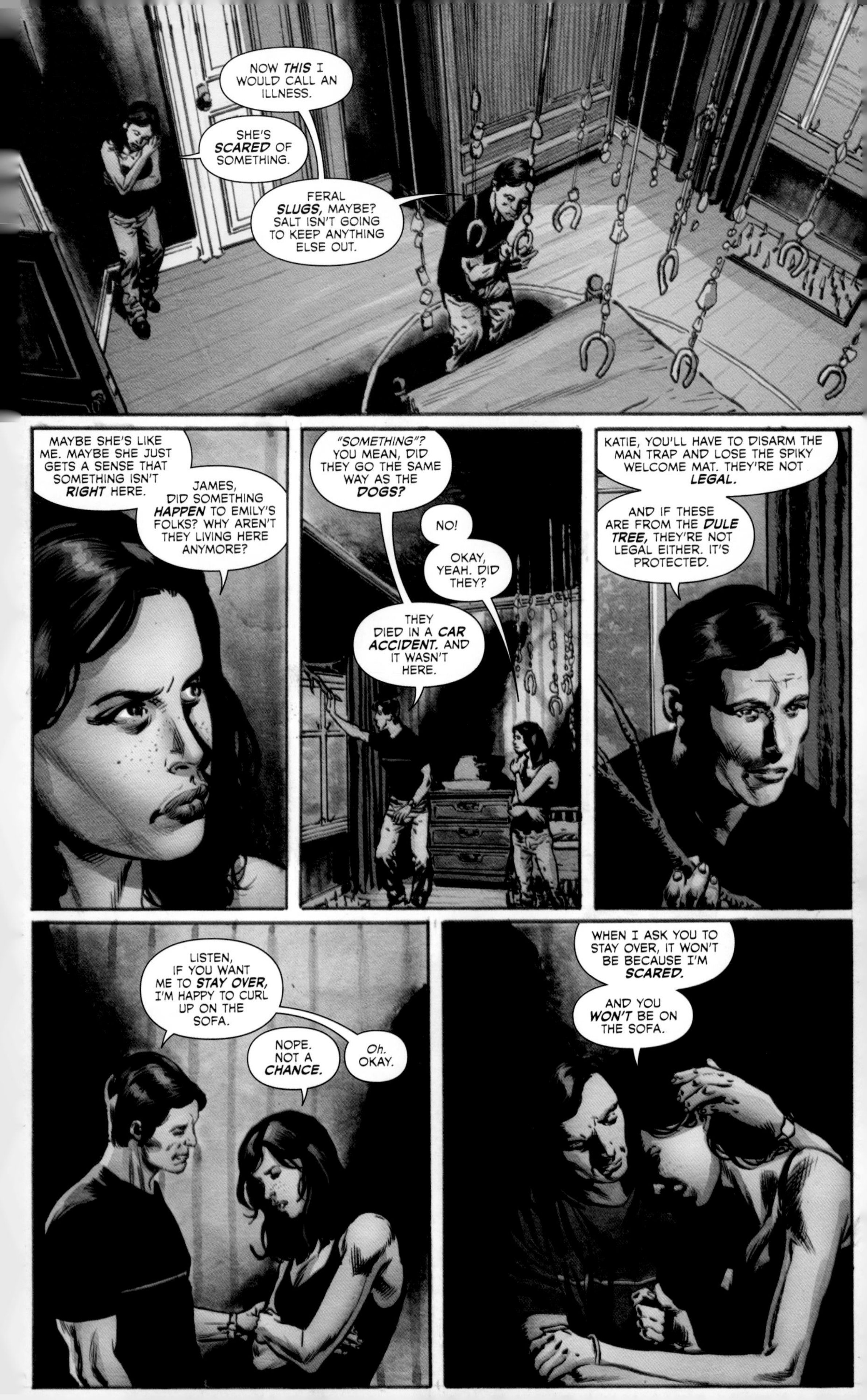
NOW THIS I WOULD CALL AN ILLNESS.
SHE'S SCARED OF SOMETHING.
FERAL SLUGS, MAYBE? SALT ISN'T GOING TO KEEP ANYTHING ELSE OUT.
MAYBE SHE'S LIKE ME. MAYBE SHE JUST GETS A SENSE THAT SOMETHING ISN'T RIGHT HERE.
JAMES, DID SOMETHING HAPPEN TO EMILY'S FOLKS? WHY AREN'T THEY LIVING HERE ANYMORE?
"SOMETHING"? YOU MEAN, DID THEY GO THE SAME WAY AS THE DOGS?
NO!
OKAY, YEAH. DID THEY?
THEY DIED IN A CAR ACCIDENT. AND IT WASN'T HERE.
KATIE, YOU'LL HAVE TO DISARM THE MAN TRAP AND LOSE THE SPIKY WELCOME MAT. THEY'RE NOT LEGAL.
AND IF THESE ARE FROM THE DULE TREE, THEY'RE NOT LEGAL EITHER. IT'S PROTECTED.
LISTEN, IF YOU WANT ME TO STAY OVER, I'M HAPPY TO CURL UP ON THE SOFA.
NOPE. NOT A CHANCE.
Oh. OKAY.
WHEN I ASK YOU TO STAY OVER, IT WON'T BE BECAUSE I'M SCARED.
AND YOU WON'T BE ON THE SOFA.

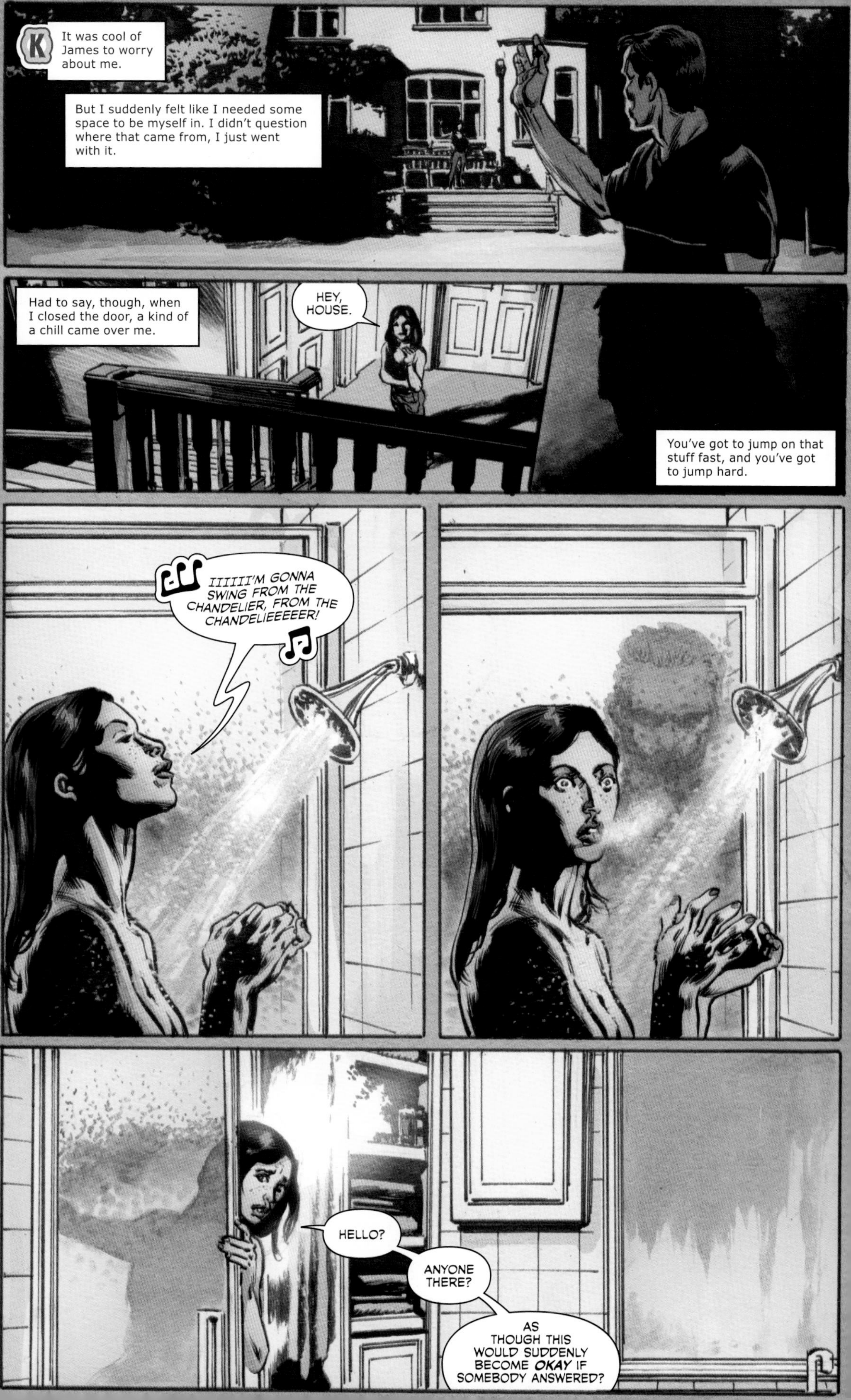
K
It was cool of James to worry about me.
But I suddenly felt like I needed some space to be myself in. I didn't question where that came from, I just went with it.
Had to say, though, when I closed the door, a kind of a chill came over me.
HEY, HOUSE.
You've got to jump on that stuff fast, and you've got to jump hard.
IIIIII'M GONNA SWING FROM THE CHANDELIER, FROM THE CHANDELIEEEEER!
HELLO?
ANYONE THERE?
AS THOUGH THIS WOULD SUDDENLY BECOME *OKAY* IF SOMEBODY ANSWERED?

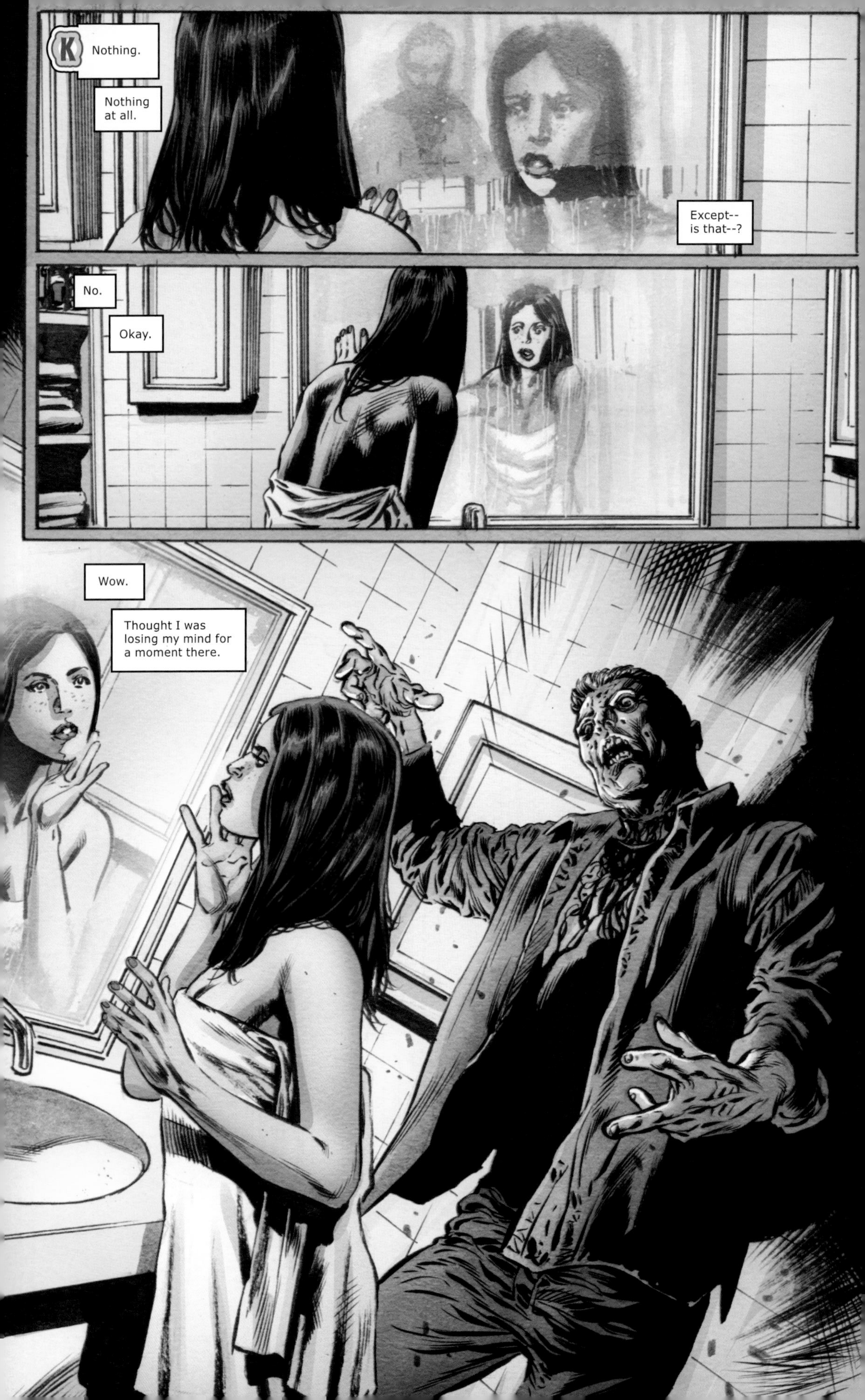
K
Nothing.
Nothing at all.
Except-- is that--?
No.
Okay.
Wow.
Thought I was losing my mind for a moment there.

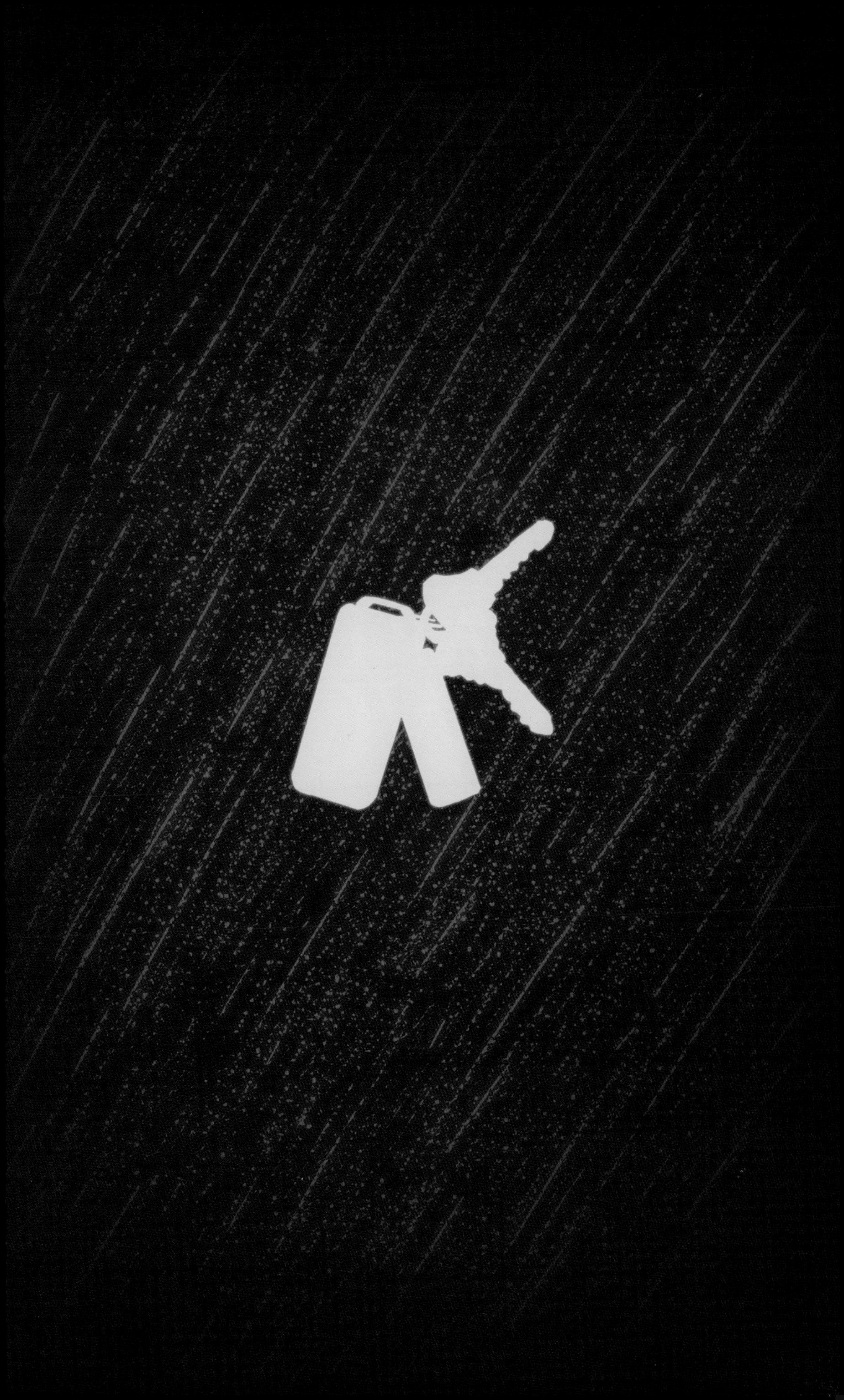

CHAPTER TWO

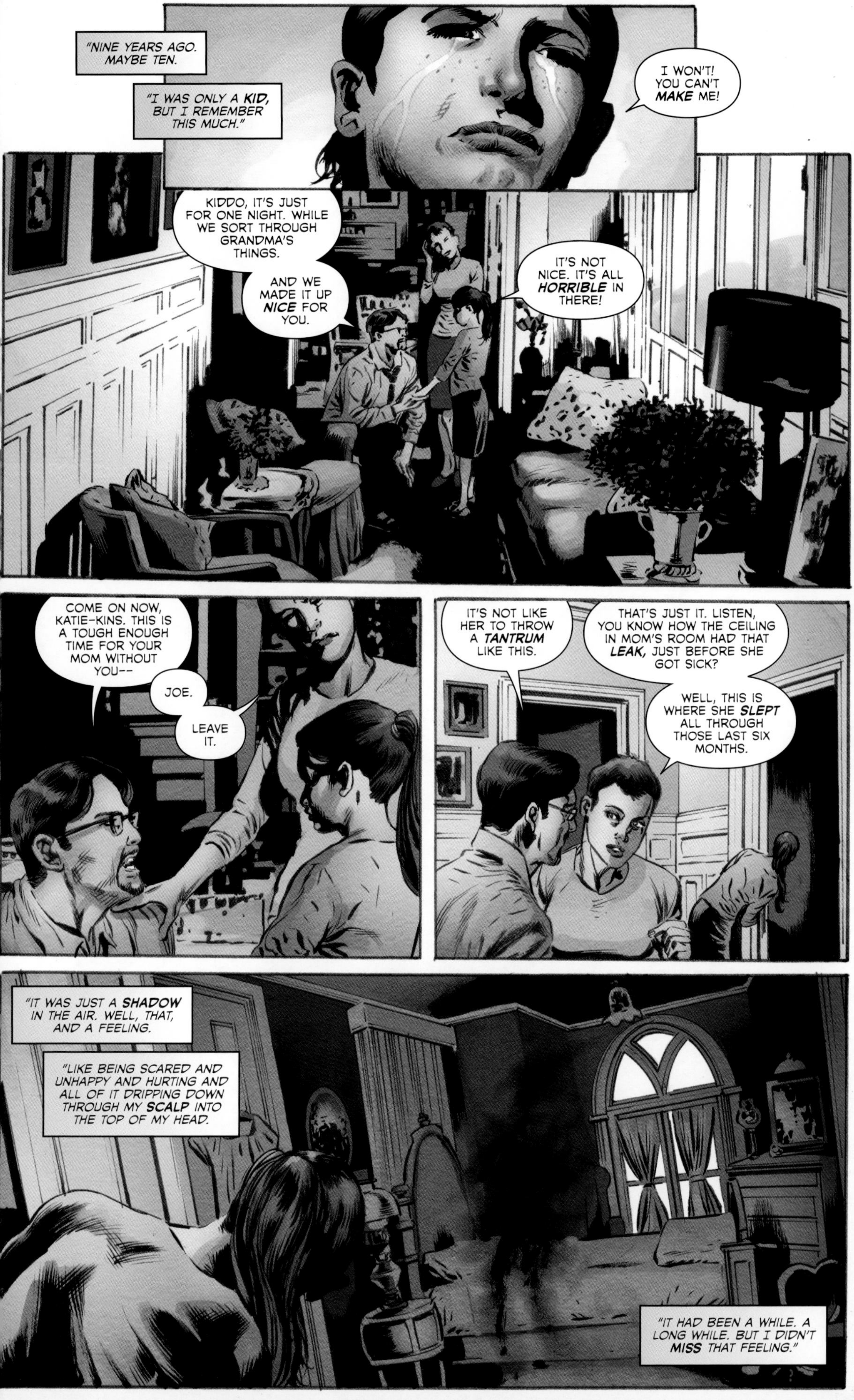
"NINE YEARS AGO. MAYBE TEN.
"I WAS ONLY A KID, BUT I REMEMBER THIS MUCH."
I WON'T! YOU CAN'T MAKE ME!
KIDDO, IT'S JUST FOR ONE NIGHT. WHILE WE SORT THROUGH GRANDMA'S THINGS.
AND WE MADE IT UP NICE FOR YOU.
IT'S NOT NICE. IT'S ALL HORRIBLE IN THERE!
COME ON NOW, KATIE-KINS. THIS IS A TOUGH ENOUGH TIME FOR YOUR MOM WITHOUT YOU--
JOE.
LEAVE IT.
IT'S NOT LIKE HER TO THROW A TANTRUM LIKE THIS.
THAT'S JUST IT. LISTEN, YOU KNOW HOW THE CEILING IN MOM'S ROOM HAD THAT LEAK, JUST BEFORE SHE GOT SICK?
WELL, THIS IS WHERE SHE SLEPT ALL THROUGH THOSE LAST SIX MONTHS.
"IT WAS JUST A SHADOW IN THE AIR. WELL, THAT, AND A FEELING.
"LIKE BEING SCARED AND UNHAPPY AND HURTING AND ALL OF IT DRIPPING DOWN THROUGH MY SCALP INTO THE TOP OF MY HEAD.
"IT HAD BEEN A WHILE. A LONG WHILE. BUT I DIDN'T MISS THAT FEELING."

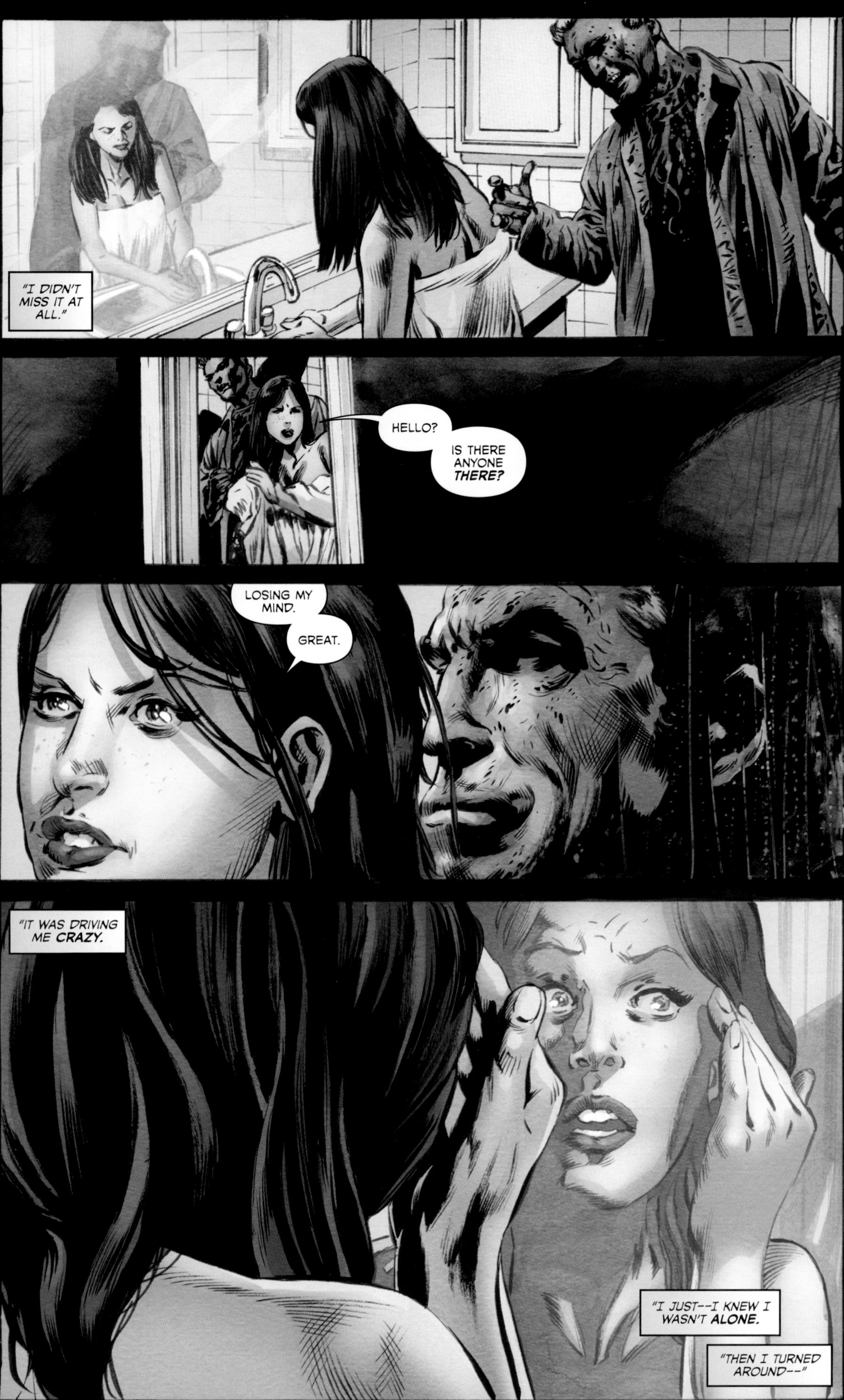
"I DIDN'T MISS IT AT ALL."
HELLO?
IS THERE ANYONE THERE?
LOSING MY MIND.
GREAT.
"IT WAS DRIVING ME CRAZY.
"I JUST--I KNEW I WASN'T ALONE.
"THEN I TURNED AROUND--"

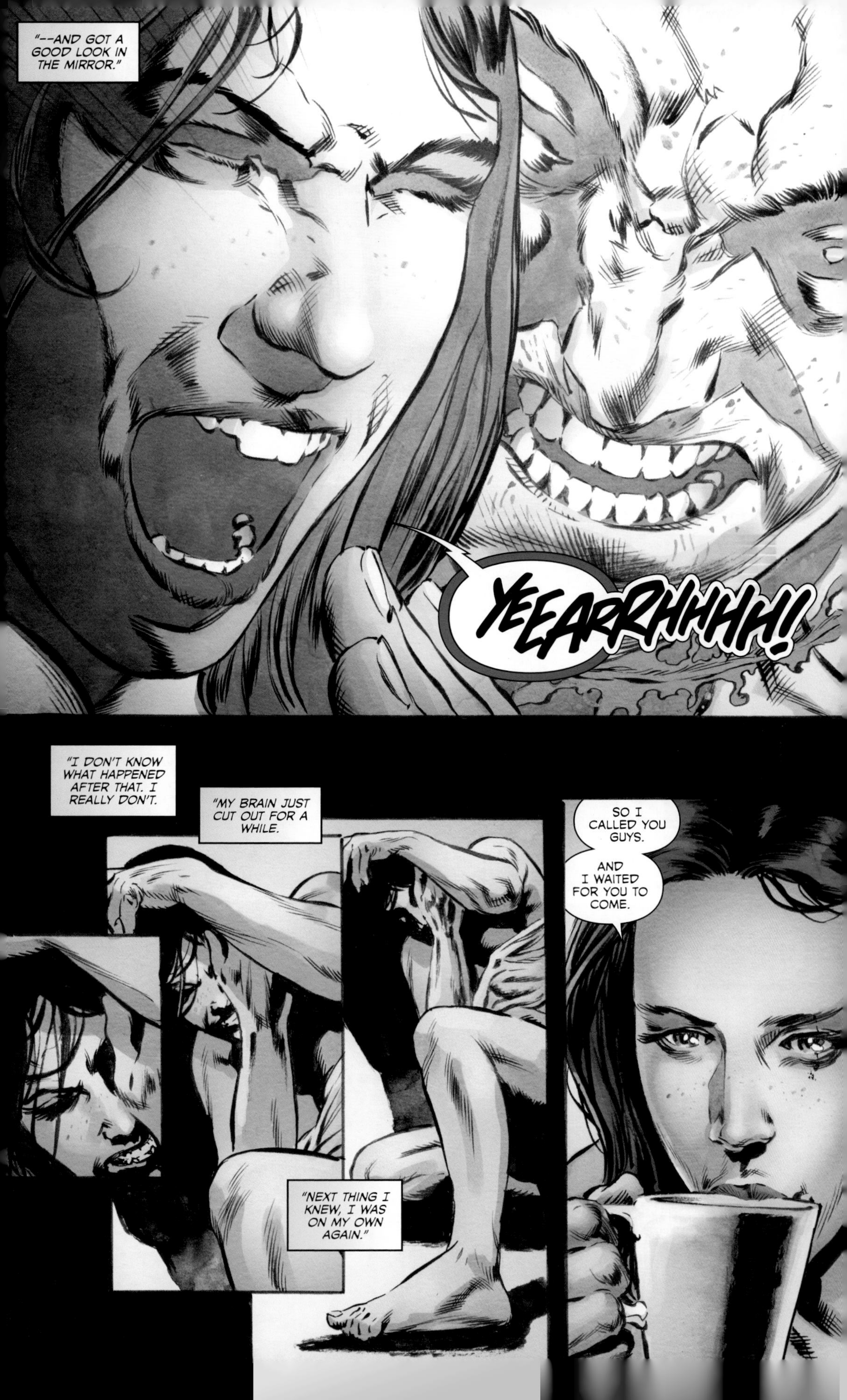
"--AND GOT A GOOD LOOK IN THE MIRROR."
YEEARRHHHH!
"I DON'T KNOW WHAT HAPPENED AFTER THAT. I REALLY DON'T.
"MY BRAIN JUST CUT OUT FOR A WHILE.
"NEXT THING I KNEW, I WAS ON MY OWN AGAIN."
SO I CALLED YOU GUYS.
AND I WAITED FOR YOU TO COME.

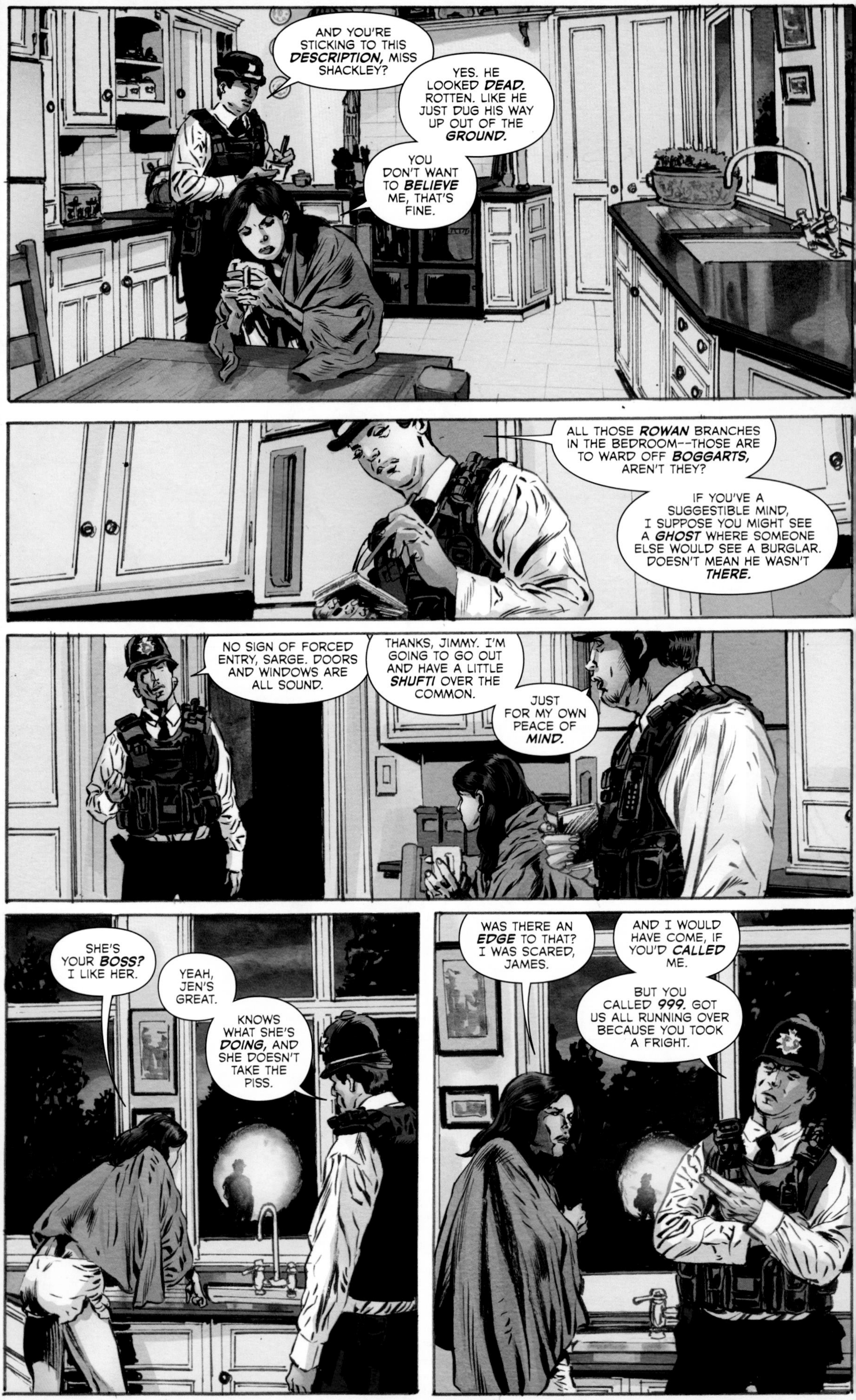
AND YOU'RE STICKING TO THIS DESCRIPTION, MISS SHACKLEY?
YES. HE LOOKED DEAD. ROTTEN. LIKE HE JUST DUG HIS WAY UP OUT OF THE GROUND.
YOU DON'T WANT TO BELIEVE ME, THAT'S FINE.
ALL THOSE ROWAN BRANCHES IN THE BEDROOM--THOSE ARE TO WARD OFF BOGGARTS, AREN'T THEY?
IF YOU'VE A SUGGESTIBLE MIND, I SUPPOSE YOU MIGHT SEE A GHOST WHERE SOMEONE ELSE WOULD SEE A BURGLAR. DOESN'T MEAN HE WASN'T THERE.
NO SIGN OF FORCED ENTRY, SARGE. DOORS AND WINDOWS ARE ALL SOUND.
THANKS, JIMMY. I'M GOING TO GO OUT AND HAVE A LITTLE SHUFTI OVER THE COMMON.
JUST FOR MY OWN PEACE OF MIND.
SHE'S YOUR BOSS? I LIKE HER.
YEAH, JEN'S GREAT.
KNOWS WHAT SHE'S DOING, AND SHE DOESN'T TAKE THE PISS.
WAS THERE AN EDGE TO THAT? I WAS SCARED, JAMES.
AND I WOULD HAVE COME, IF YOU'D CALLED ME.
BUT YOU CALLED 999. GOT US ALL RUNNING OVER BECAUSE YOU TOOK A FRIGHT.

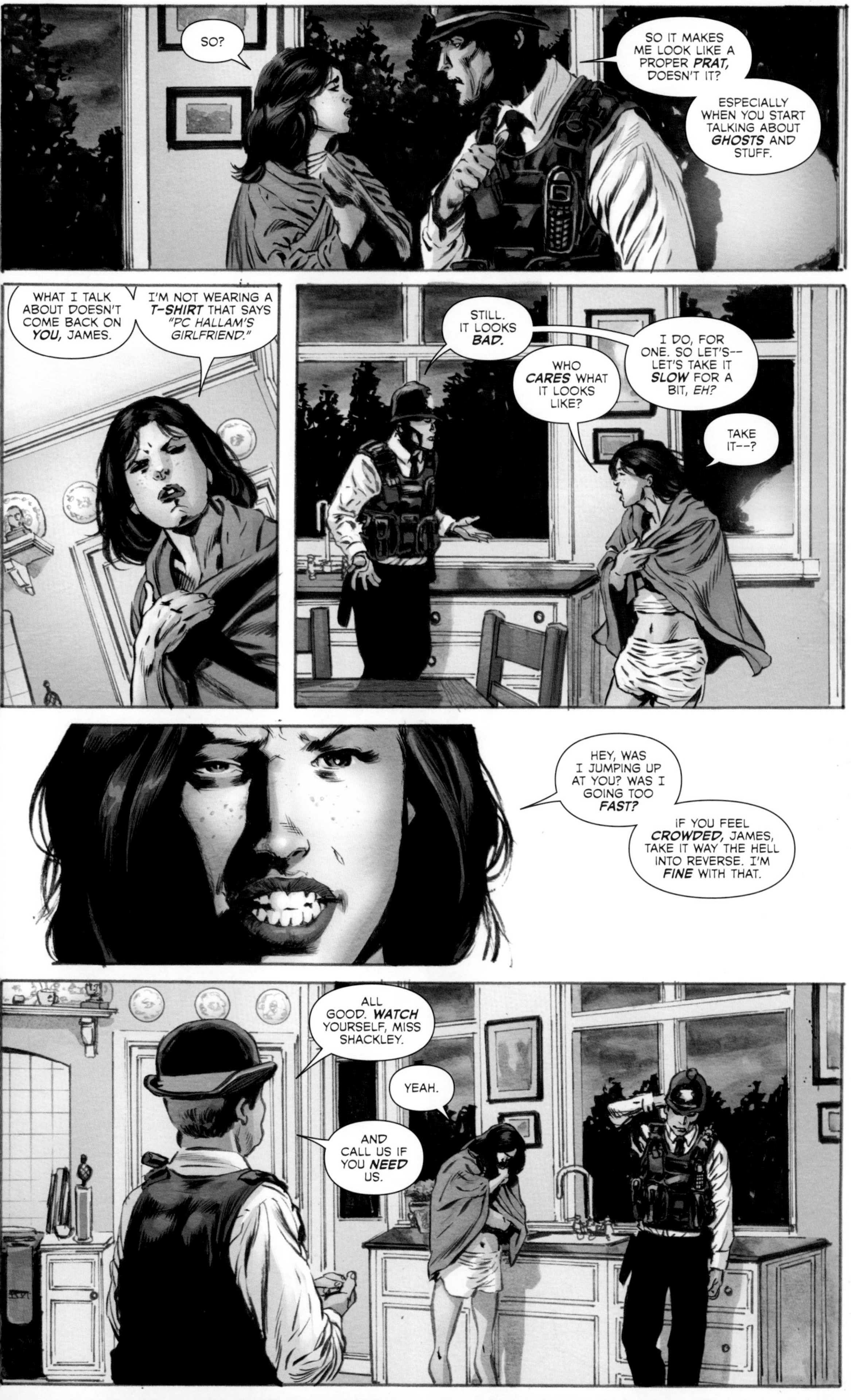
SO?
SO IT MAKES ME LOOK LIKE A PROPER PRAT, DOESN'T IT?
ESPECIALLY WHEN YOU START TALKING ABOUT GHOSTS AND STUFF.
WHAT I TALK ABOUT DOESN'T COME BACK ON YOU, JAMES.
I'M NOT WEARING A T-SHIRT THAT SAYS "PC HALLAM'S GIRLFRIEND."
STILL. IT LOOKS BAD.
WHO CARES WHAT IT LOOKS LIKE?
I DO, FOR ONE. SO LET'S-- LET'S TAKE IT SLOW FOR A BIT, EH?
TAKE IT--?
HEY, WAS I JUMPING UP AT YOU? WAS I GOING TOO FAST?
IF YOU FEEL CROWDED, JAMES, TAKE IT WAY THE HELL INTO REVERSE. I'M FINE WITH THAT.
ALL GOOD. WATCH YOURSELF, MISS SHACKLEY.
YEAH.
AND CALL US IF YOU NEED US.

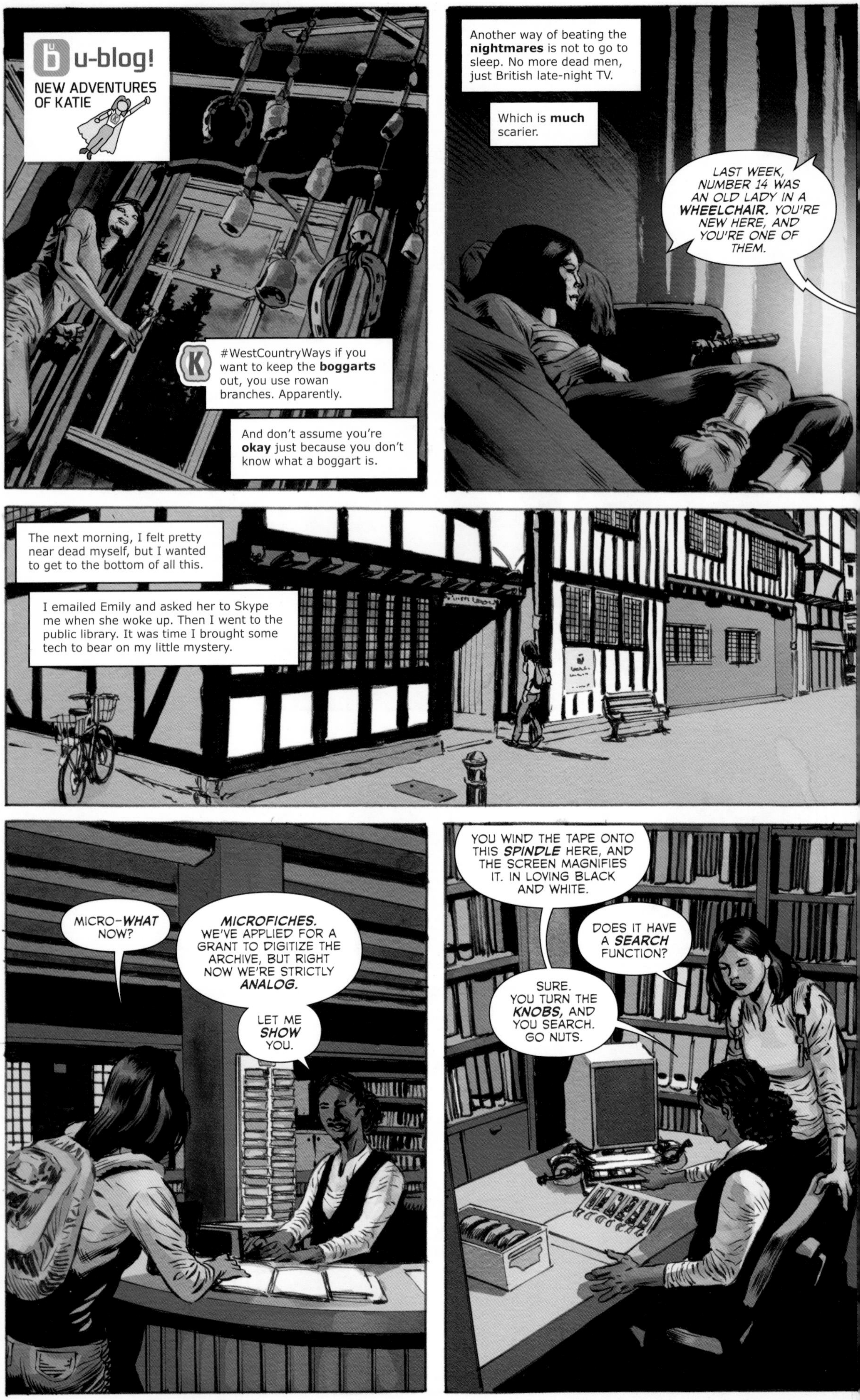
u-blog!
NEW ADVENTURES OF KATIE
#WestCountryWays if you want to keep the **boggarts** out, you use rowan branches. Apparently.
And don't assume you're **okay** just because you don't know what a boggart is.
Another way of beating the **nightmares** is not to go to sleep. No more dead men, just British late-night TV.
Which is **much** scarier.
LAST WEEK, NUMBER 14 WAS AN OLD LADY IN A **WHEELCHAIR.** YOU'RE NEW HERE, AND YOU'RE ONE OF THEM.
The next morning, I felt pretty near dead myself, but I wanted to get to the bottom of all this.
I emailed Emily and asked her to Skype me when she woke up. Then I went to the public library. It was time I brought some tech to bear on my little mystery.
MICRO-*WHAT* NOW?
MICROFICHES. WE'VE APPLIED FOR A GRANT TO DIGITIZE THE ARCHIVE, BUT RIGHT NOW WE'RE STRICTLY *ANALOG.*
LET ME *SHOW* YOU.
YOU WIND THE TAPE ONTO THIS *SPINDLE* HERE, AND THE SCREEN MAGNIFIES IT. IN LOVING BLACK AND WHITE.
DOES IT HAVE A *SEARCH* FUNCTION?
SURE. YOU TURN THE *KNOBS,* AND YOU SEARCH. GO NUTS.

K: And I pretty nearly did. News stories by the yard. Then by the mile.

It was all there. The attacks on the Coles's family dogs.

The car crash that killed Emily's mom and dad.

And--

--something else.

OH MY GOD!

Emily has a sister.

HERALD

Tragedy strikes local family - two daughters attacked

Savage attack on girls 10 and 6.

Tragedy struck a local family today as their two daughters were savagely attacked by an unknown assailant.

10-year-old Emily Coles and her younger sister Margaret (6) were playing in the garden of the family house yesterday when a stranger vaulted the fence and physically assaulted them.

The 6-year-old was beaten about the head with a blunt instrument, believed to be an ornamental bootscraper in the shape of a sausage dog, which was missing from the crime scene. When the older sister tried to intervene she was thrown aside like a rag doll, sustaining a sprained

shoulder and extensive bruising to her face and upper body.

The Coles family have lived at Rowans Rise for more than twenty years, but their tenure there has been repeatedly marred by violence. Three dogs belonging to the family were killed in separate incidents some years ago. Police have refused to rule out a link between those earlier attacks and the current tragedy.

"It's too early to speculate," detective lieutenant William Lamb of the local police told the Clarion today. "We are pursuing every avenue, but clearly it's possible that someone has been watching

this house--and targeting it--for a long time."

The brutal attack left both girls hospitalised, with the younger child reportedly in a critical condition. There was extensive fracturing to her skull, which in turn led to

intra-cranial bleeding. Staff at the Ellen Steepley Memorial Hospital say it is too early to tell whether she will make a full recovery.

The family have asked to be left alone in this trying time.

Em
and
dea

In at tinci
Pellentesq
odio, ferr
fringilla r
tellus. Se
maximus
massa se
ante. Sed
massa. U
hendrerit
rutrum p
id. Maece
sit amet
auctor vit
odio.

Nunc tinc
lorem vit
Vivamus
iaculis fe
suscipit
quis lobo
lorem ut
luctus. C
erat eget
sagittis.
augue pu
ex ac, co

Or should that be **had**?

Villagers lay seige to plans

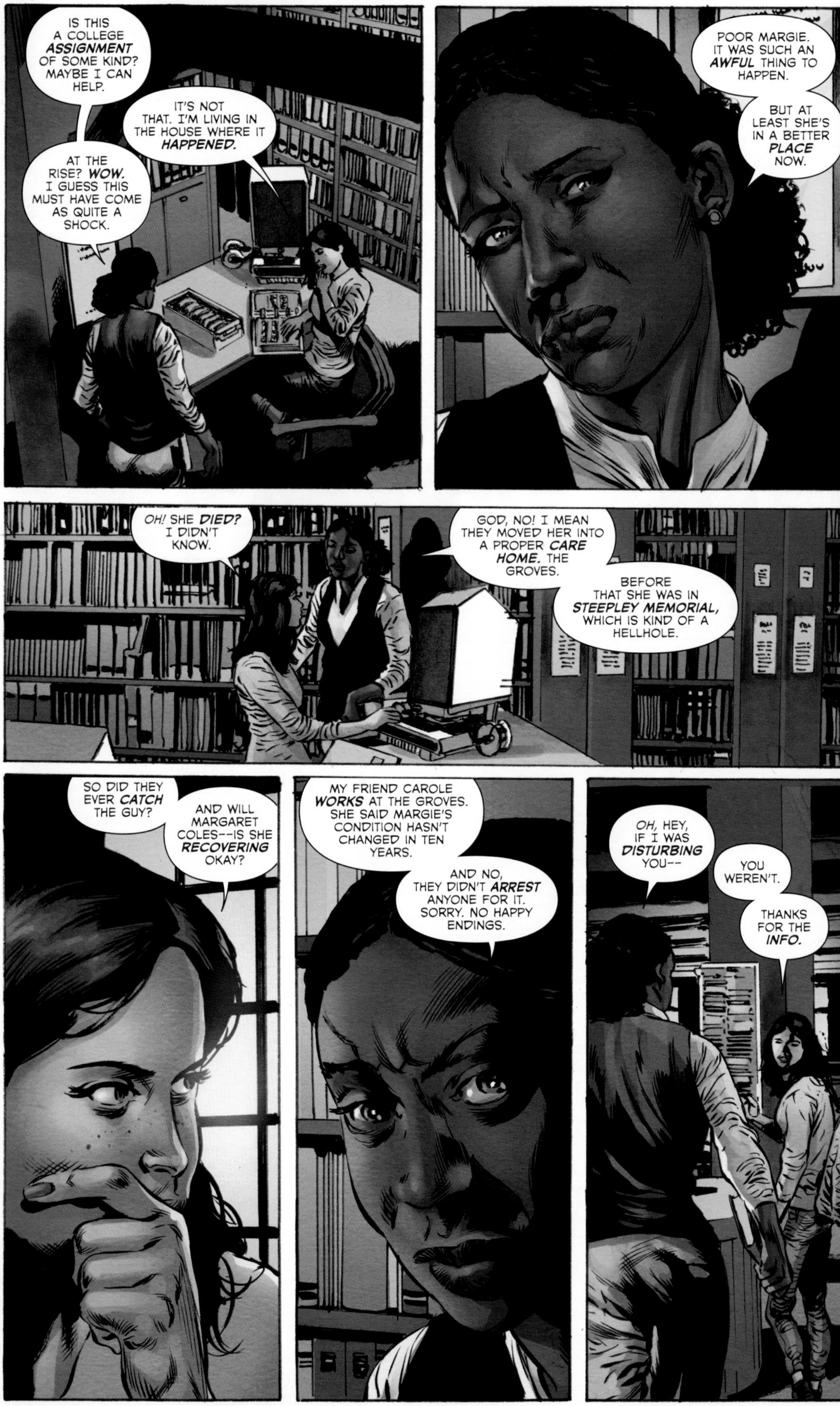

IS THIS A COLLEGE ASSIGNMENT OF SOME KIND? MAYBE I CAN HELP.
IT'S NOT THAT. I'M LIVING IN THE HOUSE WHERE IT HAPPENED.
AT THE RISE? WOW. I GUESS THIS MUST HAVE COME AS QUITE A SHOCK.
POOR MARGIE. IT WAS SUCH AN AWFUL THING TO HAPPEN.
BUT AT LEAST SHE'S IN A BETTER PLACE NOW.
OH! SHE DIED? I DIDN'T KNOW.
GOD, NO! I MEAN THEY MOVED HER INTO A PROPER CARE HOME. THE GROVES.
BEFORE THAT SHE WAS IN STEEPLEY MEMORIAL, WHICH IS KIND OF A HELLHOLE.
SO DID THEY EVER CATCH THE GUY?
AND WILL MARGARET COLES--IS SHE RECOVERING OKAY?
MY FRIEND CAROLE WORKS AT THE GROVES. SHE SAID MARGIE'S CONDITION HASN'T CHANGED IN TEN YEARS.
AND NO, THEY DIDN'T ARREST ANYONE FOR IT. SORRY. NO HAPPY ENDINGS.
OH, HEY, IF I WAS DISTURBING YOU--
YOU WEREN'T.
THANKS FOR THE INFO.

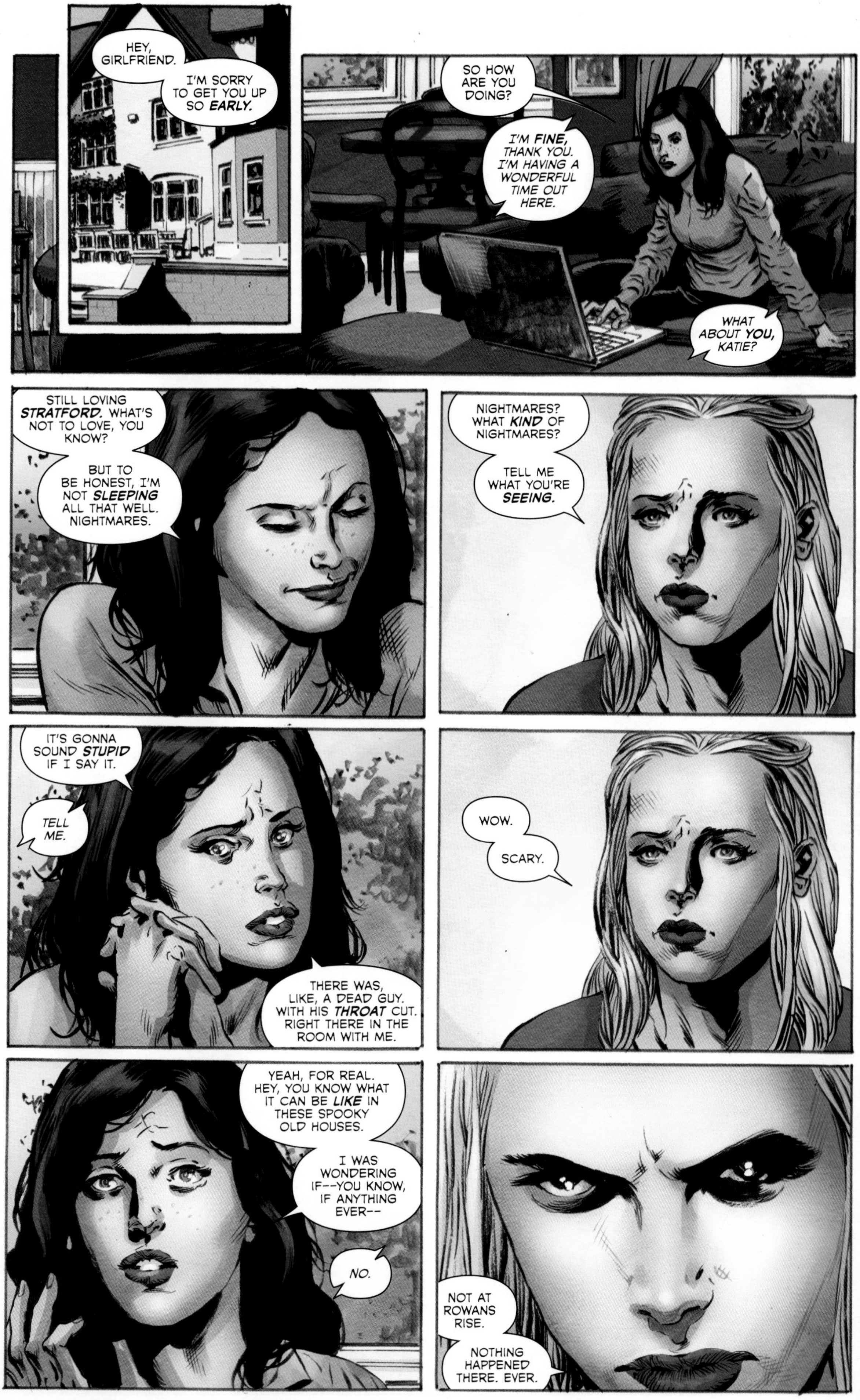
HEY, GIRLFRIEND.
I'M SORRY TO GET YOU UP SO EARLY.
SO HOW ARE YOU DOING?
I'M FINE, THANK YOU. I'M HAVING A WONDERFUL TIME OUT HERE.
WHAT ABOUT YOU, KATIE?
STILL LOVING STRATFORD. WHAT'S NOT TO LOVE, YOU KNOW?
BUT TO BE HONEST, I'M NOT SLEEPING ALL THAT WELL. NIGHTMARES.
NIGHTMARES? WHAT KIND OF NIGHTMARES?
TELL ME WHAT YOU'RE SEEING.
IT'S GONNA SOUND STUPID IF I SAY IT.
TELL ME.
THERE WAS, LIKE, A DEAD GUY. WITH HIS THROAT CUT. RIGHT THERE IN THE ROOM WITH ME.
WOW.
SCARY.
YEAH, FOR REAL. HEY, YOU KNOW WHAT IT CAN BE LIKE IN THESE SPOOKY OLD HOUSES.
I WAS WONDERING IF--YOU KNOW, IF ANYTHING EVER--
NO.
NOT AT ROWANS RISE.
NOTHING HAPPENED THERE. EVER.

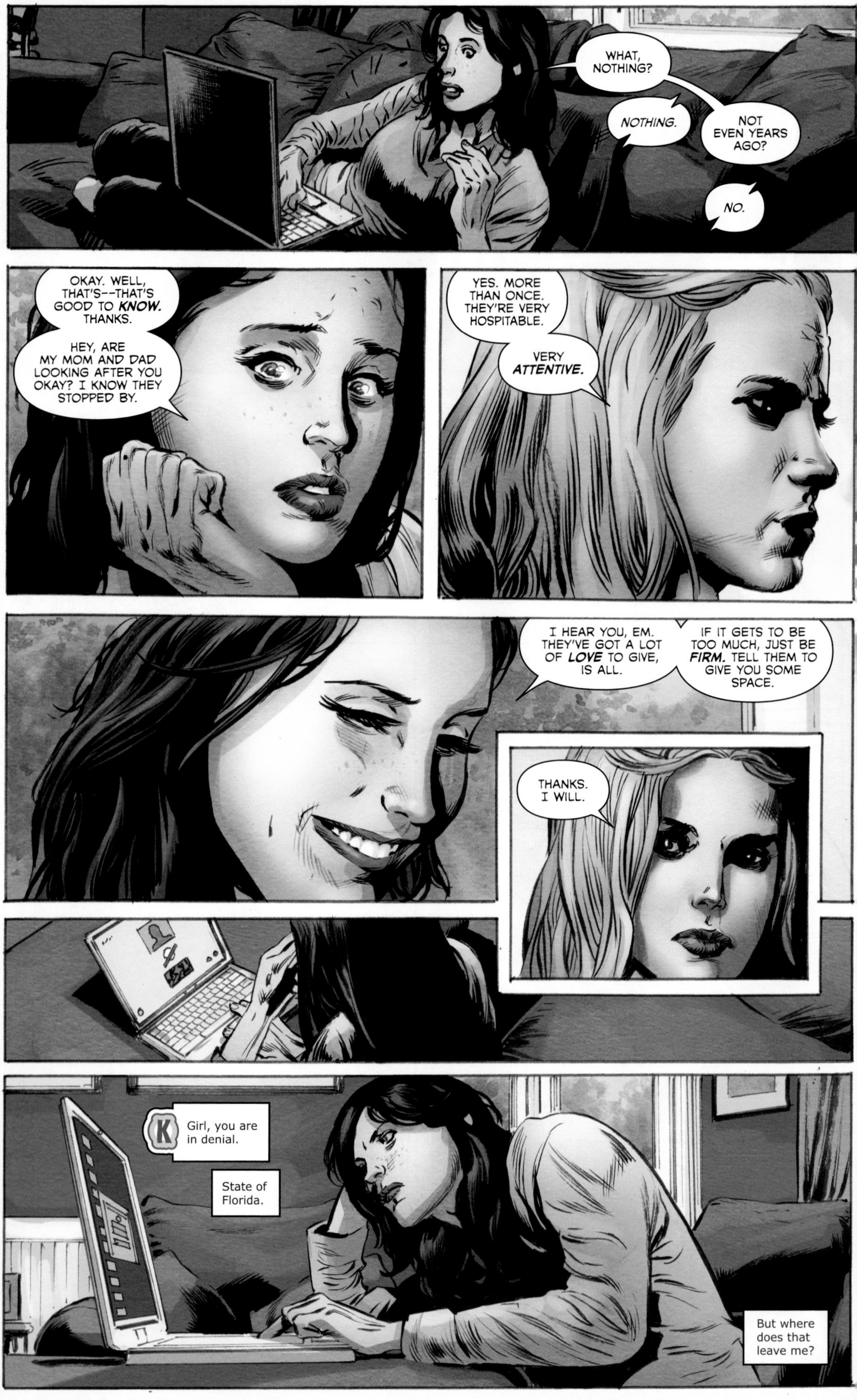
WHAT, NOTHING?
NOTHING.
NOT EVEN YEARS AGO?
NO.
OKAY. WELL, THAT'S--THAT'S GOOD TO KNOW. THANKS.
HEY, ARE MY MOM AND DAD LOOKING AFTER YOU OKAY? I KNOW THEY STOPPED BY.
YES. MORE THAN ONCE. THEY'RE VERY HOSPITABLE.
VERY ATTENTIVE.
I HEAR YOU, EM. THEY'VE GOT A LOT OF LOVE TO GIVE, IS ALL.
IF IT GETS TO BE TOO MUCH, JUST BE FIRM. TELL THEM TO GIVE YOU SOME SPACE.
THANKS. I WILL.
K
Girl, you are in denial.
State of Florida.
But where does that leave me?

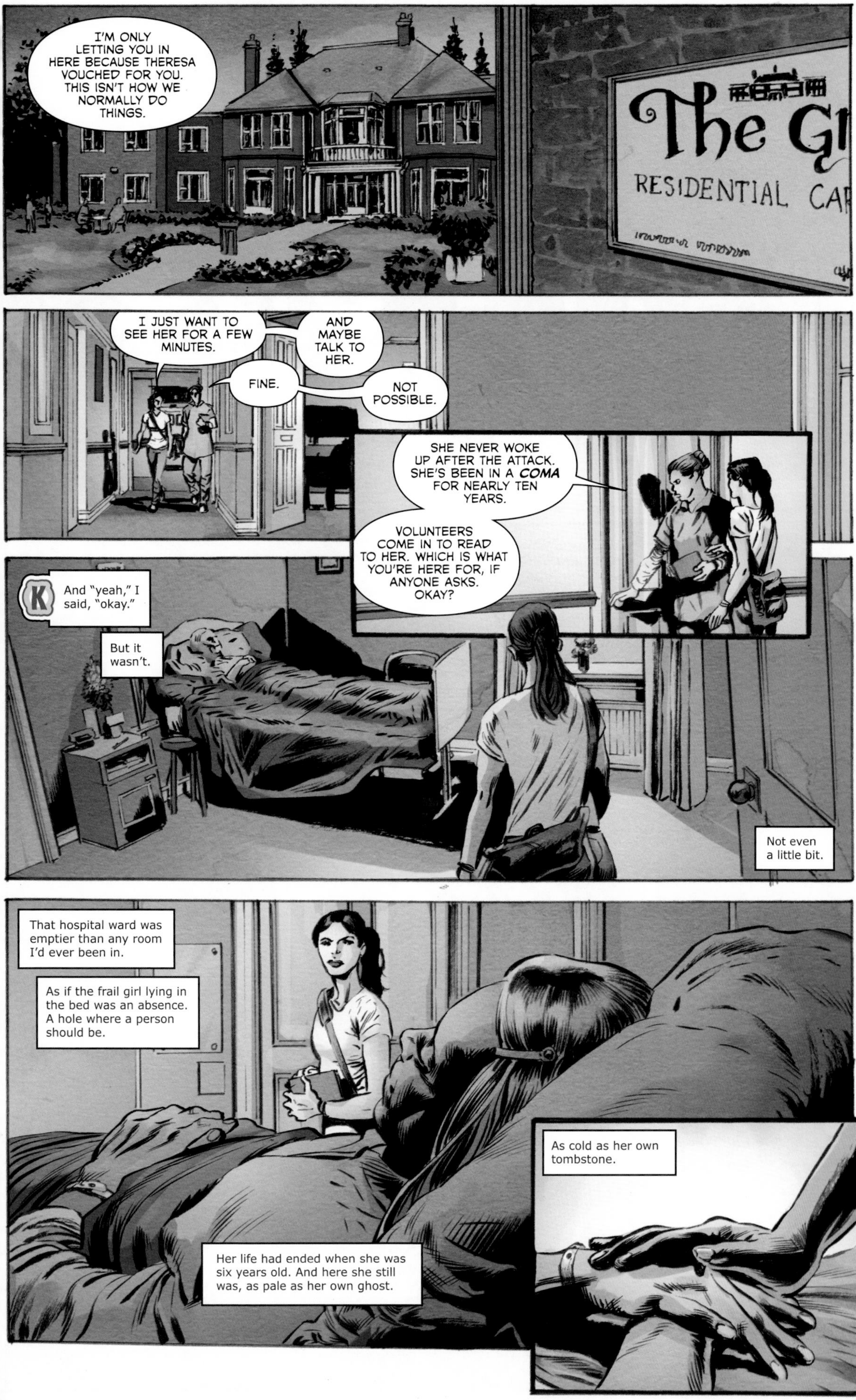

I'M ONLY LETTING YOU IN HERE BECAUSE THERESA VOUCHED FOR YOU. THIS ISN'T HOW WE NORMALLY DO THINGS.
The Gr
RESIDENTIAL CAR
I JUST WANT TO SEE HER FOR A FEW MINUTES.
AND MAYBE TALK TO HER.
FINE.
NOT POSSIBLE.
SHE NEVER WOKE UP AFTER THE ATTACK. SHE'S BEEN IN A *COMA* FOR NEARLY TEN YEARS.
VOLUNTEERS COME IN TO READ TO HER. WHICH IS WHAT YOU'RE HERE FOR, IF ANYONE ASKS. OKAY?
And "yeah," I said, "okay."
But it wasn't.
Not even a little bit.
That hospital ward was emptier than any room I'd ever been in.
As if the frail girl lying in the bed was an absence. A hole where a person should be.
Her life had ended when she was six years old. And here she still was, as pale as her own ghost.
As cold as her own tombstone.

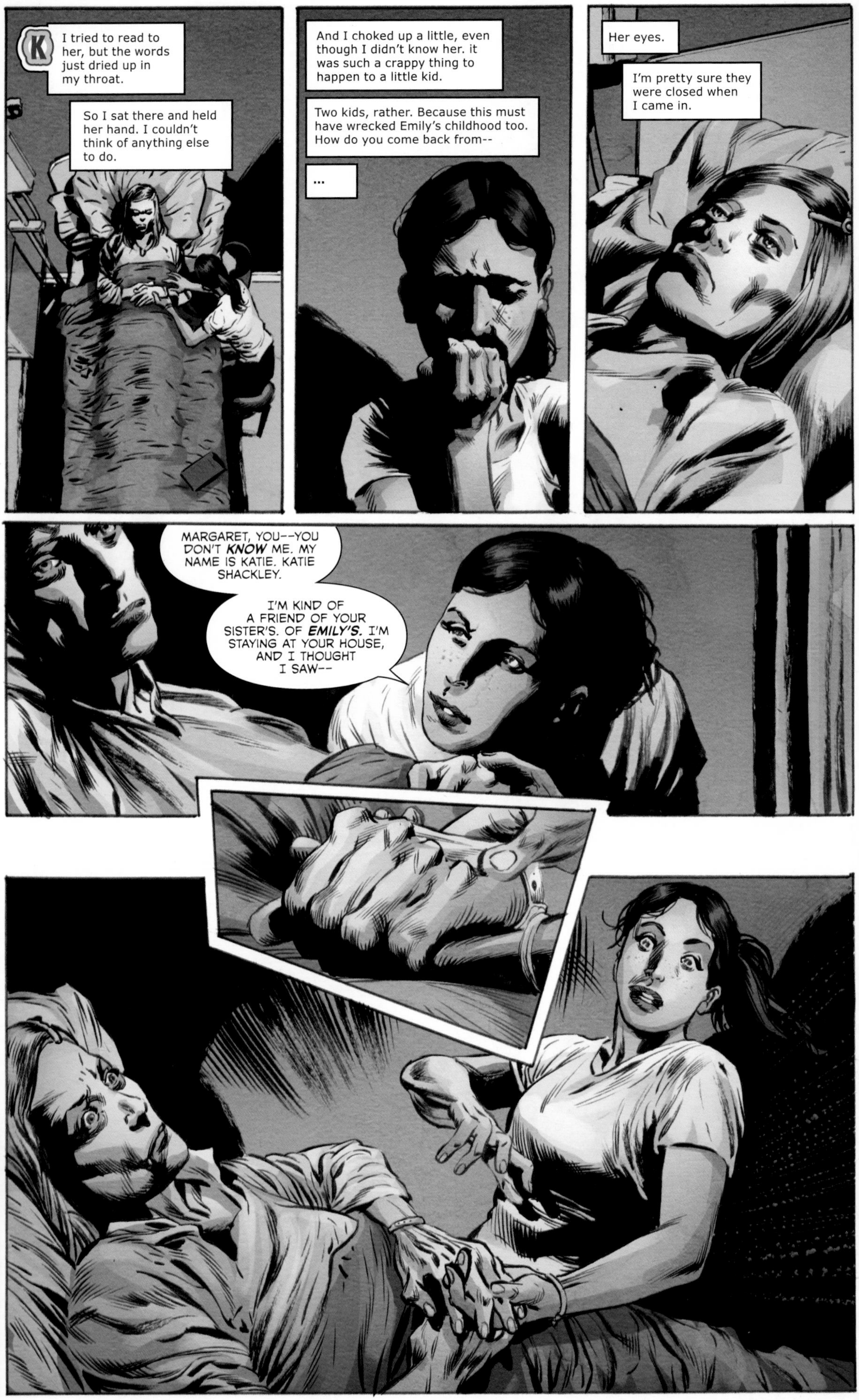
K
I tried to read to her, but the words just dried up in my throat.
So I sat there and held her hand. I couldn't think of anything else to do.
And I choked up a little, even though I didn't know her. it was such a crappy thing to happen to a little kid.
Two kids, rather. Because this must have wrecked Emily's childhood too. How do you come back from--
...
Her eyes.
I'm pretty sure they were closed when I came in.
MARGARET, YOU--YOU DON'T KNOW ME. MY NAME IS KATIE. KATIE SHACKLEY.
I'M KIND OF A FRIEND OF YOUR SISTER'S. OF EMILY'S. I'M STAYING AT YOUR HOUSE, AND I THOUGHT I SAW--

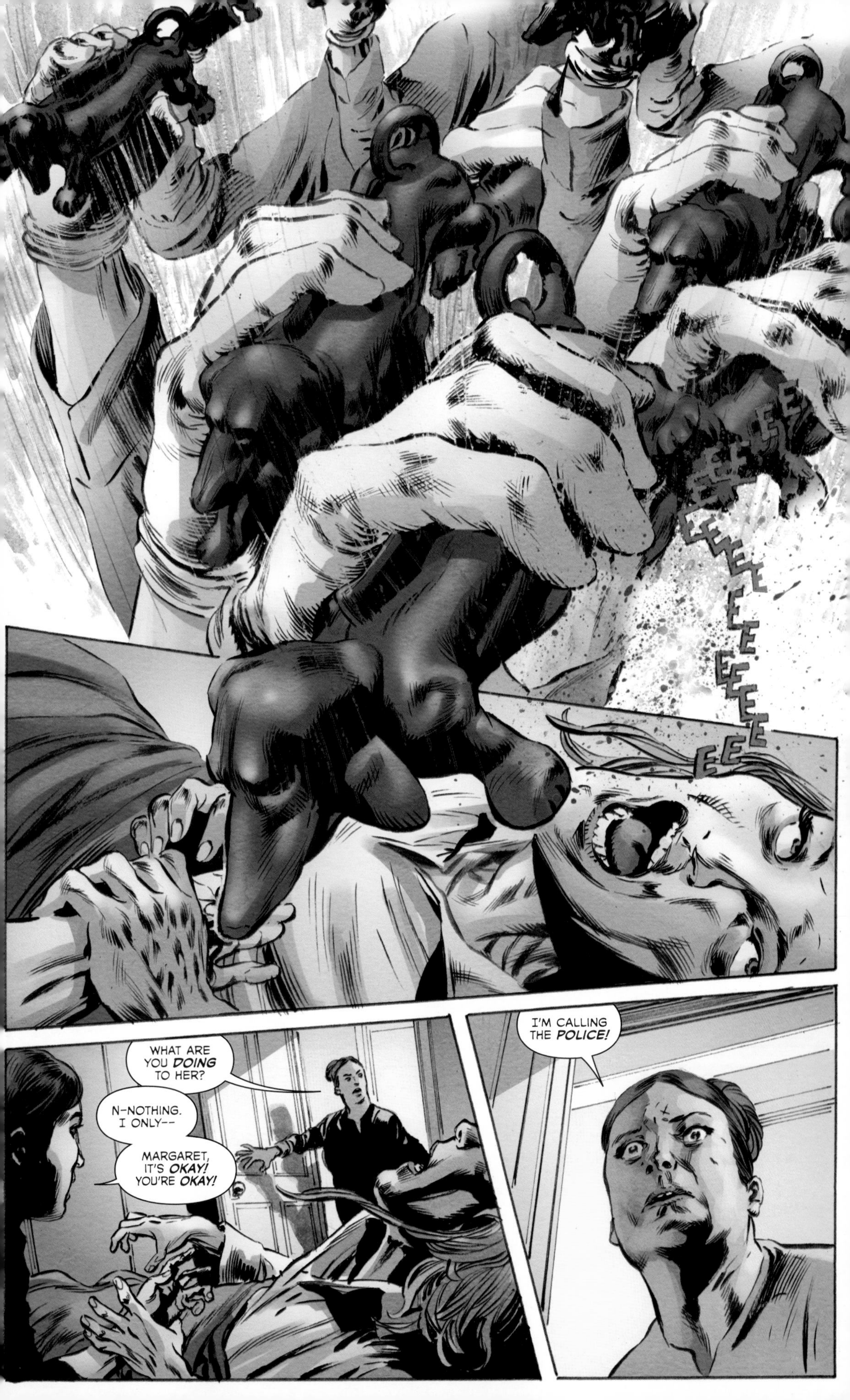
EEEEEEEEEEEEEEEE
WHAT ARE YOU DOING TO HER?
N-NOTHING. I ONLY--
MARGARET, IT'S OKAY! YOU'RE OKAY!
I'M CALLING THE POLICE!

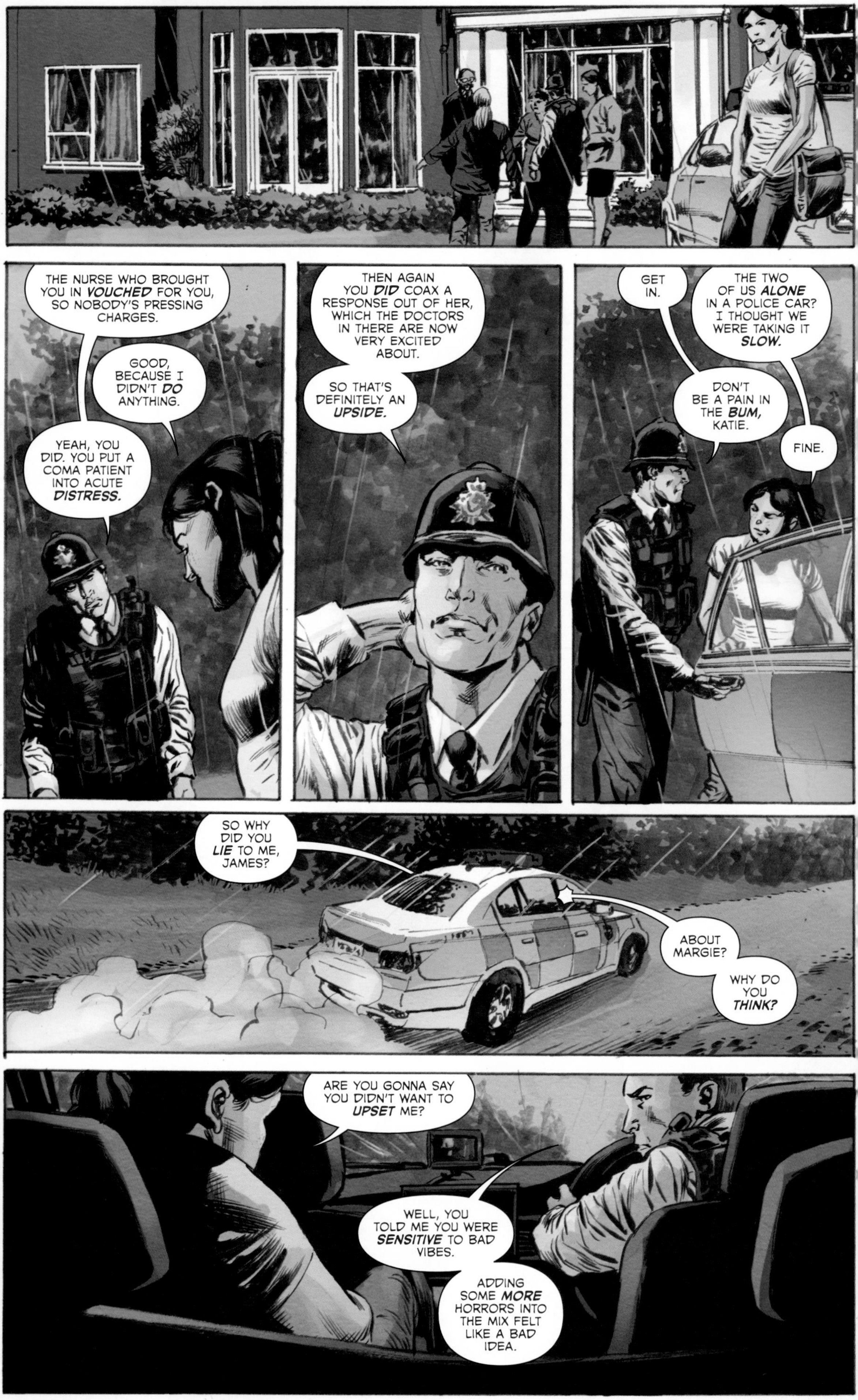
THE NURSE WHO BROUGHT YOU IN VOUCHED FOR YOU, SO NOBODY'S PRESSING CHARGES.
GOOD, BECAUSE I DIDN'T DO ANYTHING.
YEAH, YOU DID. YOU PUT A COMA PATIENT INTO ACUTE DISTRESS.
THEN AGAIN YOU DID COAX A RESPONSE OUT OF HER, WHICH THE DOCTORS IN THERE ARE NOW VERY EXCITED ABOUT.
SO THAT'S DEFINITELY AN UPSIDE.
GET IN.
THE TWO OF US ALONE IN A POLICE CAR? I THOUGHT WE WERE TAKING IT SLOW.
DON'T BE A PAIN IN THE BUM, KATIE.
FINE.
SO WHY DID YOU LIE TO ME, JAMES?
ABOUT MARGIE?
WHY DO YOU THINK?
ARE YOU GONNA SAY YOU DIDN'T WANT TO UPSET ME?
WELL, YOU TOLD ME YOU WERE SENSITIVE TO BAD VIBES.
ADDING SOME MORE HORRORS INTO THE MIX FELT LIKE A BAD IDEA.

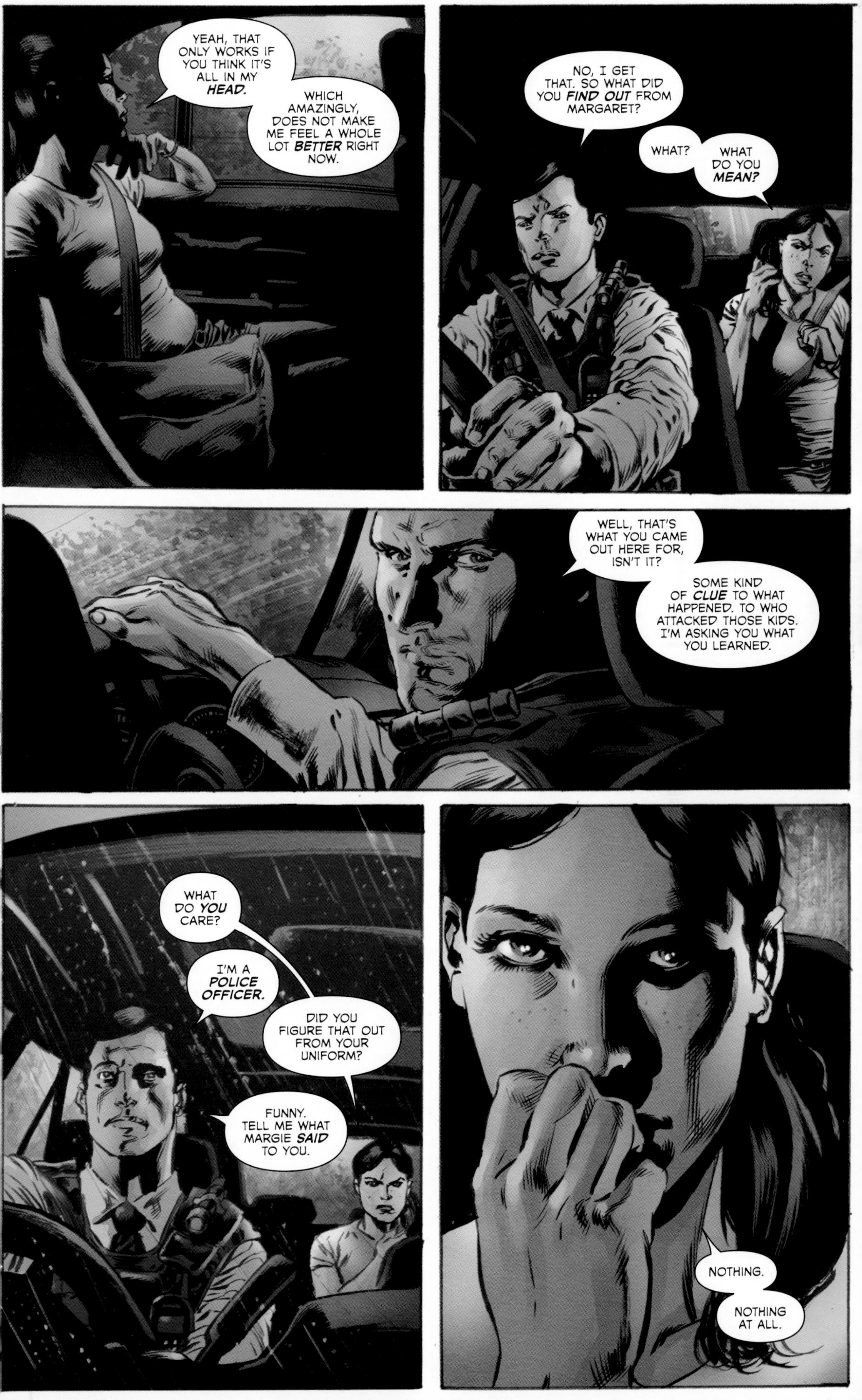
YEAH, THAT ONLY WORKS IF YOU THINK IT'S ALL IN MY **HEAD.**
WHICH AMAZINGLY, DOES NOT MAKE ME FEEL A WHOLE LOT **BETTER** RIGHT NOW.
NO, I GET THAT. SO WHAT DID YOU **FIND OUT** FROM MARGARET?
WHAT?
WHAT DO YOU **MEAN?**
WELL, THAT'S WHAT YOU CAME OUT HERE FOR, ISN'T IT?
SOME KIND OF **CLUE** TO WHAT HAPPENED. TO WHO ATTACKED THOSE KIDS. I'M ASKING YOU WHAT YOU LEARNED.
WHAT DO **YOU** CARE?
I'M A **POLICE OFFICER.**
DID YOU FIGURE THAT OUT FROM YOUR UNIFORM?
FUNNY. TELL ME WHAT MARGIE **SAID** TO YOU.
NOTHING.
NOTHING AT ALL.

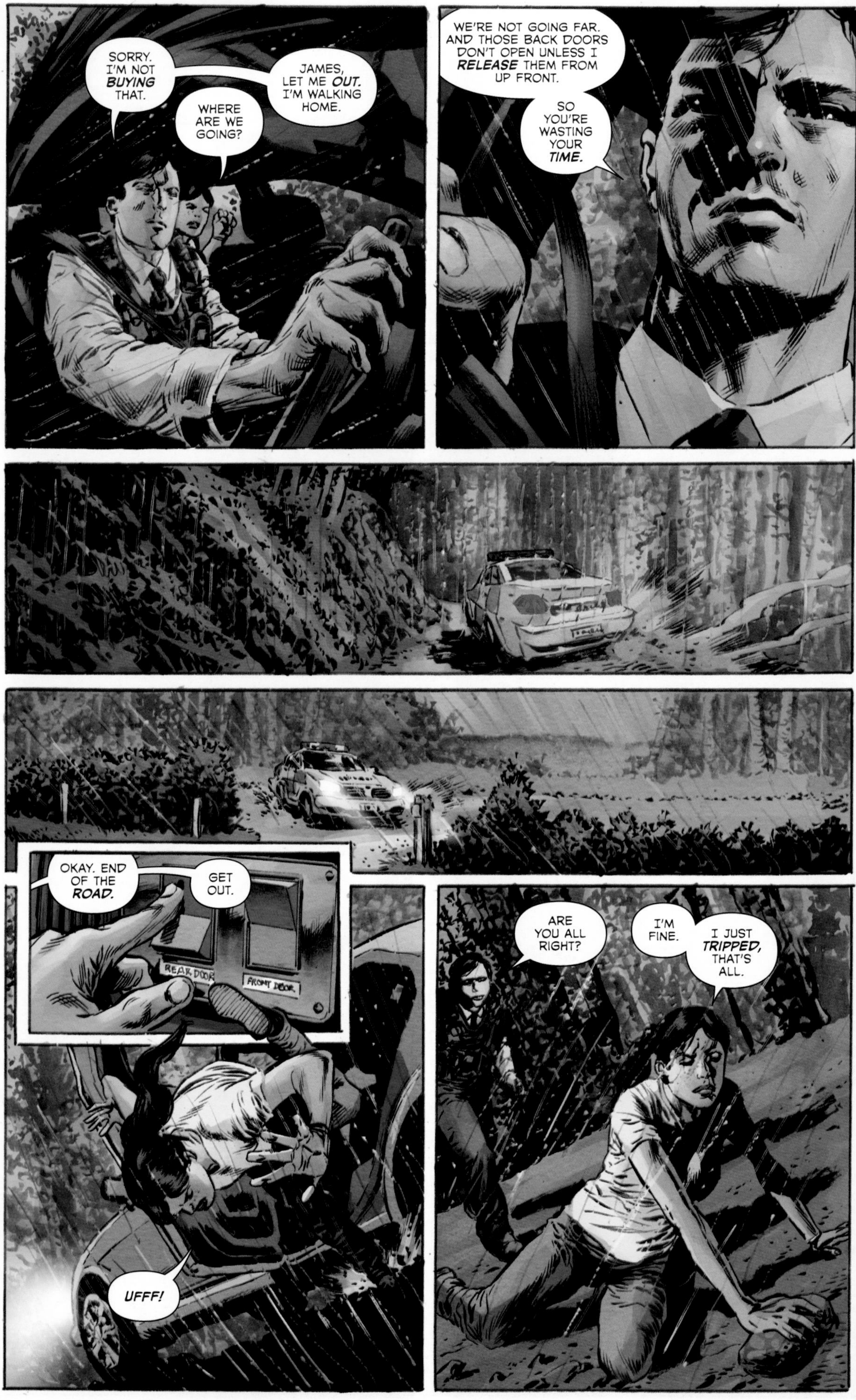
SORRY. I'M NOT **BUYING** THAT.
JAMES, LET ME **OUT.** I'M WALKING HOME.
WHERE ARE WE GOING?
WE'RE NOT GOING FAR. AND THOSE BACK DOORS DON'T OPEN UNLESS I **RELEASE** THEM FROM UP FRONT.
SO YOU'RE WASTING YOUR **TIME.**
OKAY. END OF THE **ROAD.**
GET OUT.
REAR DOOR
FRONT DOOR
UFFF!
ARE YOU ALL RIGHT?
I'M FINE.
I JUST **TRIPPED,** THAT'S ALL.

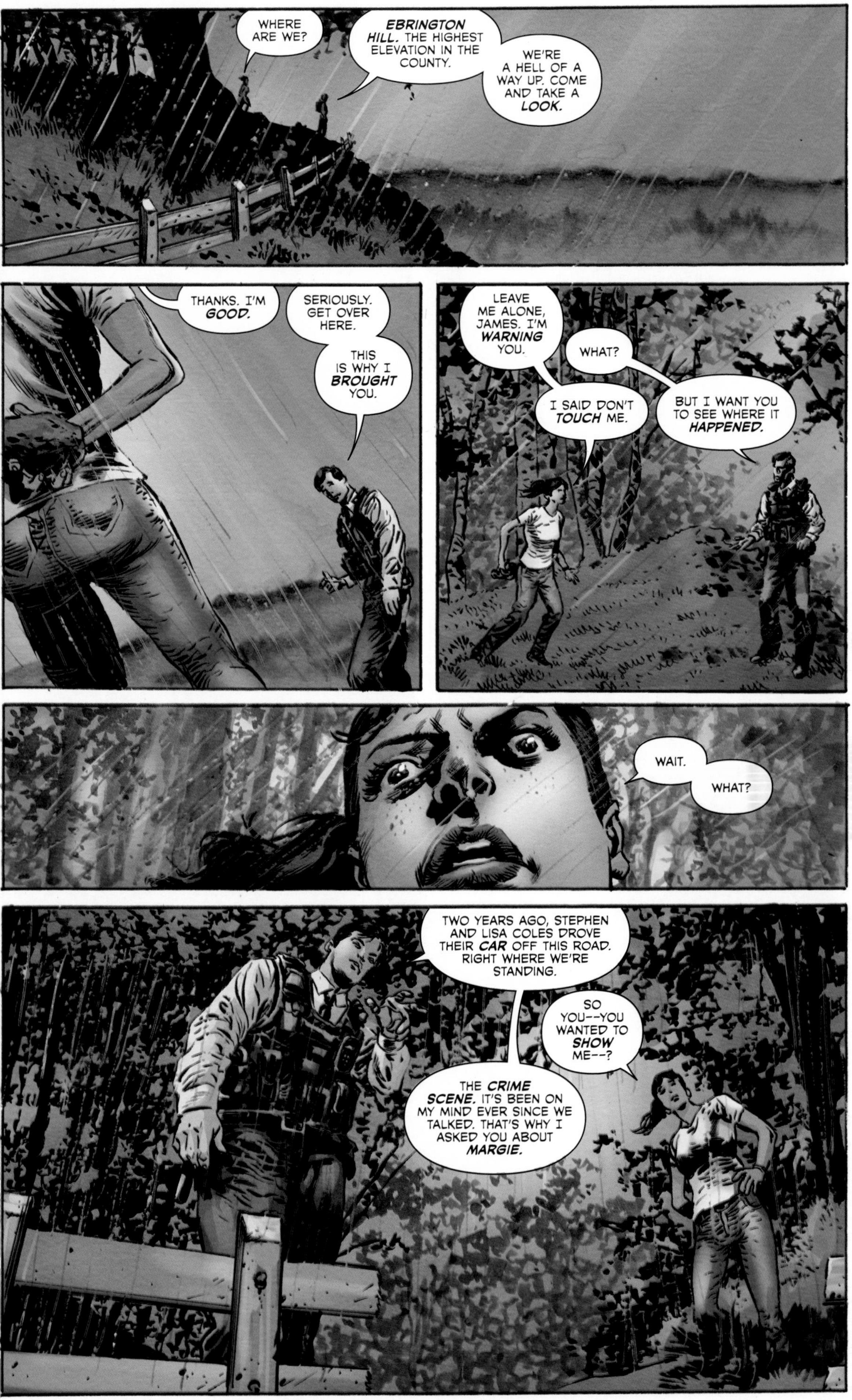
WHERE ARE WE?
EBRINGTON HILL. THE HIGHEST ELEVATION IN THE COUNTY.
WE'RE A HELL OF A WAY UP. COME AND TAKE A LOOK.
THANKS. I'M GOOD.
SERIOUSLY. GET OVER HERE.
THIS IS WHY I BROUGHT YOU.
LEAVE ME ALONE, JAMES. I'M WARNING YOU.
WHAT?
I SAID DON'T TOUCH ME.
BUT I WANT YOU TO SEE WHERE IT HAPPENED.
WAIT.
WHAT?
TWO YEARS AGO, STEPHEN AND LISA COLES DROVE THEIR CAR OFF THIS ROAD. RIGHT WHERE WE'RE STANDING.
SO YOU--YOU WANTED TO SHOW ME--?
THE CRIME SCENE. IT'S BEEN ON MY MIND EVER SINCE WE TALKED. THAT'S WHY I ASKED YOU ABOUT MARGIE.

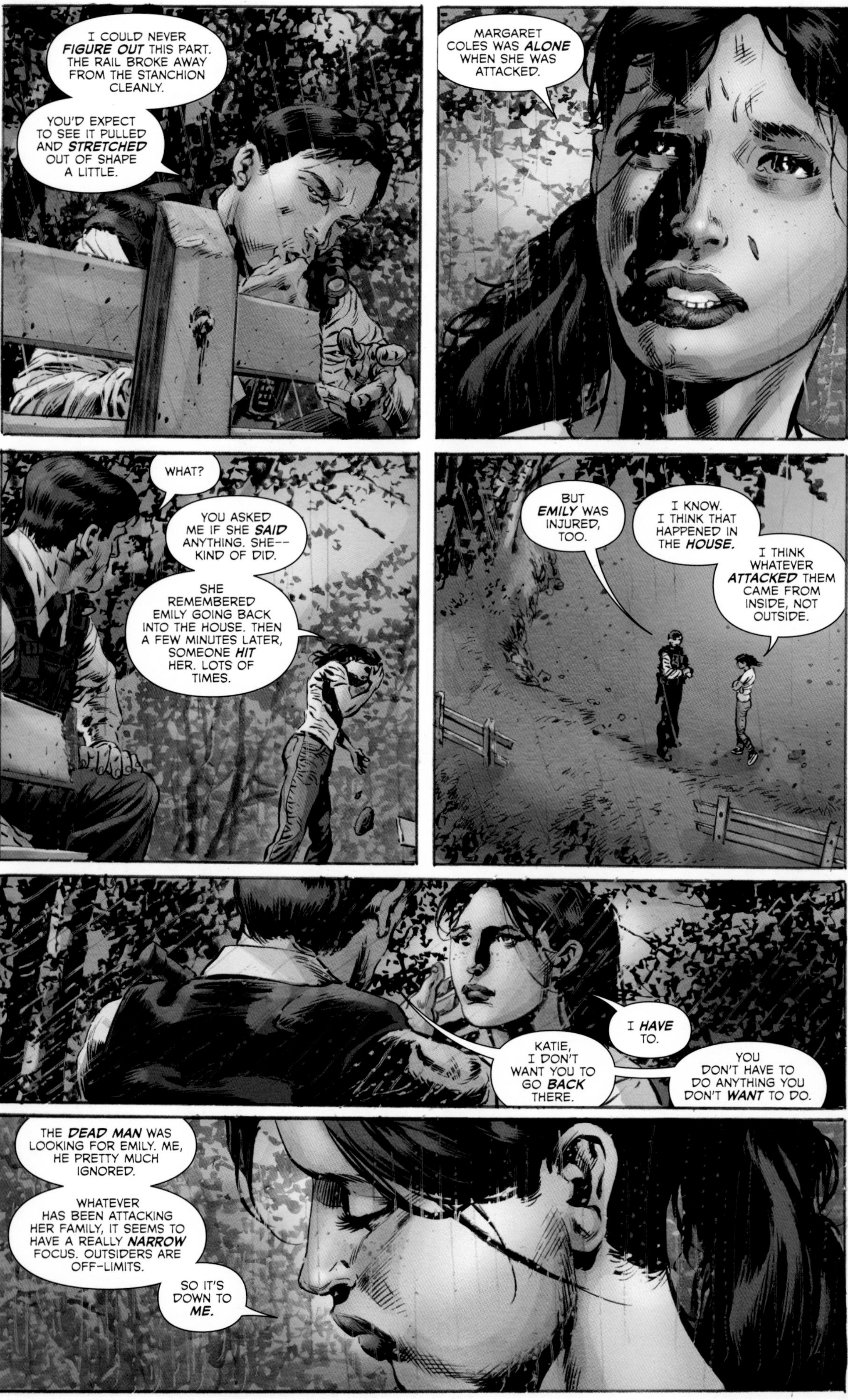
I COULD NEVER FIGURE OUT THIS PART. THE RAIL BROKE AWAY FROM THE STANCHION CLEANLY.
YOU'D EXPECT TO SEE IT PULLED AND STRETCHED OUT OF SHAPE A LITTLE.
MARGARET COLES WAS ALONE WHEN SHE WAS ATTACKED.
WHAT?
YOU ASKED ME IF SHE SAID ANYTHING. SHE-- KIND OF DID.
SHE REMEMBERED EMILY GOING BACK INTO THE HOUSE. THEN A FEW MINUTES LATER, SOMEONE HIT HER. LOTS OF TIMES.
BUT EMILY WAS INJURED, TOO.
I KNOW. I THINK THAT HAPPENED IN THE HOUSE.
I THINK WHATEVER ATTACKED THEM CAME FROM INSIDE, NOT OUTSIDE.
KATIE, I DON'T WANT YOU TO GO BACK THERE.
I HAVE TO.
YOU DON'T HAVE TO DO ANYTHING YOU DON'T WANT TO DO.
THE DEAD MAN WAS LOOKING FOR EMILY. ME, HE PRETTY MUCH IGNORED.
WHATEVER HAS BEEN ATTACKING HER FAMILY, IT SEEMS TO HAVE A REALLY NARROW FOCUS. OUTSIDERS ARE OFF-LIMITS.
SO IT'S DOWN TO ME.

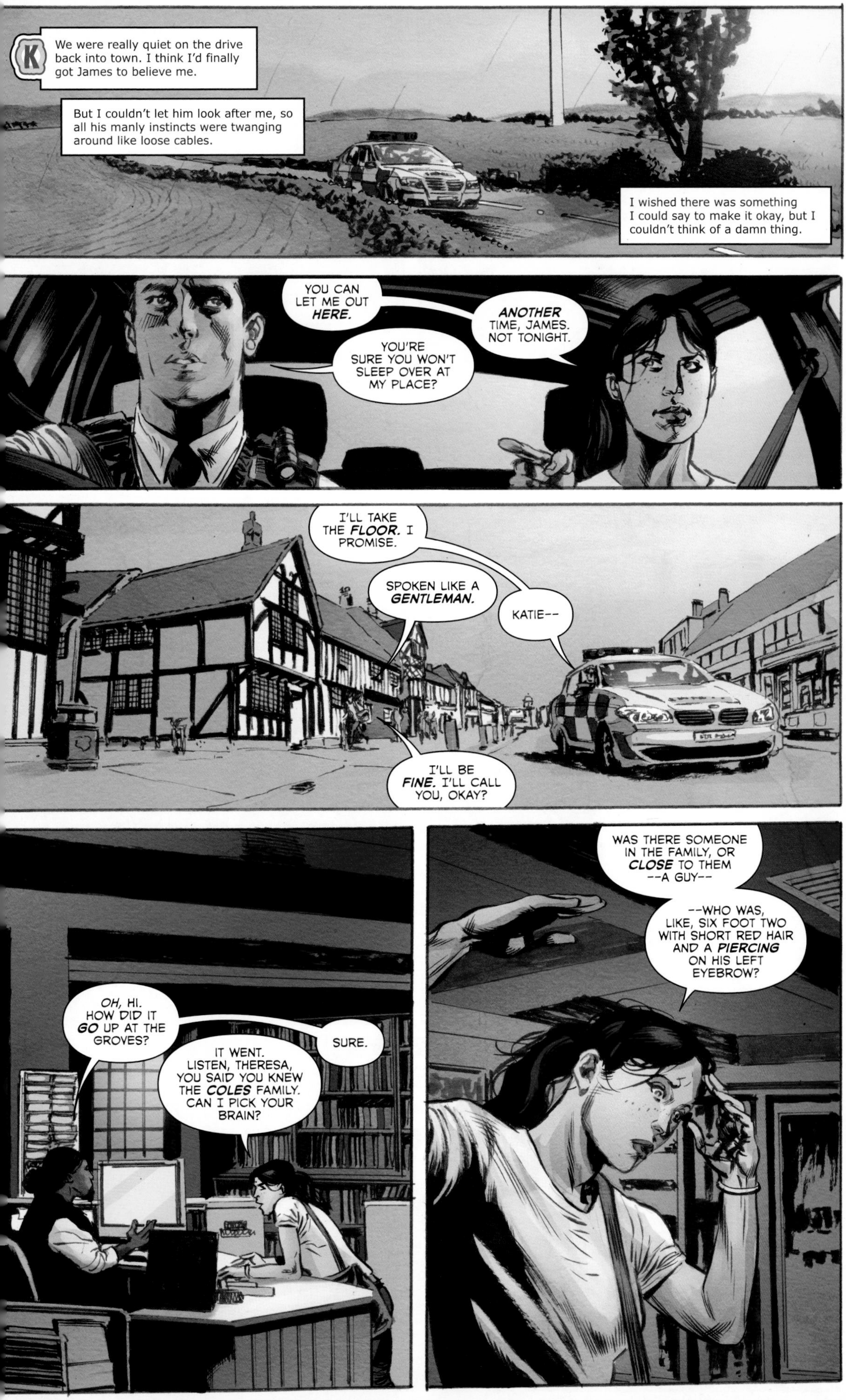

We were really quiet on the drive back into town. I think I'd finally got James to believe me.
But I couldn't let him look after me, so all his manly instincts were twanging around like loose cables.
I wished there was something I could say to make it okay, but I couldn't think of a damn thing.
YOU CAN LET ME OUT HERE.
YOU'RE SURE YOU WON'T SLEEP OVER AT MY PLACE?
ANOTHER TIME, JAMES. NOT TONIGHT.
I'LL TAKE THE FLOOR. I PROMISE.
SPOKEN LIKE A GENTLEMAN.
KATIE--
I'LL BE FINE. I'LL CALL YOU, OKAY?
OH, HI. HOW DID IT GO UP AT THE GROVES?
IT WENT. LISTEN, THERESA, YOU SAID YOU KNEW THE COLES FAMILY. CAN I PICK YOUR BRAIN?
SURE.
WAS THERE SOMEONE IN THE FAMILY, OR CLOSE TO THEM --A GUY--
--WHO WAS, LIKE, SIX FOOT TWO WITH SHORT RED HAIR AND A PIERCING ON HIS LEFT EYEBROW?

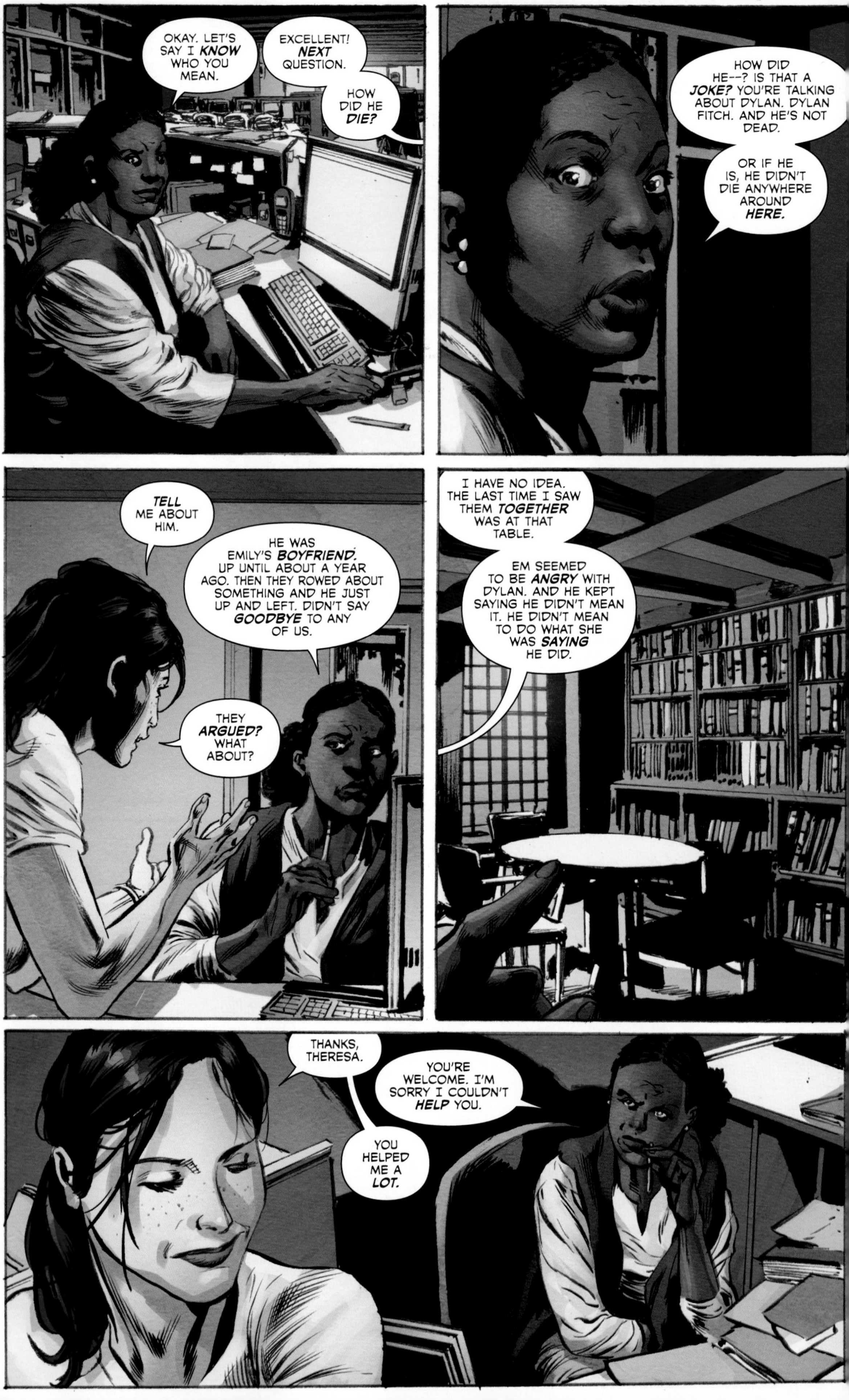
OKAY. LET'S SAY I KNOW WHO YOU MEAN.
EXCELLENT! NEXT QUESTION.
HOW DID HE DIE?
HOW DID HE--? IS THAT A JOKE? YOU'RE TALKING ABOUT DYLAN. DYLAN FITCH. AND HE'S NOT DEAD.
OR IF HE IS, HE DIDN'T DIE ANYWHERE AROUND HERE.
TELL ME ABOUT HIM.
HE WAS EMILY'S BOYFRIEND. UP UNTIL ABOUT A YEAR AGO. THEN THEY ROWED ABOUT SOMETHING AND HE JUST UP AND LEFT. DIDN'T SAY GOODBYE TO ANY OF US.
THEY ARGUED? WHAT ABOUT?
I HAVE NO IDEA. THE LAST TIME I SAW THEM TOGETHER WAS AT THAT TABLE.
EM SEEMED TO BE ANGRY WITH DYLAN. AND HE KEPT SAYING HE DIDN'T MEAN IT. HE DIDN'T MEAN TO DO WHAT SHE WAS SAYING HE DID.
THANKS, THERESA.
YOU'RE WELCOME. I'M SORRY I COULDN'T HELP YOU.
YOU HELPED ME A LOT.

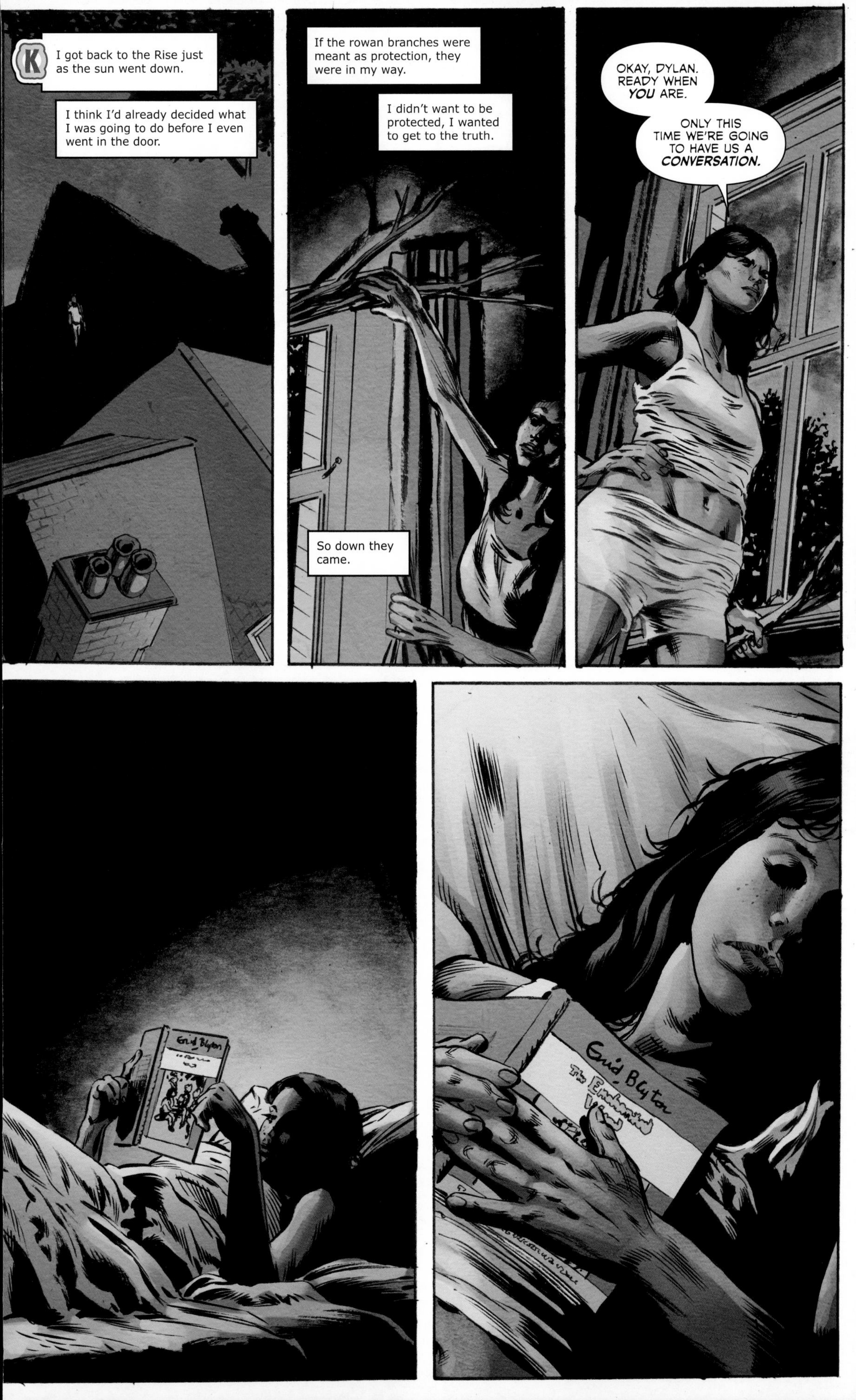
I got back to the Rise just as the sun went down.
I think I'd already decided what I was going to do before I even went in the door.
If the rowan branches were meant as protection, they were in my way.
I didn't want to be protected, I wanted to get to the truth.
So down they came.
OKAY, DYLAN. READY WHEN *YOU* ARE.
ONLY THIS TIME WE'RE GOING TO HAVE US A *CONVERSATION.*
Enid Blyton

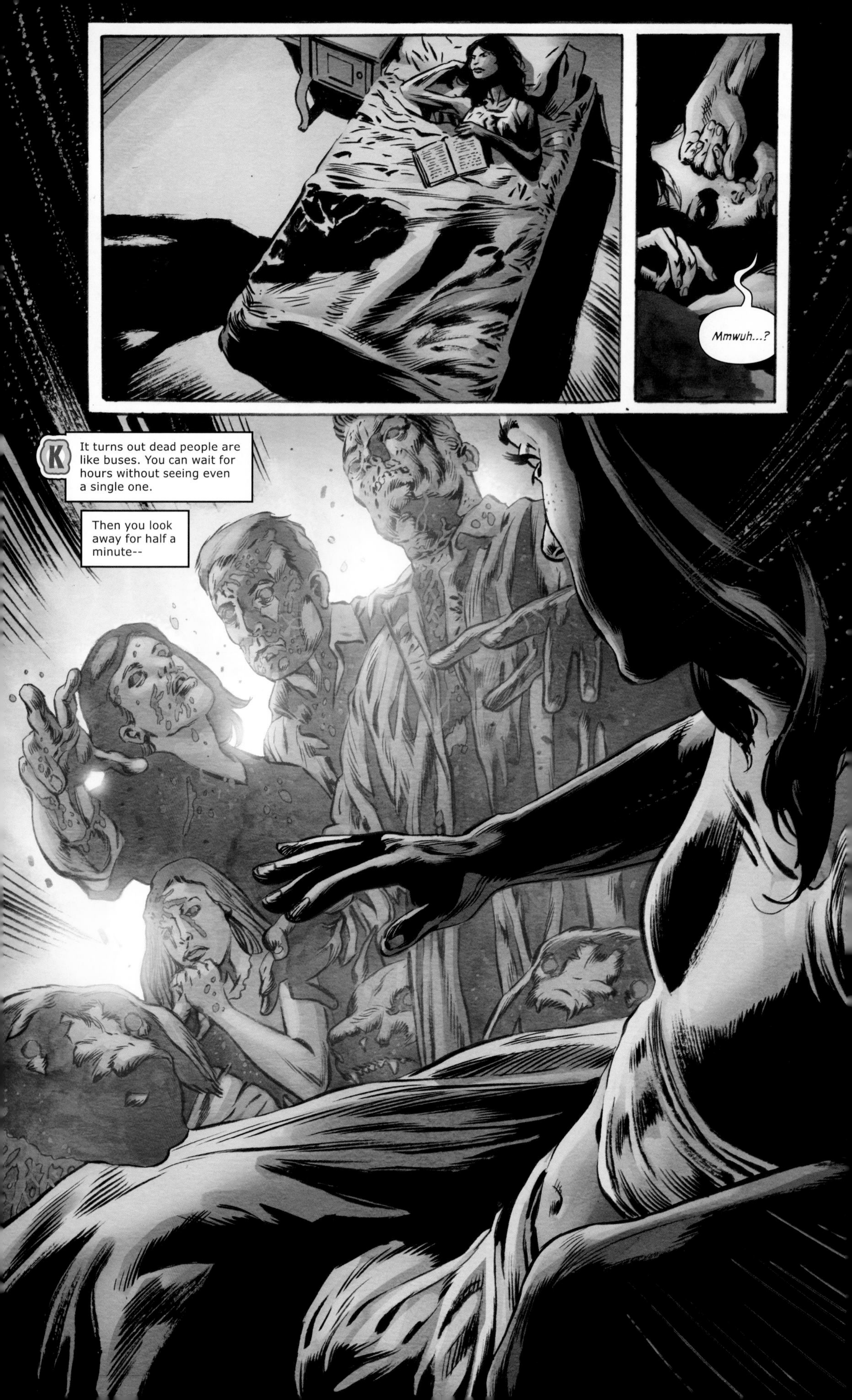
Mmwuh...?
It turns out dead people are like buses. You can wait for hours without seeing even a single one.
Then you look away for half a minute--

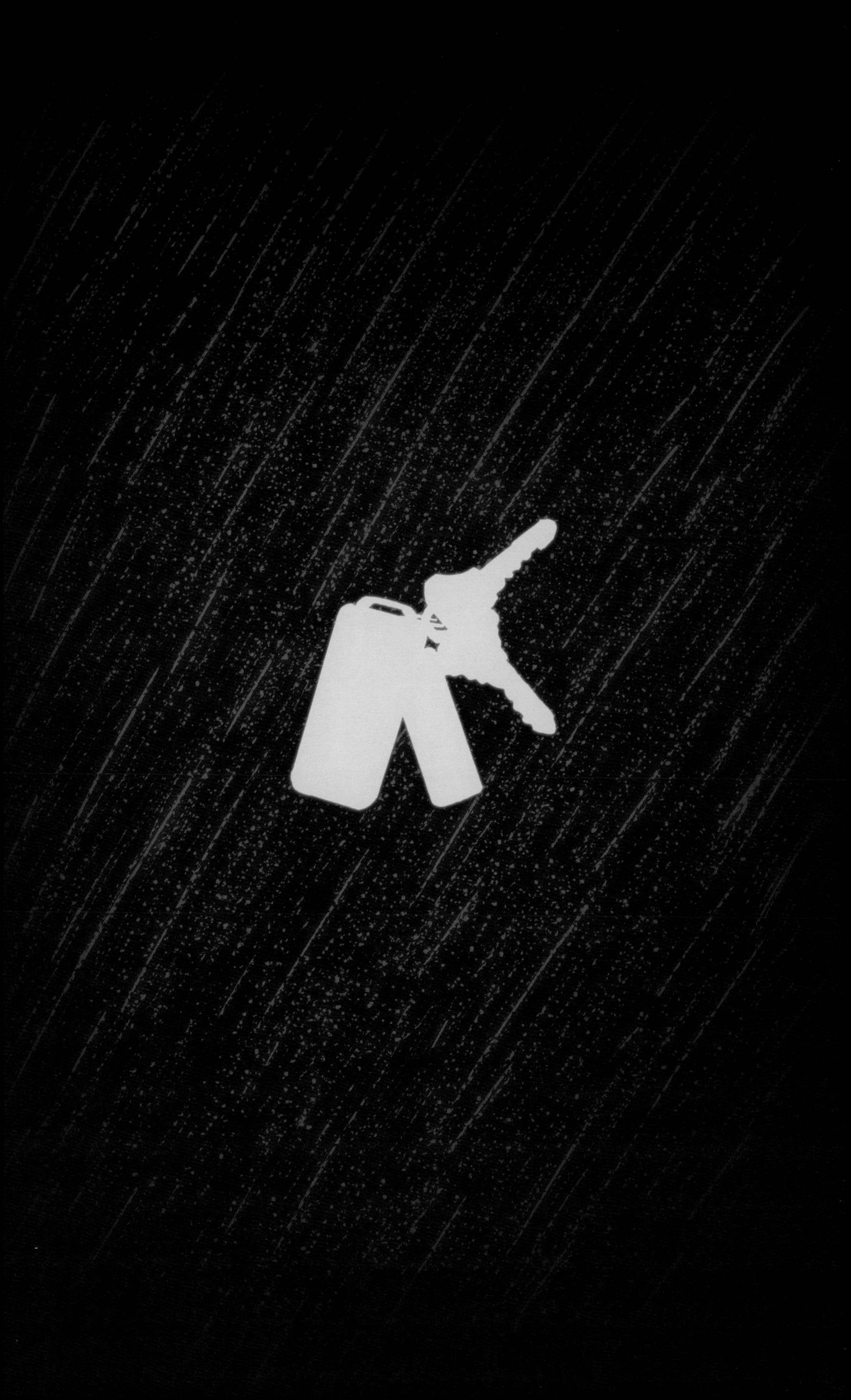

CHAPTER THREE

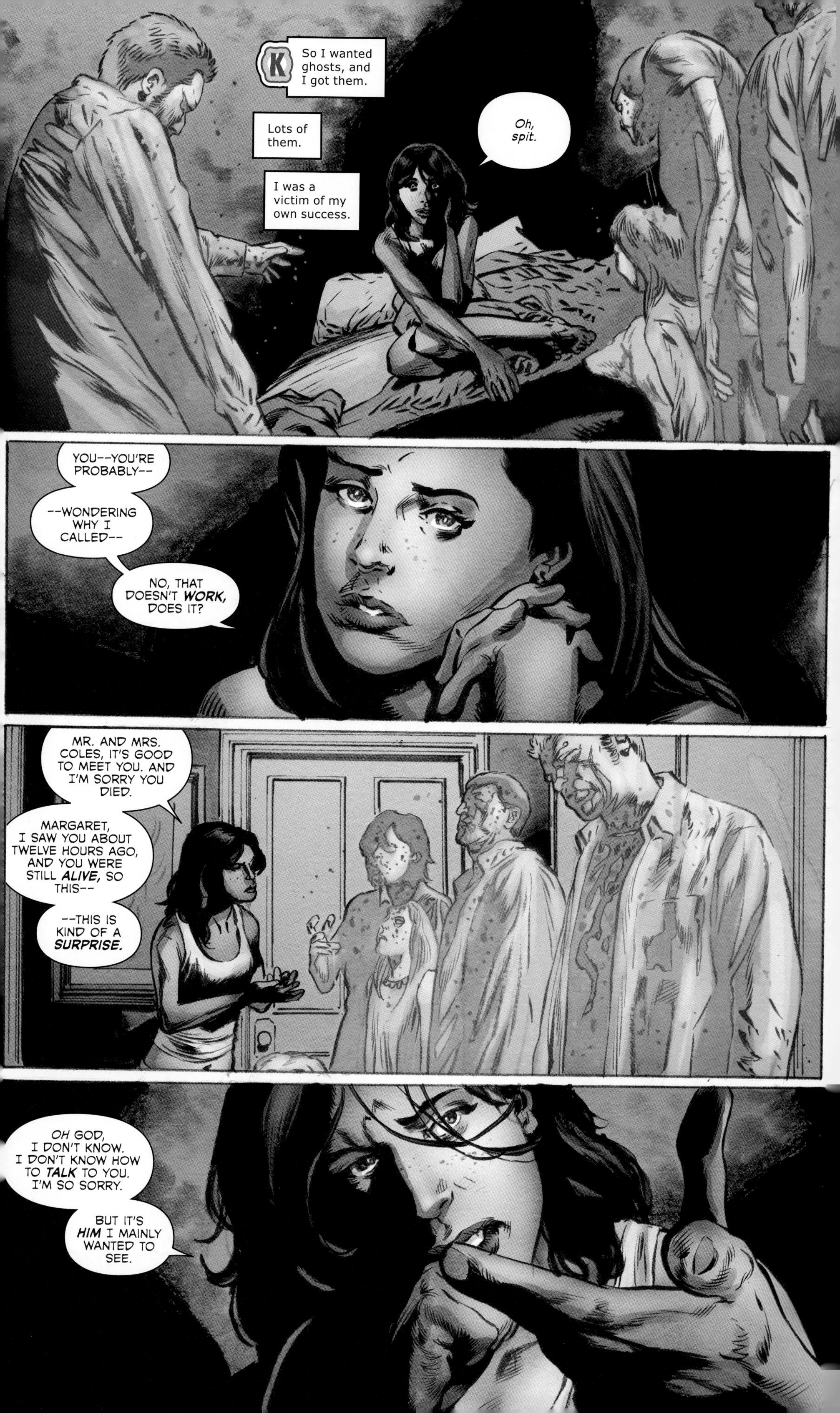
So I wanted ghosts, and I got them.
Lots of them.
I was a victim of my own success.
Oh, spit.
YOU--YOU'RE PROBABLY--
--WONDERING WHY I CALLED--
NO, THAT DOESN'T WORK, DOES IT?
MR. AND MRS. COLES, IT'S GOOD TO MEET YOU. AND I'M SORRY YOU DIED.
MARGARET, I SAW YOU ABOUT TWELVE HOURS AGO, AND YOU WERE STILL ALIVE, SO THIS--
--THIS IS KIND OF A SURPRISE.
OH GOD, I DON'T KNOW. I DON'T KNOW HOW TO TALK TO YOU. I'M SO SORRY.
BUT IT'S HIM I MAINLY WANTED TO SEE.

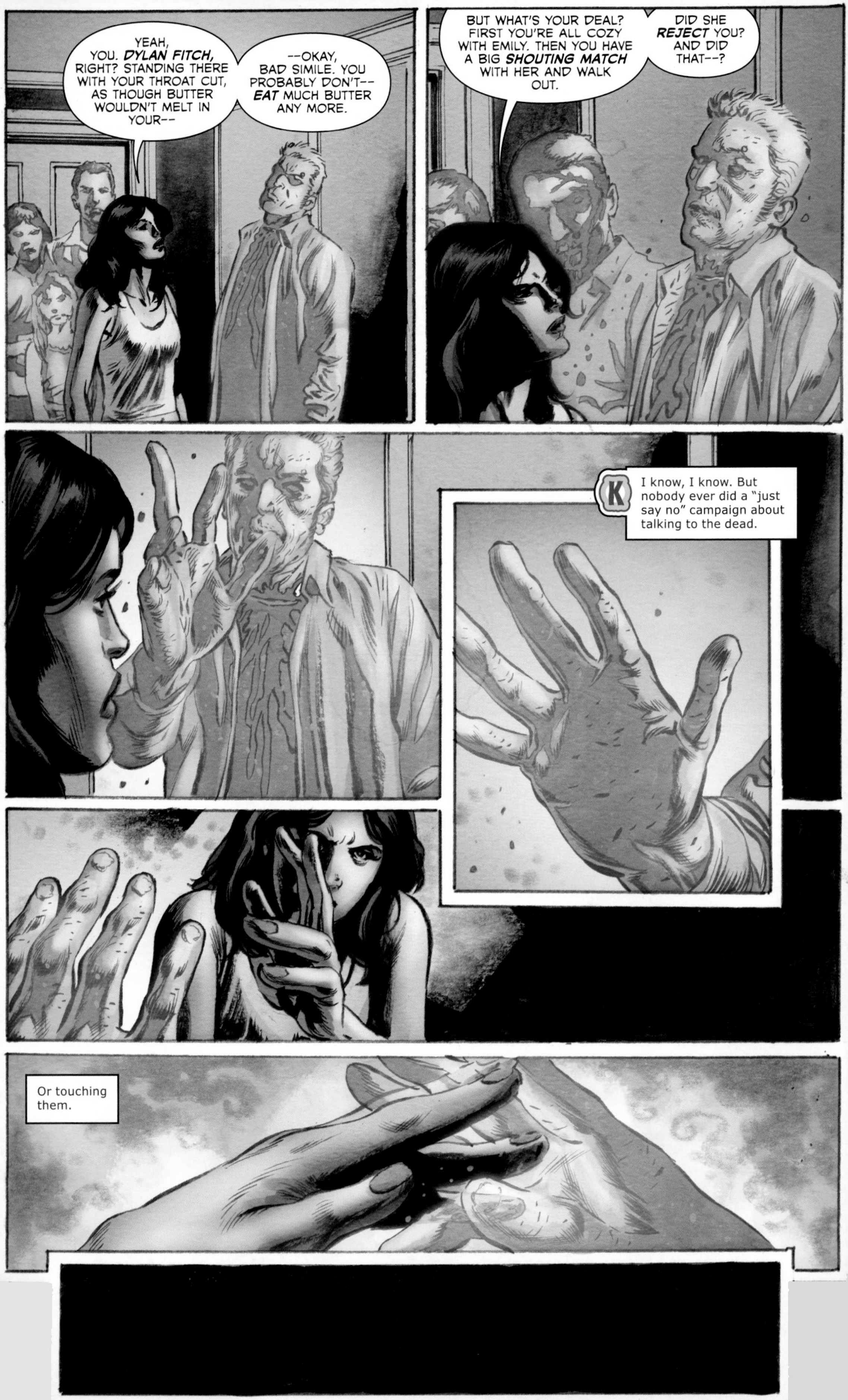
YEAH, YOU. DYLAN FITCH, RIGHT? STANDING THERE WITH YOUR THROAT CUT, AS THOUGH BUTTER WOULDN'T MELT IN YOUR--
--OKAY, BAD SIMILE. YOU PROBABLY DON'T-- EAT MUCH BUTTER ANY MORE.
BUT WHAT'S YOUR DEAL? FIRST YOU'RE ALL COZY WITH EMILY. THEN YOU HAVE A BIG SHOUTING MATCH WITH HER AND WALK OUT.
DID SHE REJECT YOU? AND DID THAT--?
K
I know, I know. But nobody ever did a "just say no" campaign about talking to the dead.
Or touching them.

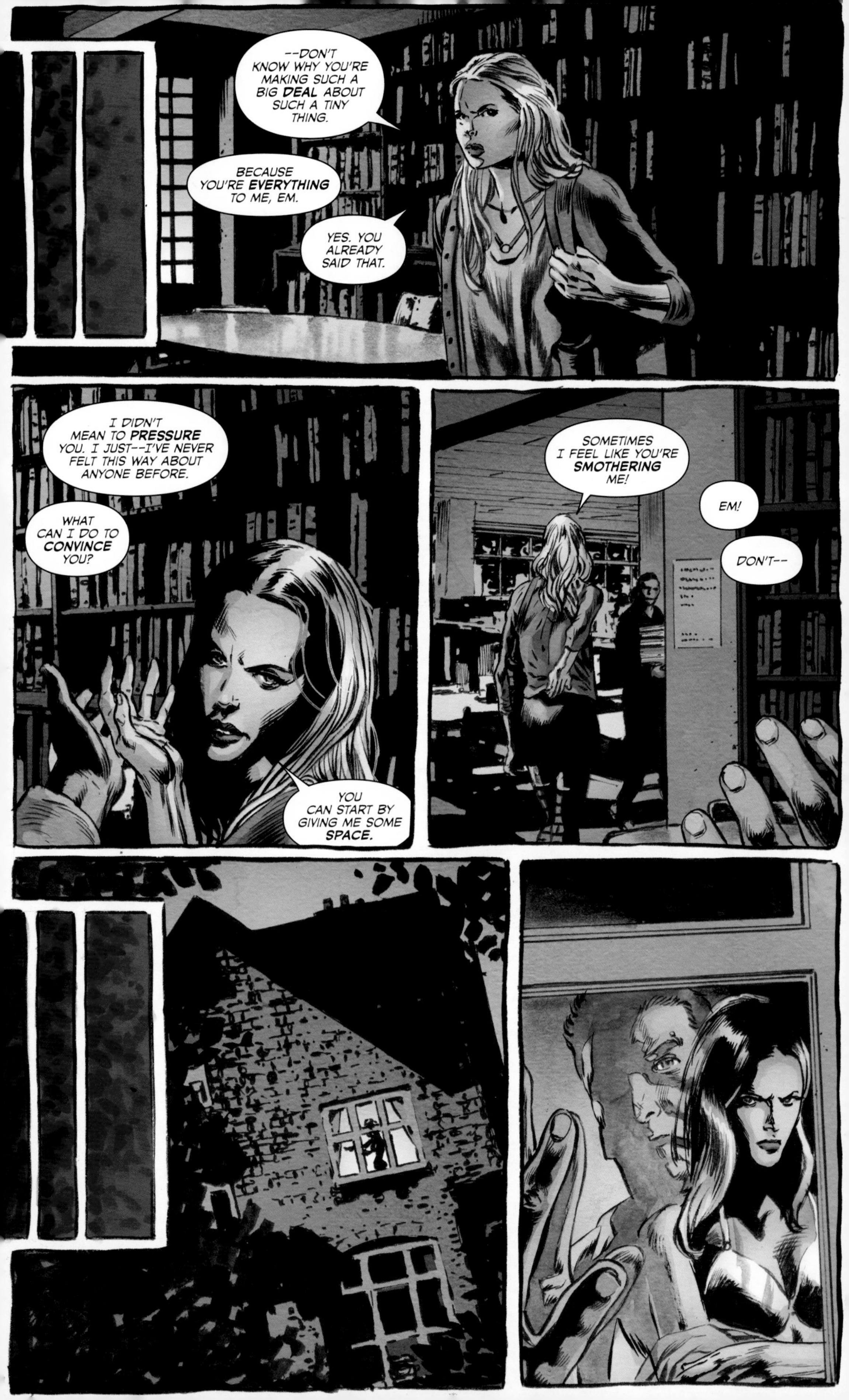

--DON'T KNOW WHY YOU'RE MAKING SUCH A BIG DEAL ABOUT SUCH A TINY THING.
BECAUSE YOU'RE EVERYTHING TO ME, EM.
YES. YOU ALREADY SAID THAT.
I DIDN'T MEAN TO PRESSURE YOU. I JUST--I'VE NEVER FELT THIS WAY ABOUT ANYONE BEFORE.
WHAT CAN I DO TO CONVINCE YOU?
YOU CAN START BY GIVING ME SOME SPACE.
SOMETIMES I FEEL LIKE YOU'RE SMOTHERING ME!
EM!
DON'T--

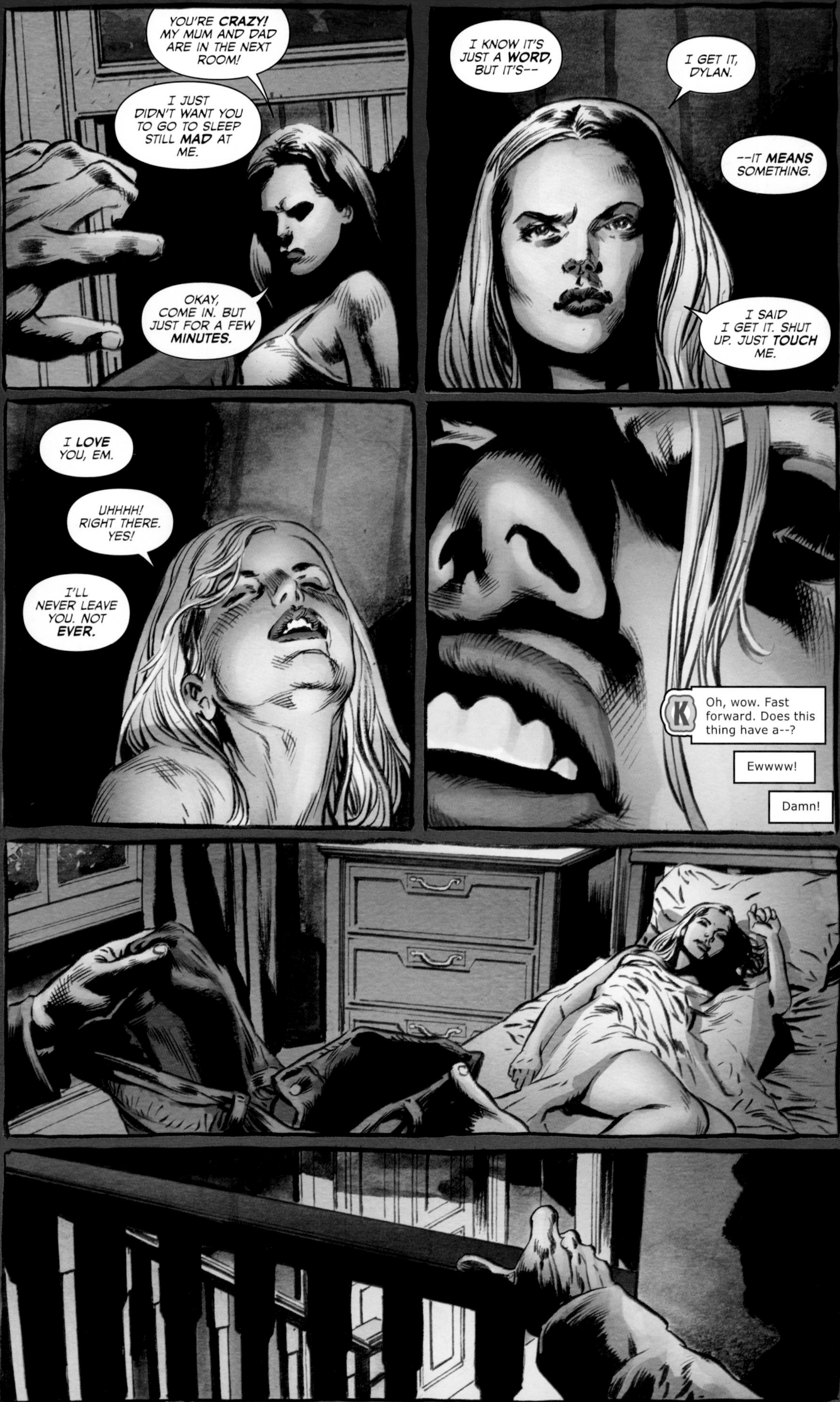
YOU'RE CRAZY! MY MUM AND DAD ARE IN THE NEXT ROOM!
I JUST DIDN'T WANT YOU TO GO TO SLEEP STILL MAD AT ME.
OKAY, COME IN. BUT JUST FOR A FEW MINUTES.
I KNOW IT'S JUST A WORD, BUT IT'S--
I GET IT, DYLAN.
--IT MEANS SOMETHING.
I SAID I GET IT. SHUT UP. JUST TOUCH ME.
I LOVE YOU, EM.
UHHHH! RIGHT THERE. YES!
I'LL NEVER LEAVE YOU. NOT EVER.
K
Oh, wow. Fast forward. Does this thing have a--?
Ewwww!
Damn!

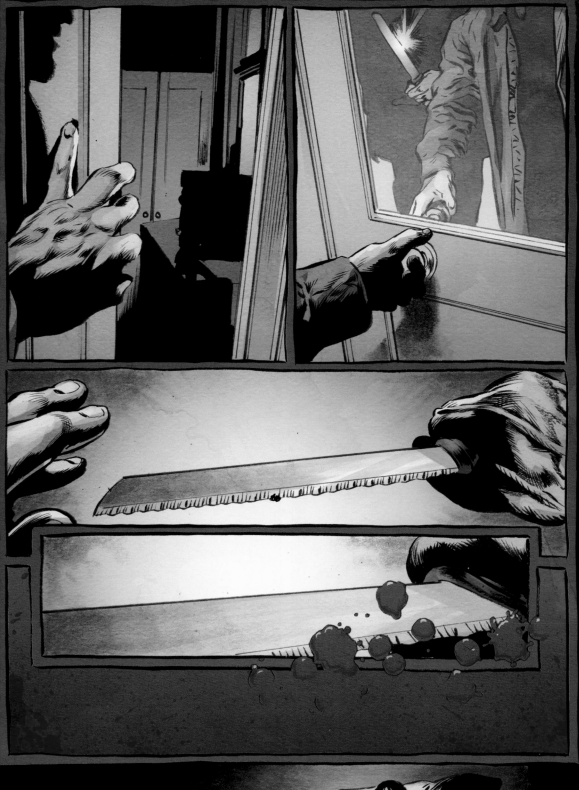

...

Ow?

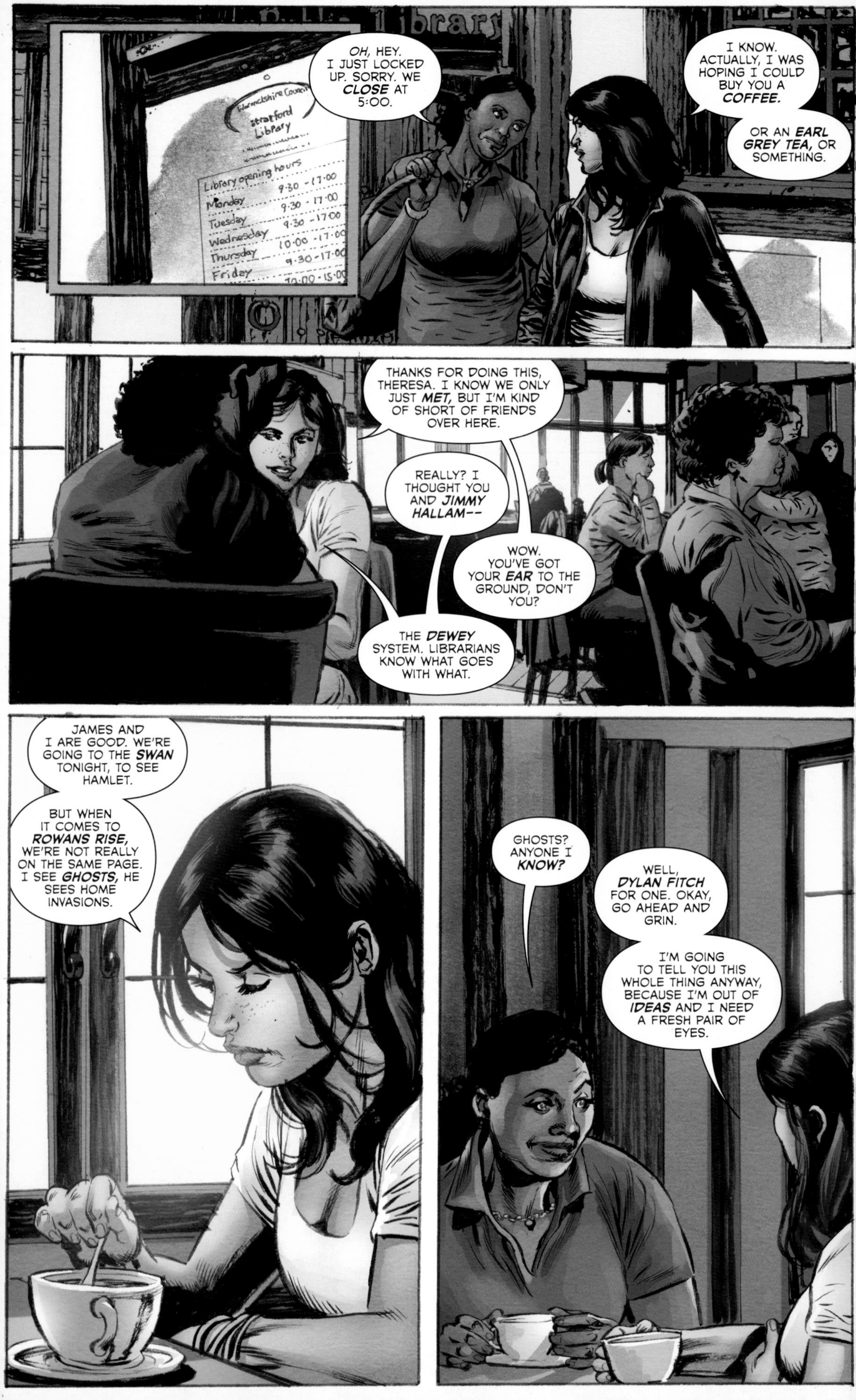
stratford Library
Library opening hours
Monday
Tuesday
Wednesday
Thursday
Friday
OH, HEY. I JUST LOCKED UP. SORRY. WE CLOSE AT 5:00.
I KNOW. ACTUALLY, I WAS HOPING I COULD BUY YOU A COFFEE.
OR AN EARL GREY TEA, OR SOMETHING.
THANKS FOR DOING THIS, THERESA. I KNOW WE ONLY JUST MET, BUT I'M KIND OF SHORT OF FRIENDS OVER HERE.
REALLY? I THOUGHT YOU AND JIMMY HALLAM--
WOW. YOU'VE GOT YOUR EAR TO THE GROUND, DON'T YOU?
THE DEWEY SYSTEM. LIBRARIANS KNOW WHAT GOES WITH WHAT.
JAMES AND I ARE GOOD. WE'RE GOING TO THE SWAN TONIGHT, TO SEE HAMLET.
BUT WHEN IT COMES TO ROWANS RISE, WE'RE NOT REALLY ON THE SAME PAGE. I SEE GHOSTS, HE SEES HOME INVASIONS.
GHOSTS? ANYONE I KNOW?
WELL, DYLAN FITCH FOR ONE. OKAY, GO AHEAD AND GRIN.
I'M GOING TO TELL YOU THIS WHOLE THING ANYWAY, BECAUSE I'M OUT OF IDEAS AND I NEED A FRESH PAIR OF EYES.

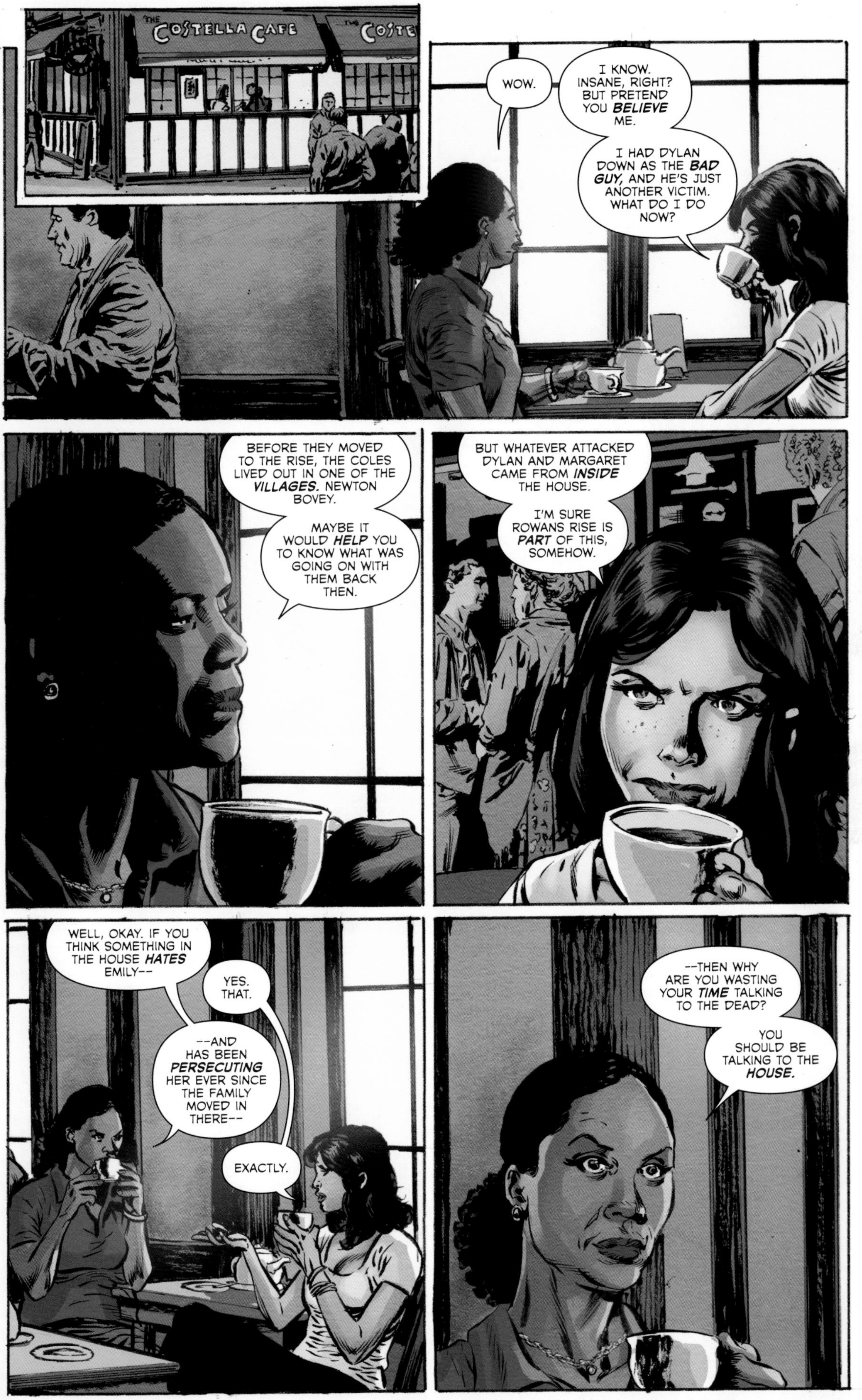
THE COSTELLA CAFE
WOW.
I KNOW. INSANE, RIGHT? BUT PRETEND YOU BELIEVE ME.
I HAD DYLAN DOWN AS THE BAD GUY, AND HE'S JUST ANOTHER VICTIM. WHAT DO I DO NOW?
BEFORE THEY MOVED TO THE RISE, THE COLES LIVED OUT IN ONE OF THE VILLAGES. NEWTON BOVEY.
MAYBE IT WOULD HELP YOU TO KNOW WHAT WAS GOING ON WITH THEM BACK THEN.
BUT WHATEVER ATTACKED DYLAN AND MARGARET CAME FROM INSIDE THE HOUSE.
I'M SURE ROWANS RISE IS PART OF THIS, SOMEHOW.
WELL, OKAY. IF YOU THINK SOMETHING IN THE HOUSE HATES EMILY--
YES. THAT.
--AND HAS BEEN PERSECUTING HER EVER SINCE THE FAMILY MOVED IN THERE--
EXACTLY.
--THEN WHY ARE YOU WASTING YOUR TIME TALKING TO THE DEAD?
YOU SHOULD BE TALKING TO THE HOUSE.

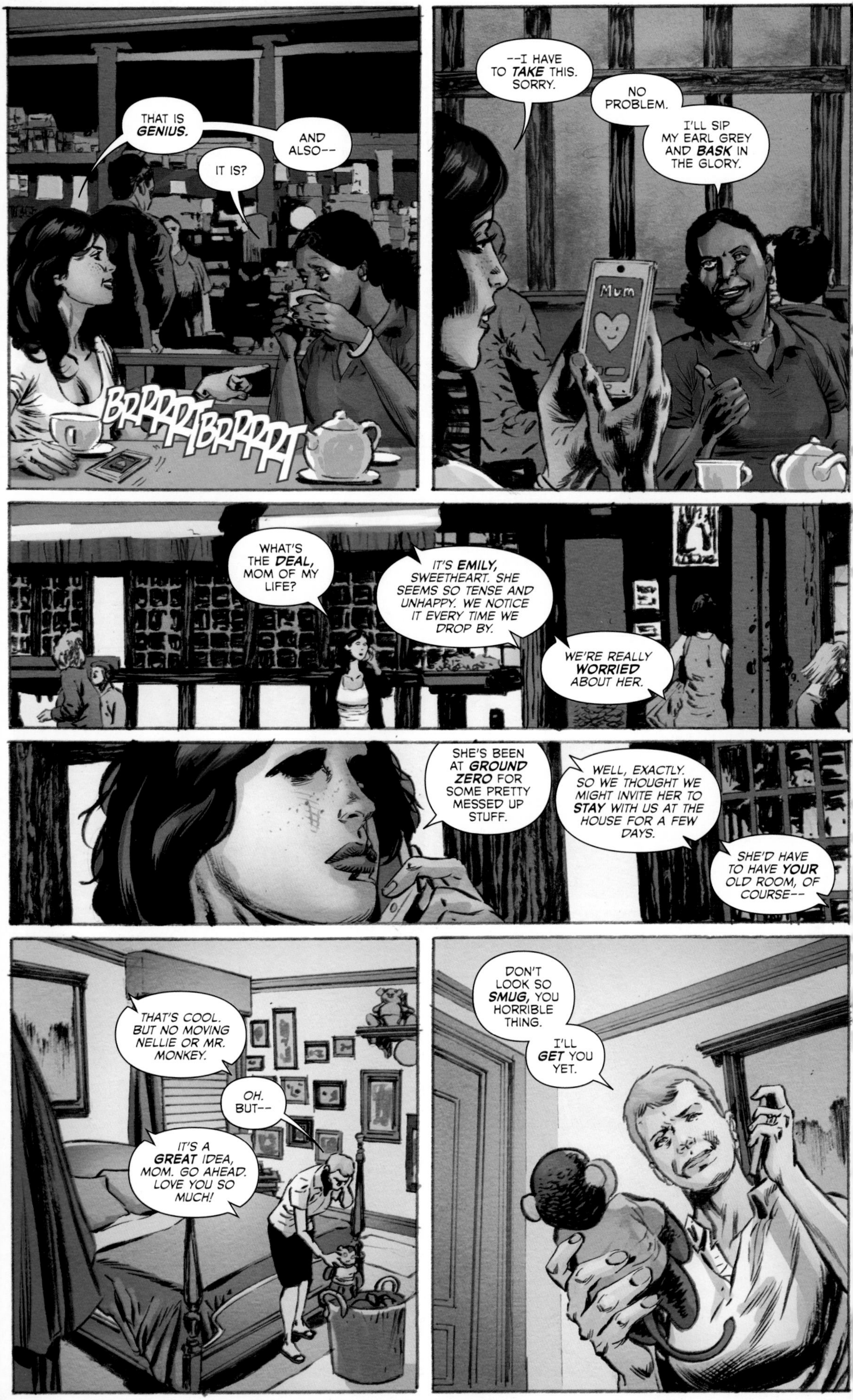
THAT IS GENIUS.
AND ALSO--
IT IS?
BRRRRT BRRRRT
--I HAVE TO TAKE THIS. SORRY.
NO PROBLEM.
I'LL SIP MY EARL GREY AND BASK IN THE GLORY.
Mum
WHAT'S THE DEAL, MOM OF MY LIFE?
IT'S EMILY, SWEETHEART. SHE SEEMS SO TENSE AND UNHAPPY. WE NOTICE IT EVERY TIME WE DROP BY.
WE'RE REALLY WORRIED ABOUT HER.
SHE'S BEEN AT GROUND ZERO FOR SOME PRETTY MESSED UP STUFF.
WELL, EXACTLY. SO WE THOUGHT WE MIGHT INVITE HER TO STAY WITH US AT THE HOUSE FOR A FEW DAYS.
SHE'D HAVE TO HAVE YOUR OLD ROOM, OF COURSE--
THAT'S COOL. BUT NO MOVING NELLIE OR MR. MONKEY.
OH. BUT--
IT'S A GREAT IDEA, MOM. GO AHEAD. LOVE YOU SO MUCH!
DON'T LOOK SO SMUG, YOU HORRIBLE THING.
I'LL GET YOU YET.

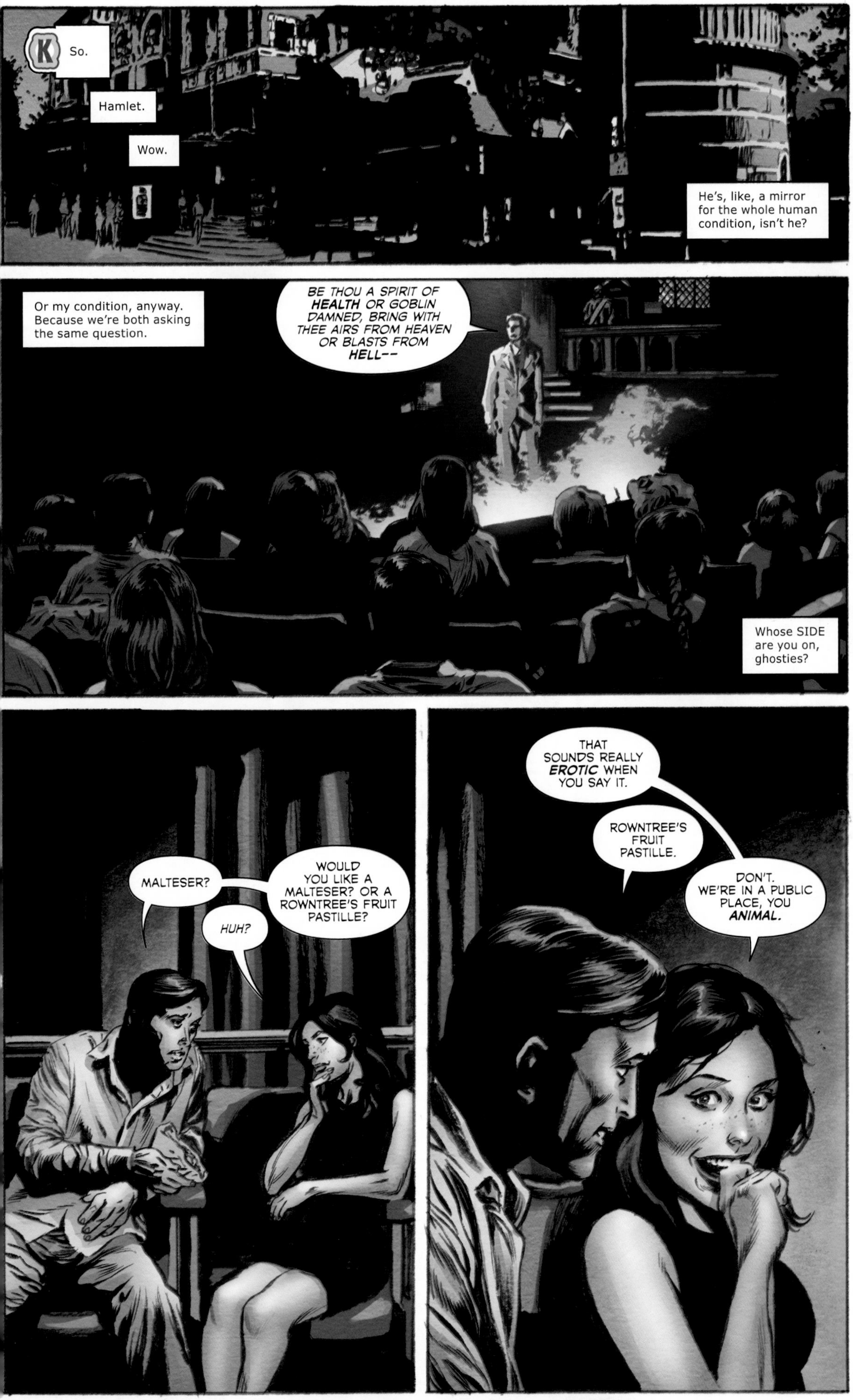
So.
Hamlet.
Wow.
He's, like, a mirror for the whole human condition, isn't he?
Or my condition, anyway. Because we're both asking the same question.
BE THOU A SPIRIT OF HEALTH OR GOBLIN DAMNED, BRING WITH THEE AIRS FROM HEAVEN OR BLASTS FROM HELL--
Whose SIDE are you on, ghosties?
WOULD YOU LIKE A MALTESER? OR A ROWNTREE'S FRUIT PASTILLE?
HUH?
MALTESER?
ROWNTREE'S FRUIT PASTILLE.
THAT SOUNDS REALLY EROTIC WHEN YOU SAY IT.
DON'T. WE'RE IN A PUBLIC PLACE, YOU ANIMAL.

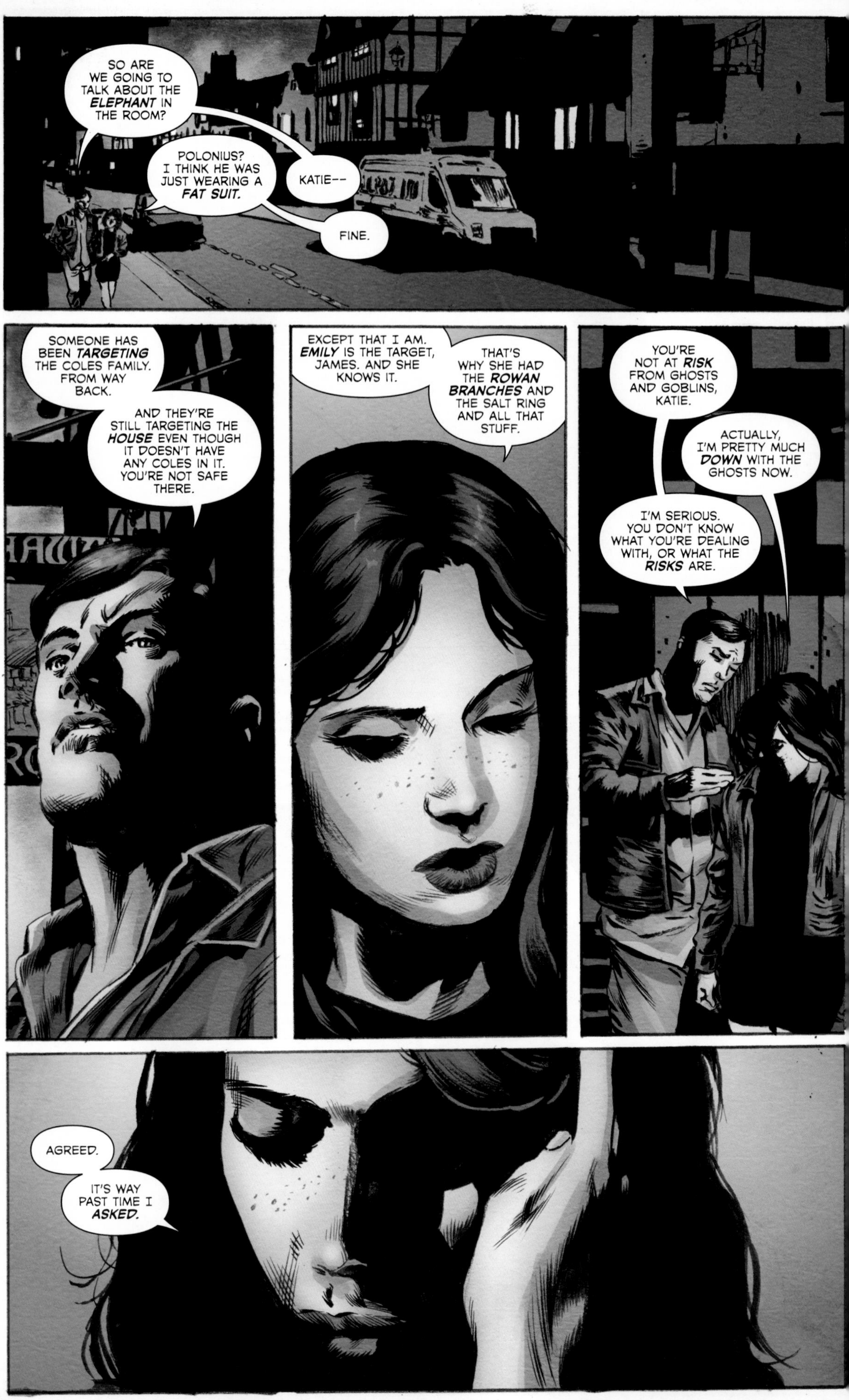
SO ARE WE GOING TO TALK ABOUT THE *ELEPHANT* IN THE ROOM?
POLONIUS? I THINK HE WAS JUST WEARING A *FAT SUIT.*
KATIE--
FINE.
SOMEONE HAS BEEN *TARGETING* THE COLES FAMILY. FROM WAY BACK.
AND THEY'RE STILL TARGETING THE *HOUSE* EVEN THOUGH IT DOESN'T HAVE ANY COLES IN IT. YOU'RE NOT SAFE THERE.
EXCEPT THAT I AM. *EMILY* IS THE TARGET, JAMES. AND SHE KNOWS IT.
THAT'S WHY SHE HAD THE *ROWAN BRANCHES* AND THE SALT RING AND ALL THAT STUFF.
YOU'RE NOT AT *RISK* FROM GHOSTS AND GOBLINS, KATIE.
ACTUALLY, I'M PRETTY MUCH *DOWN* WITH THE GHOSTS NOW.
I'M SERIOUS. YOU DON'T KNOW WHAT YOU'RE DEALING WITH, OR WHAT THE *RISKS* ARE.
AGREED.
IT'S WAY PAST TIME I *ASKED.*

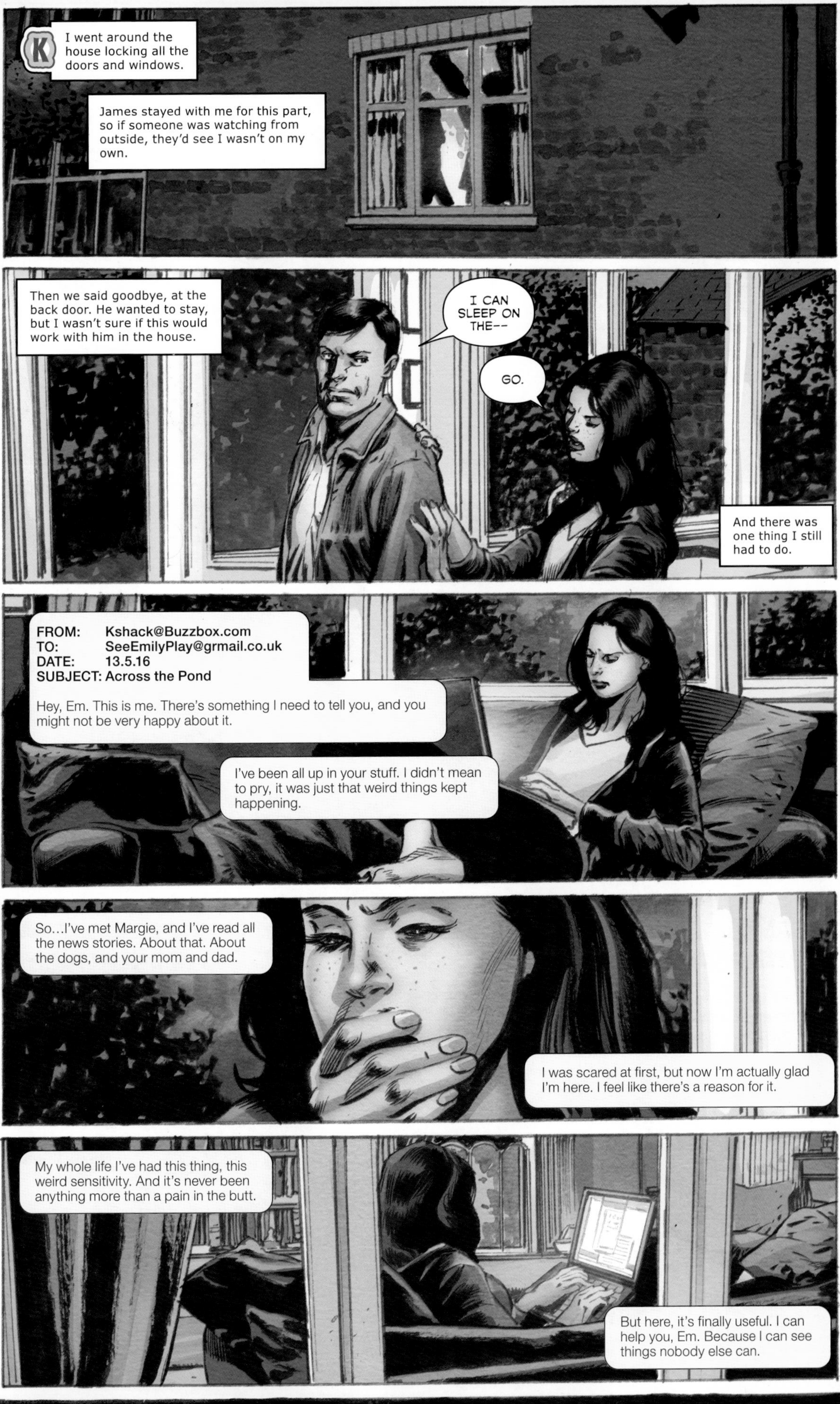
K
I went around the house locking all the doors and windows.
James stayed with me for this part, so if someone was watching from outside, they'd see I wasn't on my own.
Then we said goodbye, at the back door. He wanted to stay, but I wasn't sure if this would work with him in the house.
I CAN SLEEP ON THE--
GO.
And there was one thing I still had to do.
FROM: Kshack@Buzzbox.com
TO: SeeEmilyPlay@grmail.co.uk
DATE: 13.5.16
SUBJECT: Across the Pond
Hey, Em. This is me. There's something I need to tell you, and you might not be very happy about it.
I've been all up in your stuff. I didn't mean to pry, it was just that weird things kept happening.
So…I've met Margie, and I've read all the news stories. About that. About the dogs, and your mom and dad.
I was scared at first, but now I'm actually glad I'm here. I feel like there's a reason for it.
My whole life I've had this thing, this weird sensitivity. And it's never been anything more than a pain in the butt.
But here, it's finally useful. I can help you, Em. Because I can see things nobody else can.

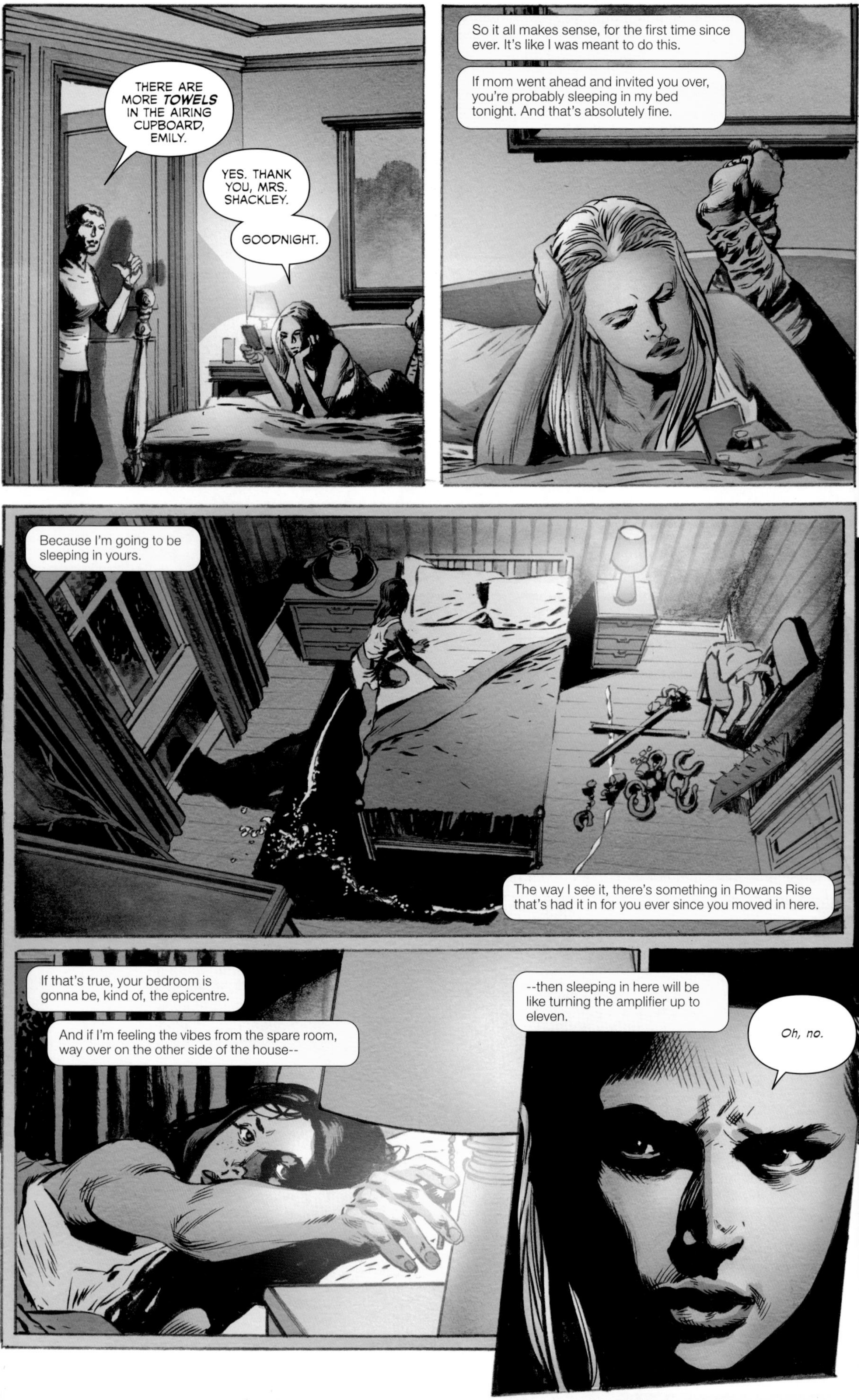
THERE ARE MORE *TOWELS* IN THE AIRING CUPBOARD, EMILY.
YES. THANK YOU, MRS. SHACKLEY.
GOODNIGHT.
So it all makes sense, for the first time since ever. It's like I was meant to do this.
If mom went ahead and invited you over, you're probably sleeping in my bed tonight. And that's absolutely fine.
Because I'm going to be sleeping in yours.
The way I see it, there's something in Rowans Rise that's had it in for you ever since you moved in here.
If that's true, your bedroom is gonna be, kind of, the epicentre.
And if I'm feeling the vibes from the spare room, way over on the other side of the house--
--then sleeping in here will be like turning the amplifier up to eleven.
Oh, no.

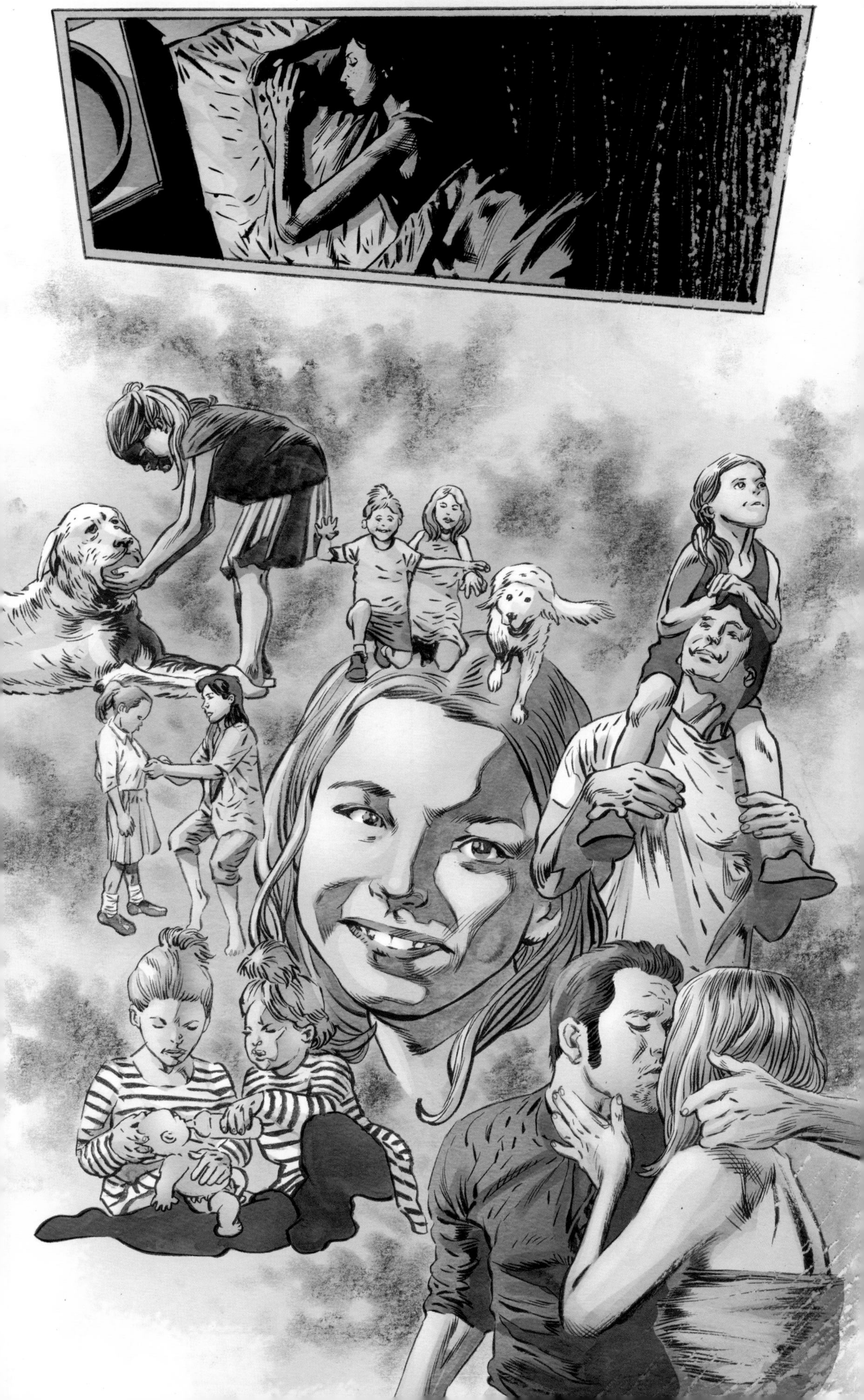

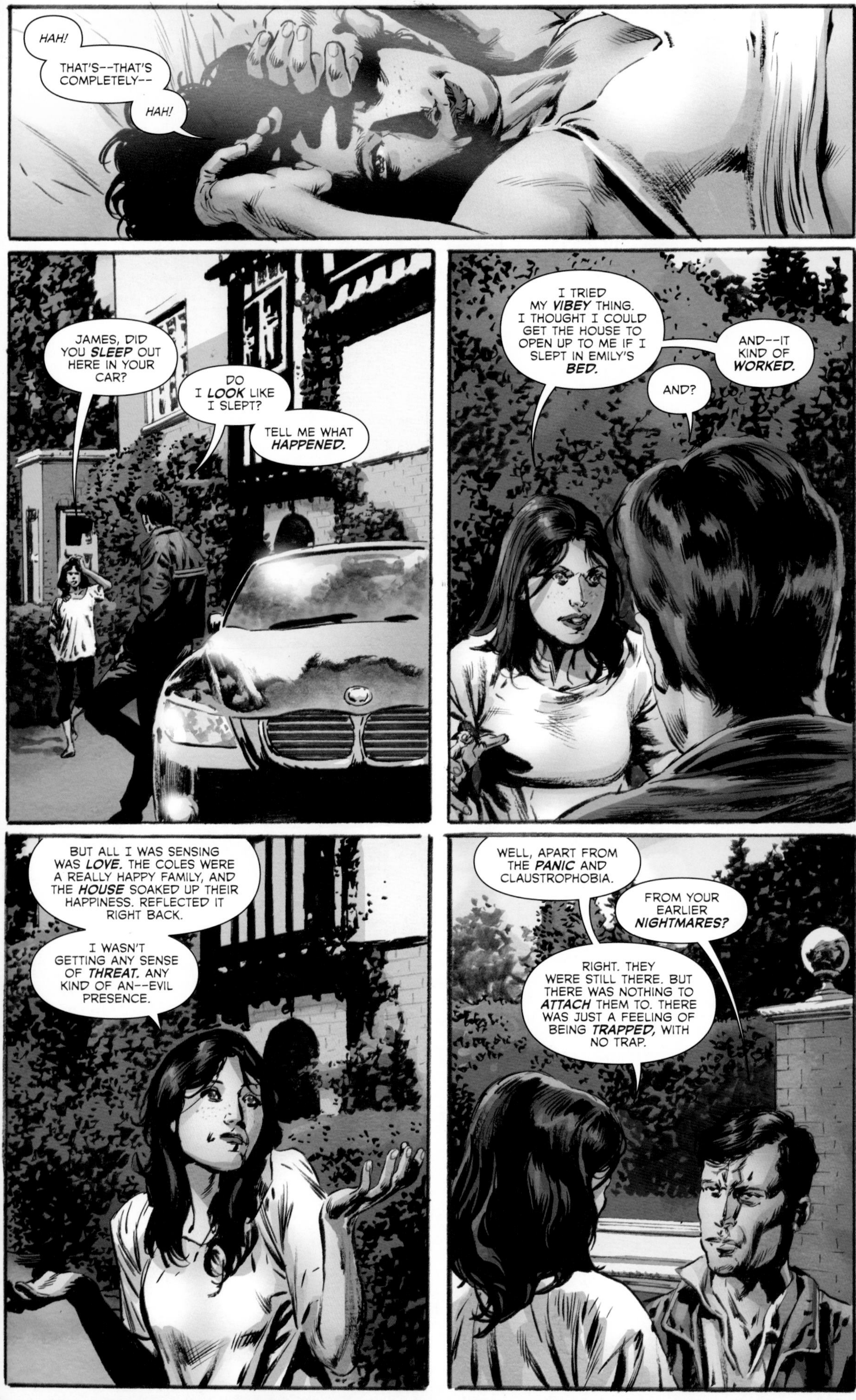
HAH!
THAT'S--THAT'S COMPLETELY--
HAH!
JAMES, DID YOU SLEEP OUT HERE IN YOUR CAR?
DO I LOOK LIKE I SLEPT?
TELL ME WHAT HAPPENED.
I TRIED MY VIBEY THING. I THOUGHT I COULD GET THE HOUSE TO OPEN UP TO ME IF I SLEPT IN EMILY'S BED.
AND--IT KIND OF WORKED.
AND?
BUT ALL I WAS SENSING WAS LOVE. THE COLES WERE A REALLY HAPPY FAMILY, AND THE HOUSE SOAKED UP THEIR HAPPINESS. REFLECTED IT RIGHT BACK.
I WASN'T GETTING ANY SENSE OF THREAT. ANY KIND OF AN--EVIL PRESENCE.
WELL, APART FROM THE PANIC AND CLAUSTROPHOBIA.
FROM YOUR EARLIER NIGHTMARES?
RIGHT. THEY WERE STILL THERE. BUT THERE WAS NOTHING TO ATTACH THEM TO. THERE WAS JUST A FEELING OF BEING TRAPPED, WITH NO TRAP.

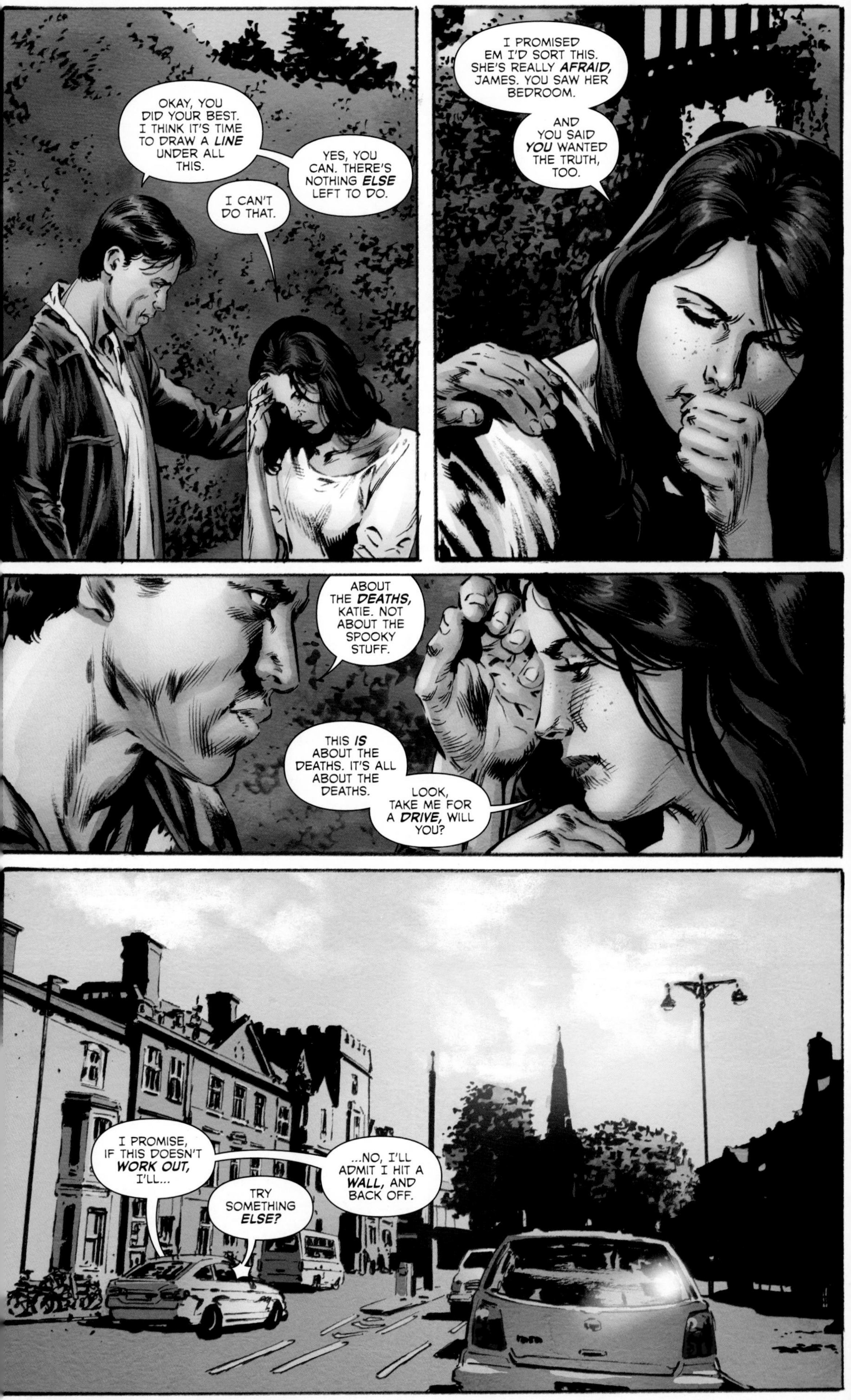

OKAY, YOU DID YOUR BEST. I THINK IT'S TIME TO DRAW A *LINE* UNDER ALL THIS.
I CAN'T DO THAT.
YES, YOU CAN. THERE'S NOTHING *ELSE* LEFT TO DO.
I PROMISED EM I'D SORT THIS. SHE'S REALLY *AFRAID,* JAMES. YOU SAW HER BEDROOM.
AND YOU SAID *YOU* WANTED THE TRUTH, TOO.
ABOUT THE *DEATHS,* KATIE. NOT ABOUT THE SPOOKY STUFF.
THIS *IS* ABOUT THE DEATHS. IT'S ALL ABOUT THE DEATHS.
LOOK, TAKE ME FOR A *DRIVE,* WILL YOU?
I PROMISE, IF THIS DOESN'T *WORK OUT,* I'LL...
TRY SOMETHING *ELSE?*
...NO, I'LL ADMIT I HIT A *WALL,* AND BACK OFF.

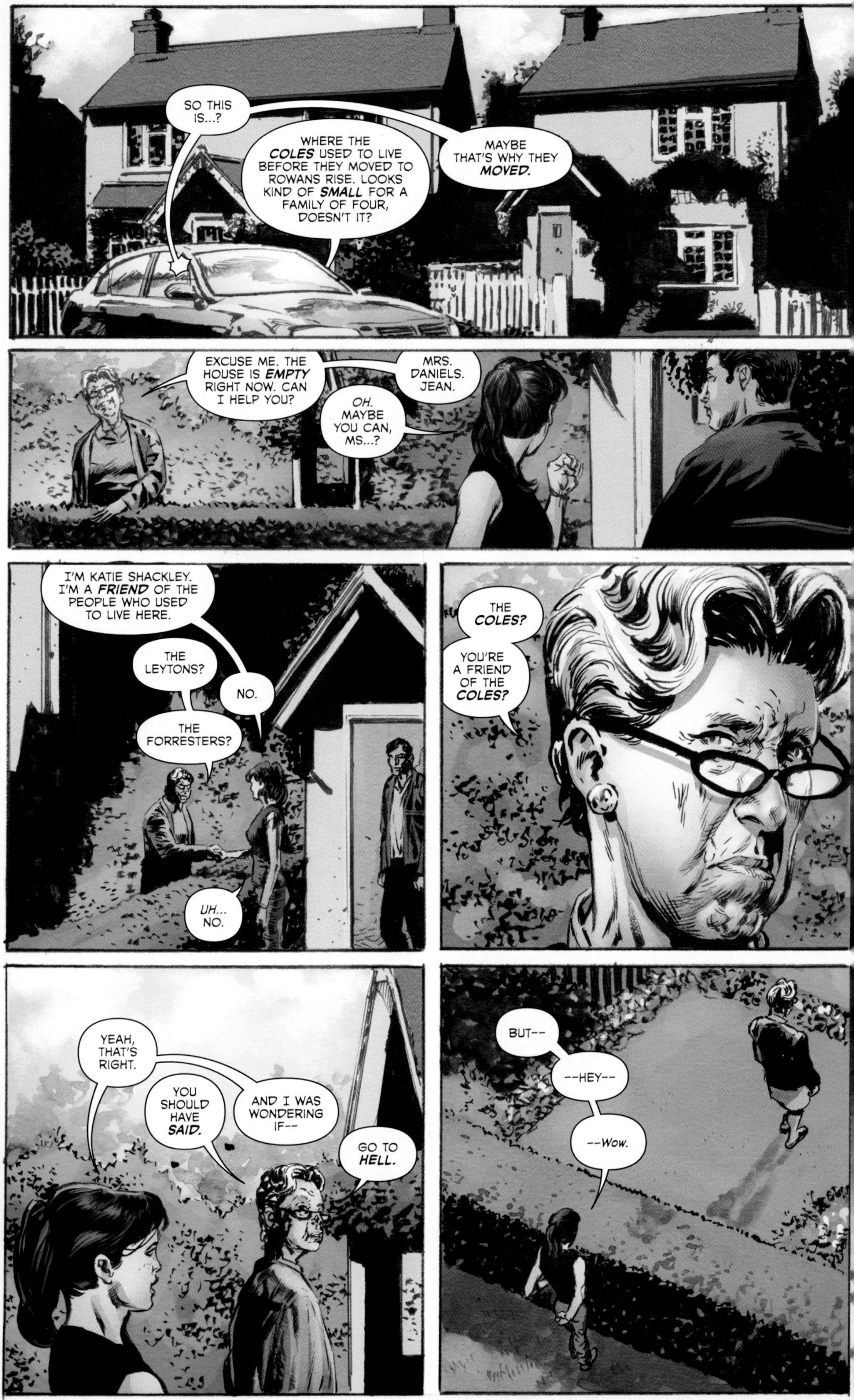
SO THIS IS...?
WHERE THE COLES USED TO LIVE BEFORE THEY MOVED TO ROWANS RISE. LOOKS KIND OF SMALL FOR A FAMILY OF FOUR, DOESN'T IT?
MAYBE THAT'S WHY THEY MOVED.
EXCUSE ME. THE HOUSE IS EMPTY RIGHT NOW. CAN I HELP YOU?
OH. MAYBE YOU CAN, MS...?
MRS. DANIELS. JEAN.
I'M KATIE SHACKLEY. I'M A FRIEND OF THE PEOPLE WHO USED TO LIVE HERE.
THE LEYTONS?
NO.
THE FORRESTERS?
UH... NO.
THE COLES?
YOU'RE A FRIEND OF THE COLES?
YEAH, THAT'S RIGHT.
YOU SHOULD HAVE SAID.
AND I WAS WONDERING IF--
GO TO HELL.
BUT--
--HEY--
--WOW.

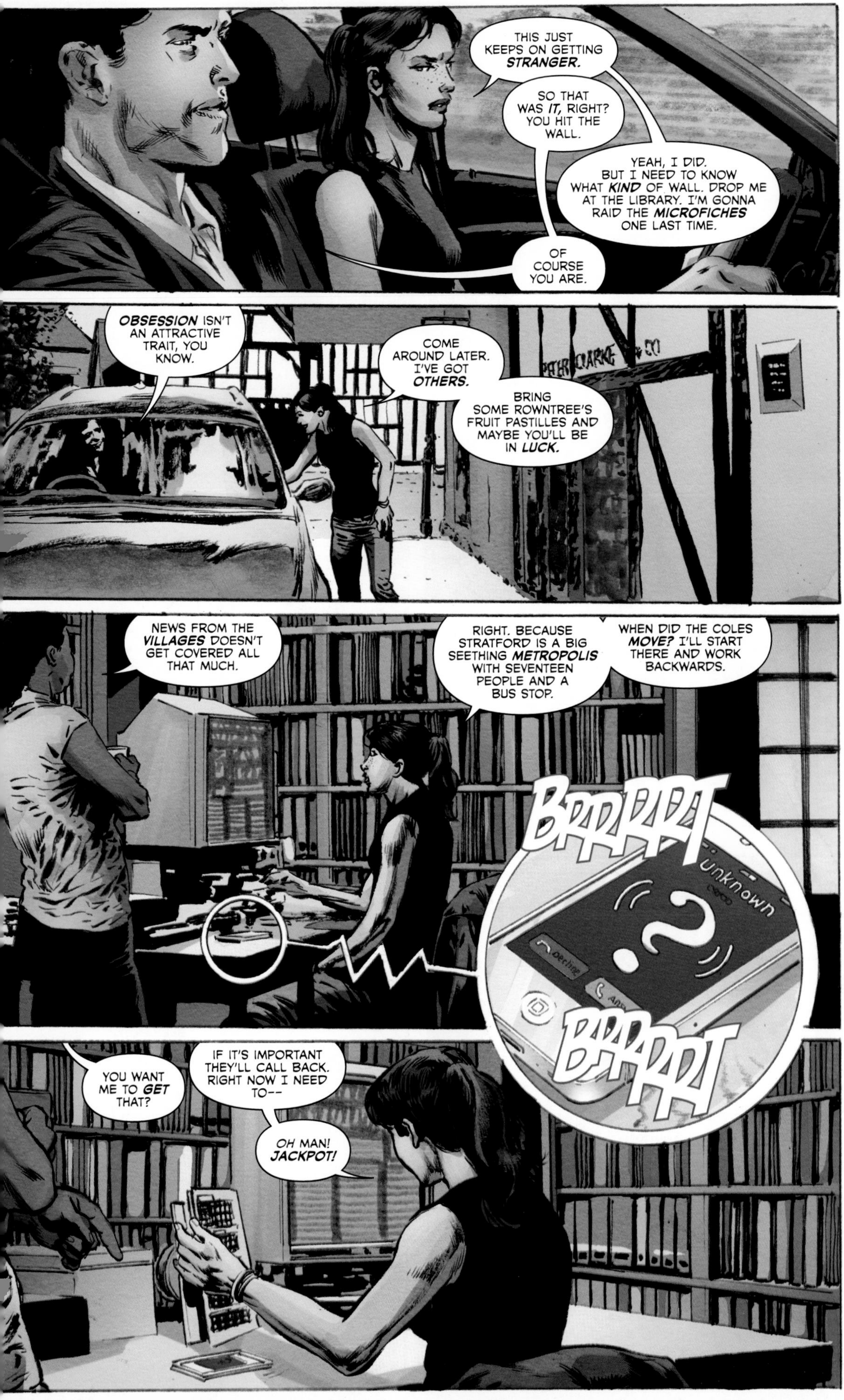

THIS JUST KEEPS ON GETTING STRANGER.
SO THAT WAS IT, RIGHT? YOU HIT THE WALL.
YEAH, I DID. BUT I NEED TO KNOW WHAT KIND OF WALL. DROP ME AT THE LIBRARY. I'M GONNA RAID THE MICROFICHES ONE LAST TIME.
OF COURSE YOU ARE.
OBSESSION ISN'T AN ATTRACTIVE TRAIT, YOU KNOW.
COME AROUND LATER. I'VE GOT OTHERS.
BRING SOME ROWNTREE'S FRUIT PASTILLES AND MAYBE YOU'LL BE IN LUCK.
PETER CLARKE & CO
NEWS FROM THE VILLAGES DOESN'T GET COVERED ALL THAT MUCH.
RIGHT. BECAUSE STRATFORD IS A BIG SEETHING METROPOLIS WITH SEVENTEEN PEOPLE AND A BUS STOP.
WHEN DID THE COLES MOVE? I'LL START THERE AND WORK BACKWARDS.
BRRRRRT
unknown
BRRRRRT
YOU WANT ME TO GET THAT?
IF IT'S IMPORTANT THEY'LL CALL BACK. RIGHT NOW I NEED TO--
OH MAN! JACKPOT!

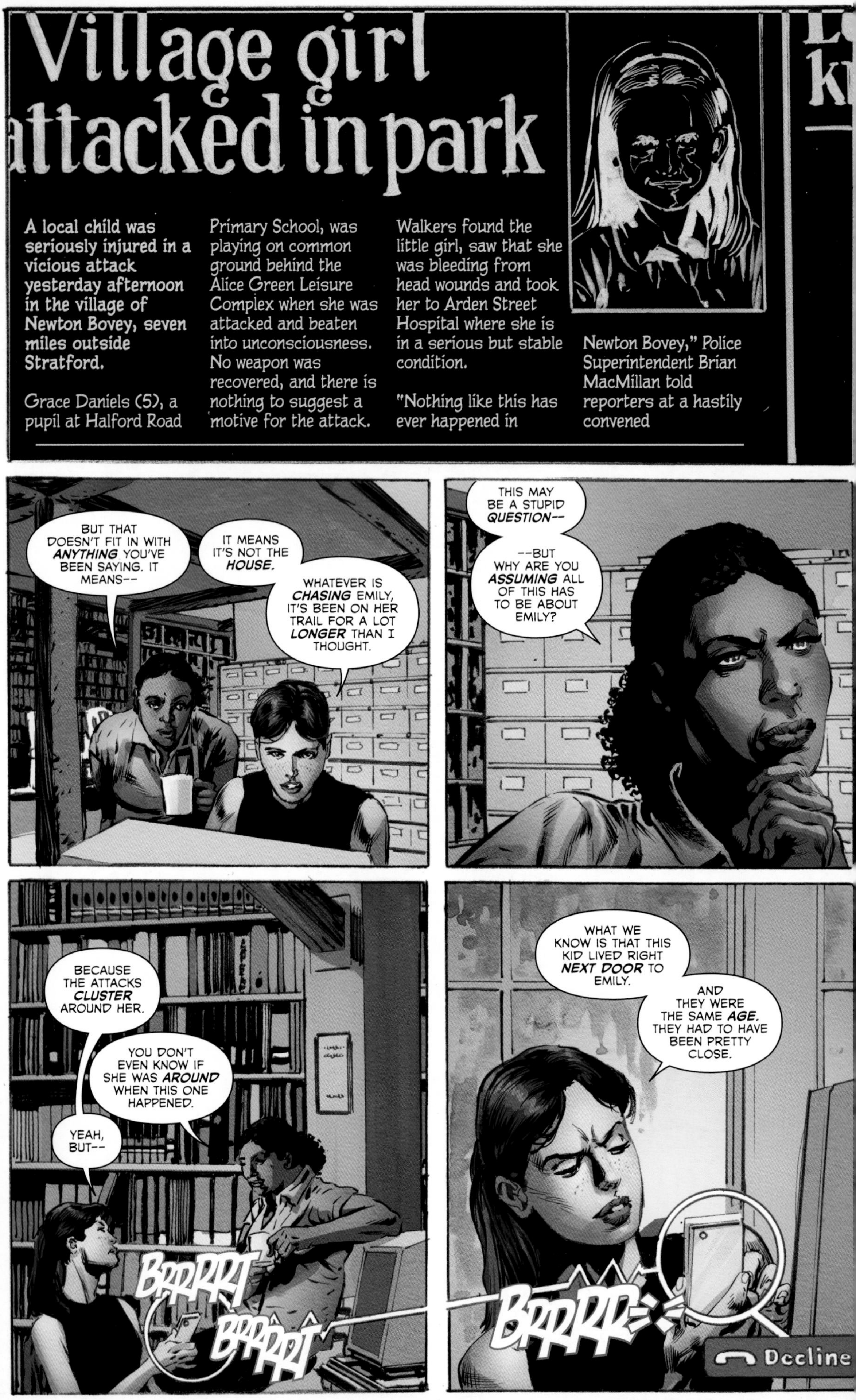
Village girl attacked in park
A local child was seriously injured in a vicious attack yesterday afternoon in the village of Newton Bovey, seven miles outside Stratford.
Grace Daniels (5), a pupil at Halford Road Primary School, was playing on common ground behind the Alice Green Leisure Complex when she was attacked and beaten into unconsciousness. No weapon was recovered, and there is nothing to suggest a motive for the attack.
Walkers found the little girl, saw that she was bleeding from head wounds and took her to Arden Street Hospital where she is in a serious but stable condition.
"Nothing like this has ever happened in Newton Bovey," Police Superintendent Brian MacMillan told reporters at a hastily convened
BUT THAT DOESN'T FIT IN WITH ANYTHING YOU'VE BEEN SAYING. IT MEANS--
IT MEANS IT'S NOT THE HOUSE.
WHATEVER IS CHASING EMILY, IT'S BEEN ON HER TRAIL FOR A LOT LONGER THAN I THOUGHT.
THIS MAY BE A STUPID QUESTION--
--BUT WHY ARE YOU ASSUMING ALL OF THIS HAS TO BE ABOUT EMILY?
BECAUSE THE ATTACKS CLUSTER AROUND HER.
YOU DON'T EVEN KNOW IF SHE WAS AROUND WHEN THIS ONE HAPPENED.
YEAH, BUT--
BRRRRRT
BRRRRRT
WHAT WE KNOW IS THAT THIS KID LIVED RIGHT NEXT DOOR TO EMILY.
AND THEY WERE THE SAME AGE. THEY HAD TO HAVE BEEN PRETTY CLOSE.
BRRRRR
Decline

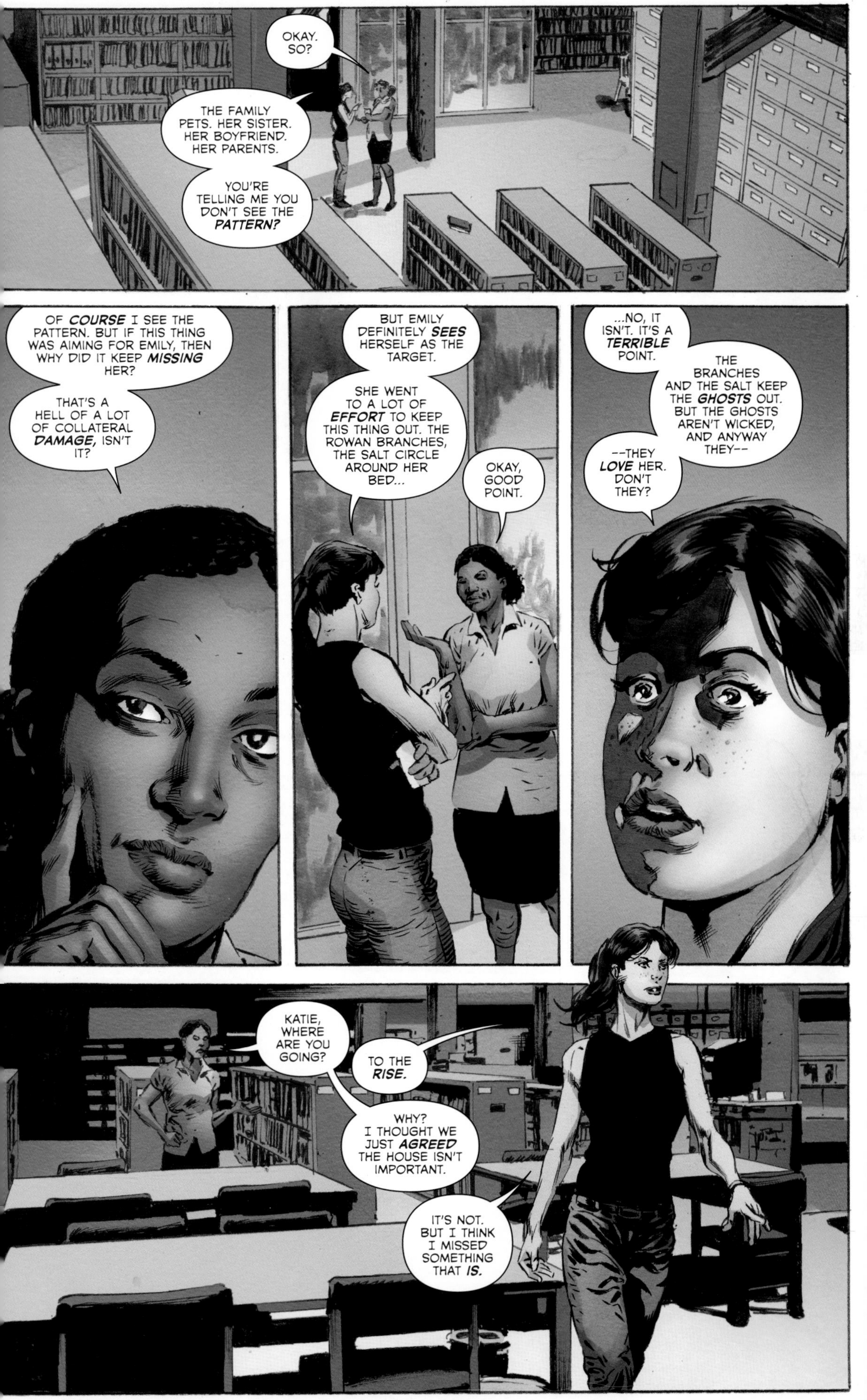
OKAY. SO?
THE FAMILY PETS. HER SISTER. HER BOYFRIEND. HER PARENTS.
YOU'RE TELLING ME YOU DON'T SEE THE PATTERN?
OF COURSE I SEE THE PATTERN. BUT IF THIS THING WAS AIMING FOR EMILY, THEN WHY DID IT KEEP MISSING HER?
THAT'S A HELL OF A LOT OF COLLATERAL DAMAGE, ISN'T IT?
BUT EMILY DEFINITELY SEES HERSELF AS THE TARGET.
SHE WENT TO A LOT OF EFFORT TO KEEP THIS THING OUT. THE ROWAN BRANCHES, THE SALT CIRCLE AROUND HER BED...
OKAY, GOOD POINT.
...NO, IT ISN'T. IT'S A TERRIBLE POINT.
THE BRANCHES AND THE SALT KEEP THE GHOSTS OUT. BUT THE GHOSTS AREN'T WICKED, AND ANYWAY THEY--
--THEY LOVE HER. DON'T THEY?
KATIE, WHERE ARE YOU GOING?
TO THE RISE.
WHY? I THOUGHT WE JUST AGREED THE HOUSE ISN'T IMPORTANT.
IT'S NOT. BUT I THINK I MISSED SOMETHING THAT IS.

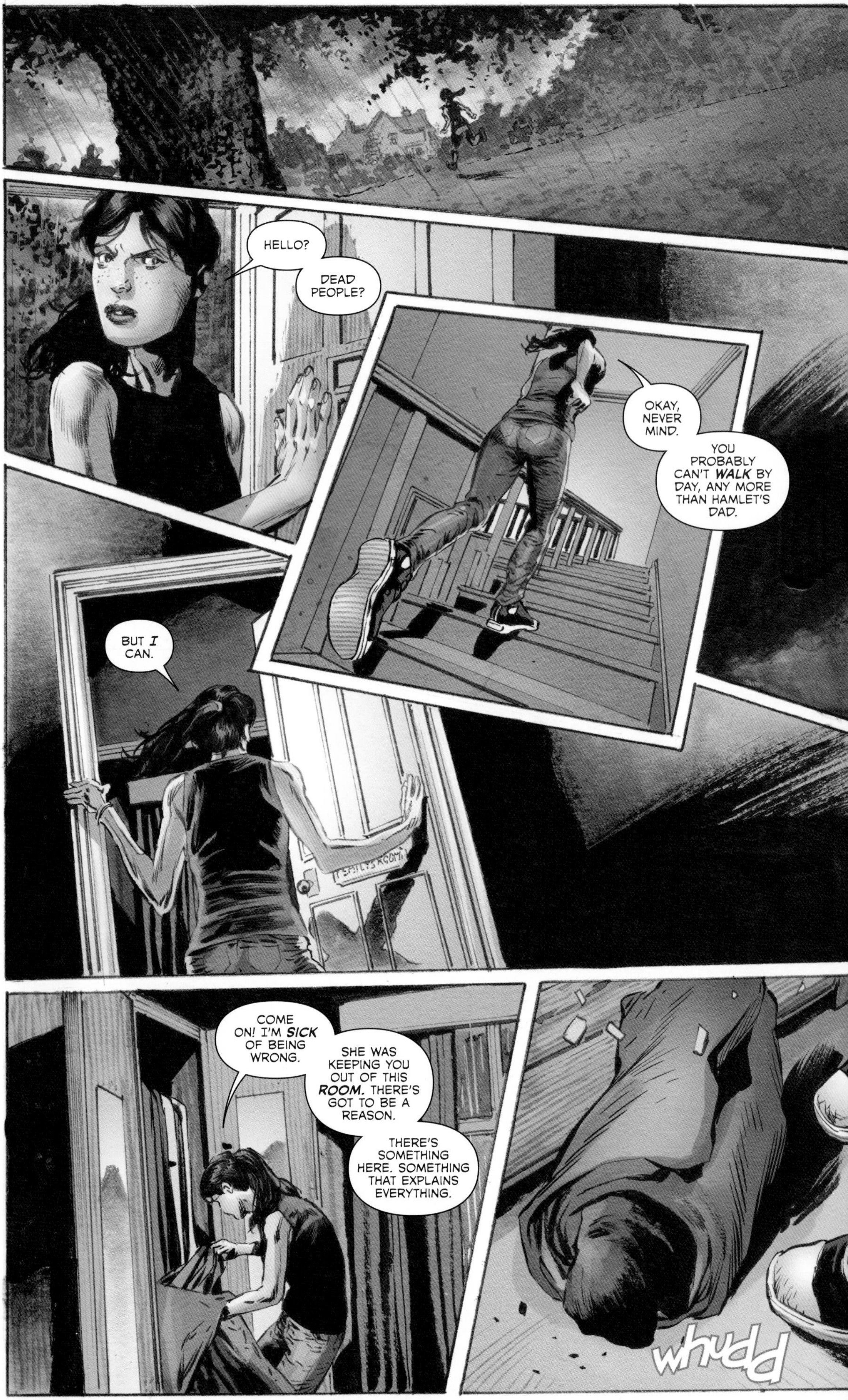
HELLO?
DEAD PEOPLE?
OKAY, NEVER MIND.
YOU PROBABLY CAN'T WALK BY DAY, ANY MORE THAN HAMLET'S DAD.
BUT I CAN.
COME ON! I'M SICK OF BEING WRONG.
SHE WAS KEEPING YOU OUT OF THIS ROOM. THERE'S GOT TO BE A REASON.
THERE'S SOMETHING HERE. SOMETHING THAT EXPLAINS EVERYTHING.
whudd

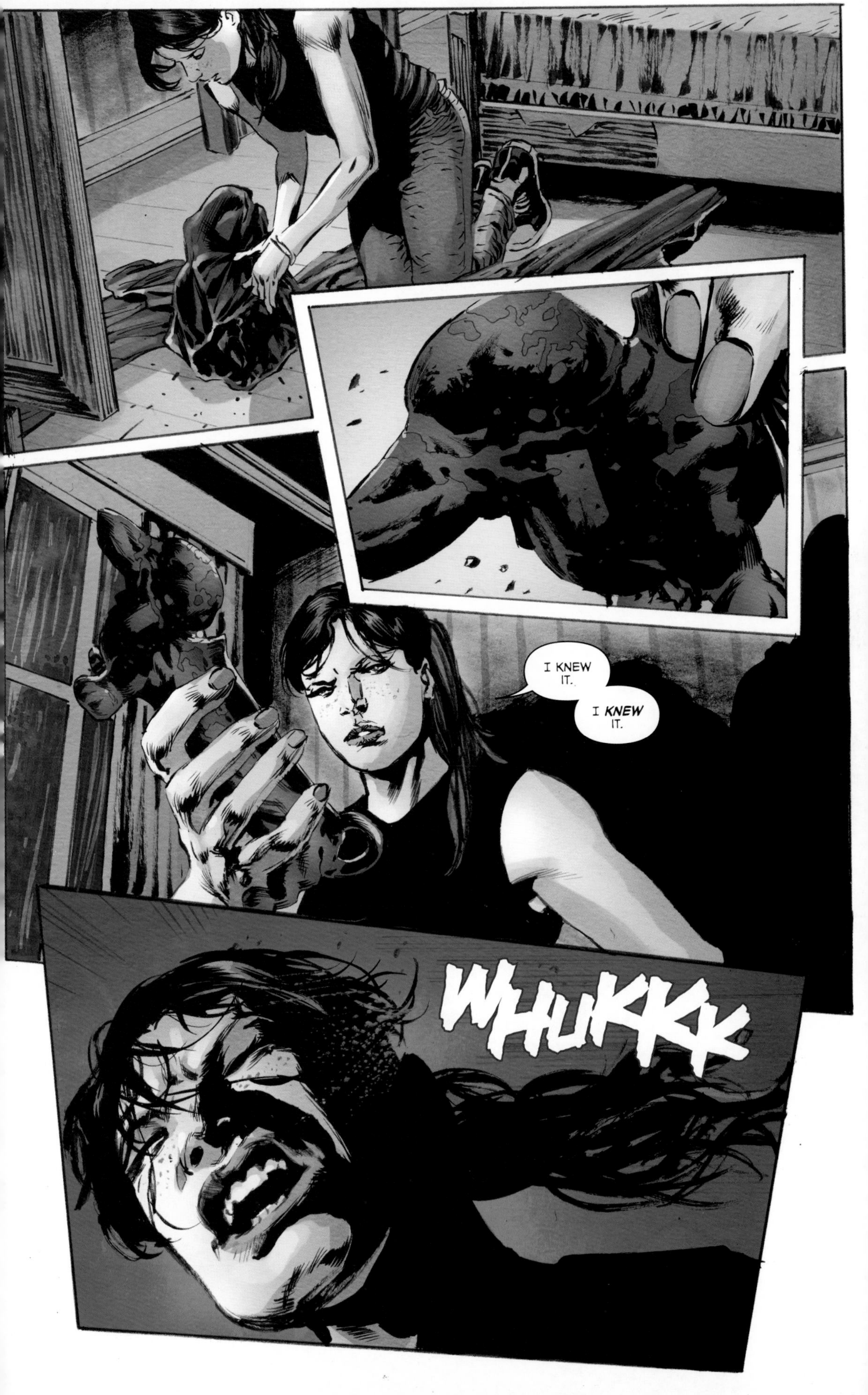
I KNEW IT.
I KNEW IT.
WHUKKK

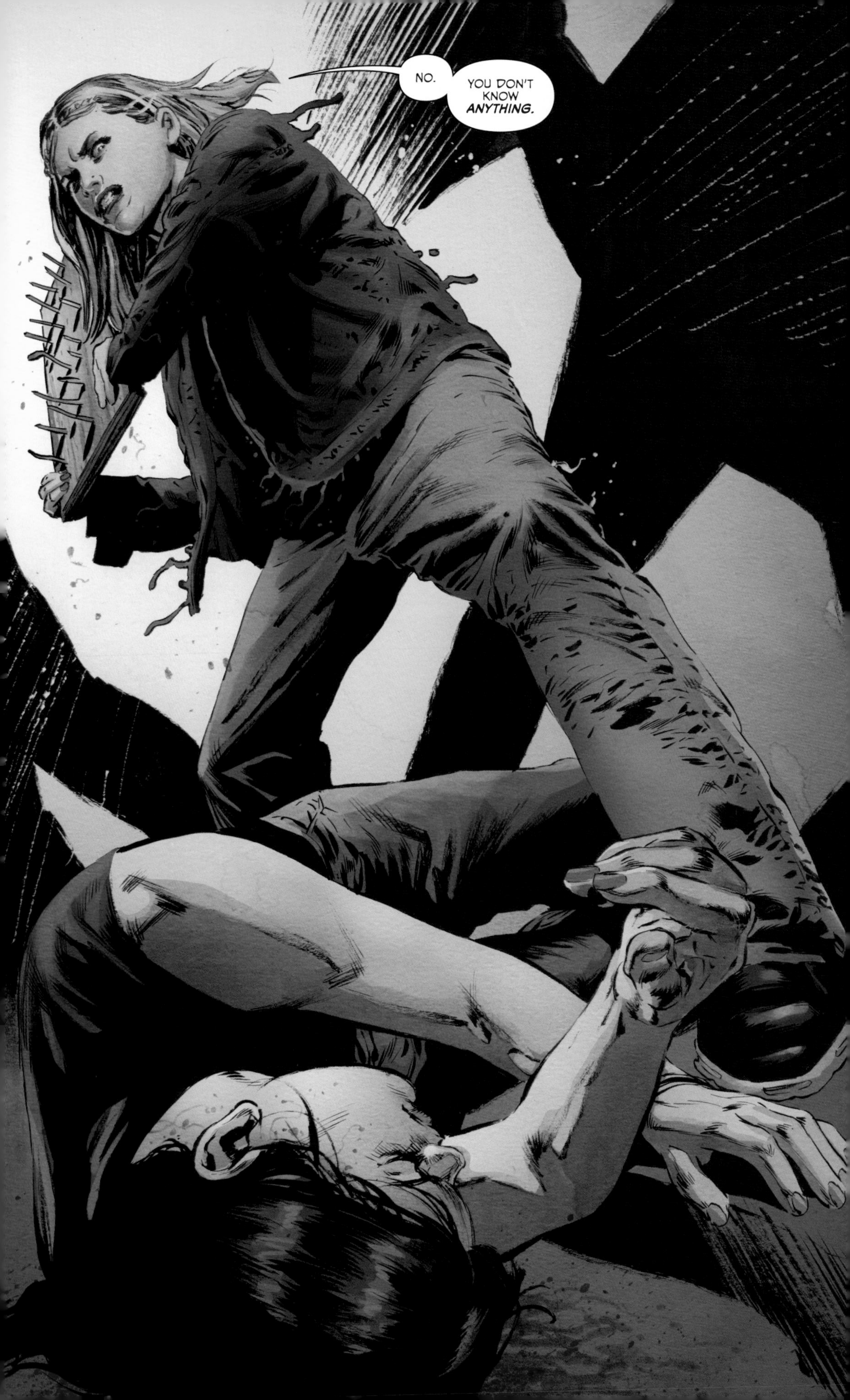
NO.
YOU DON'T KNOW ANYTHING.

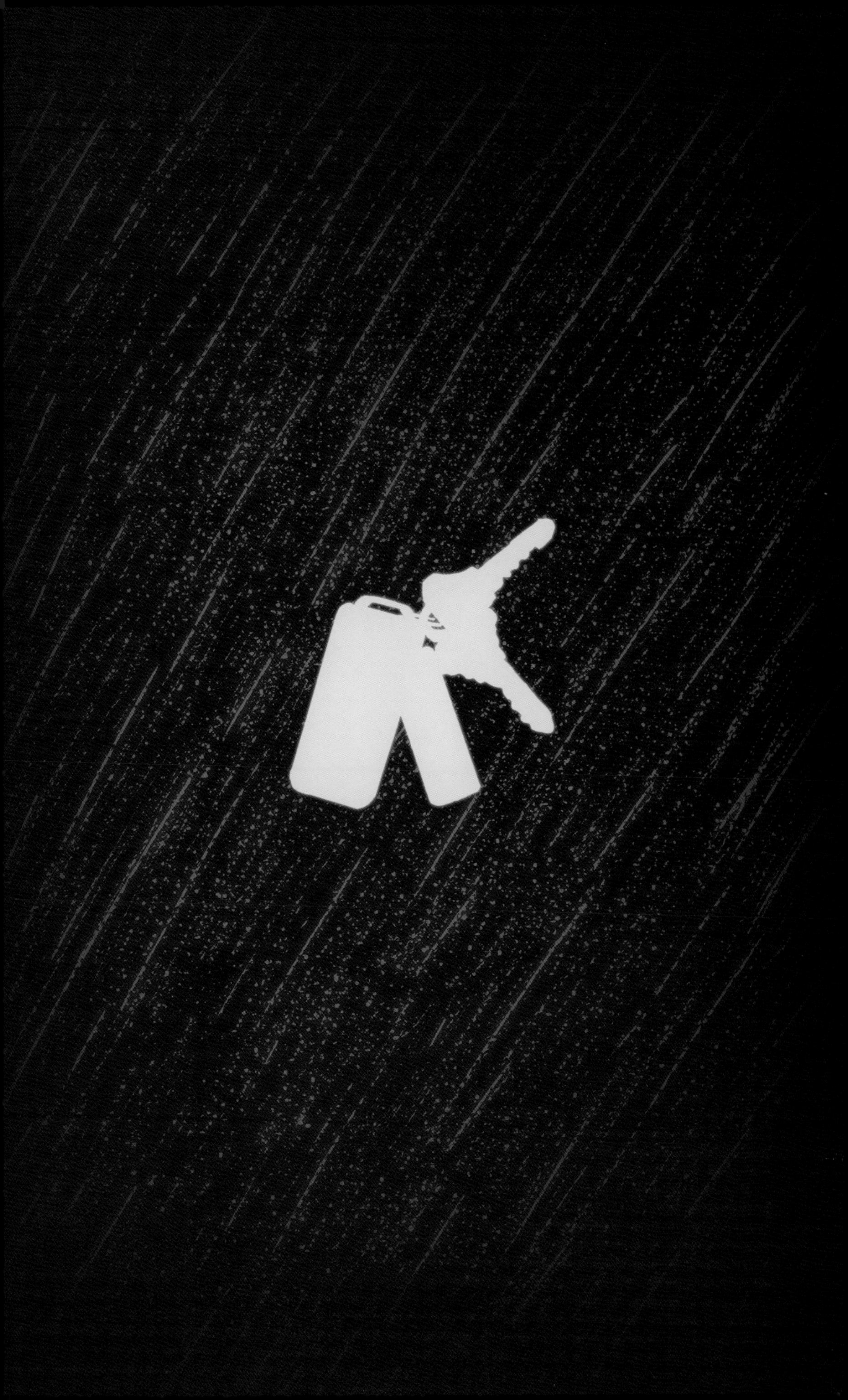

CHAPTER FOUR

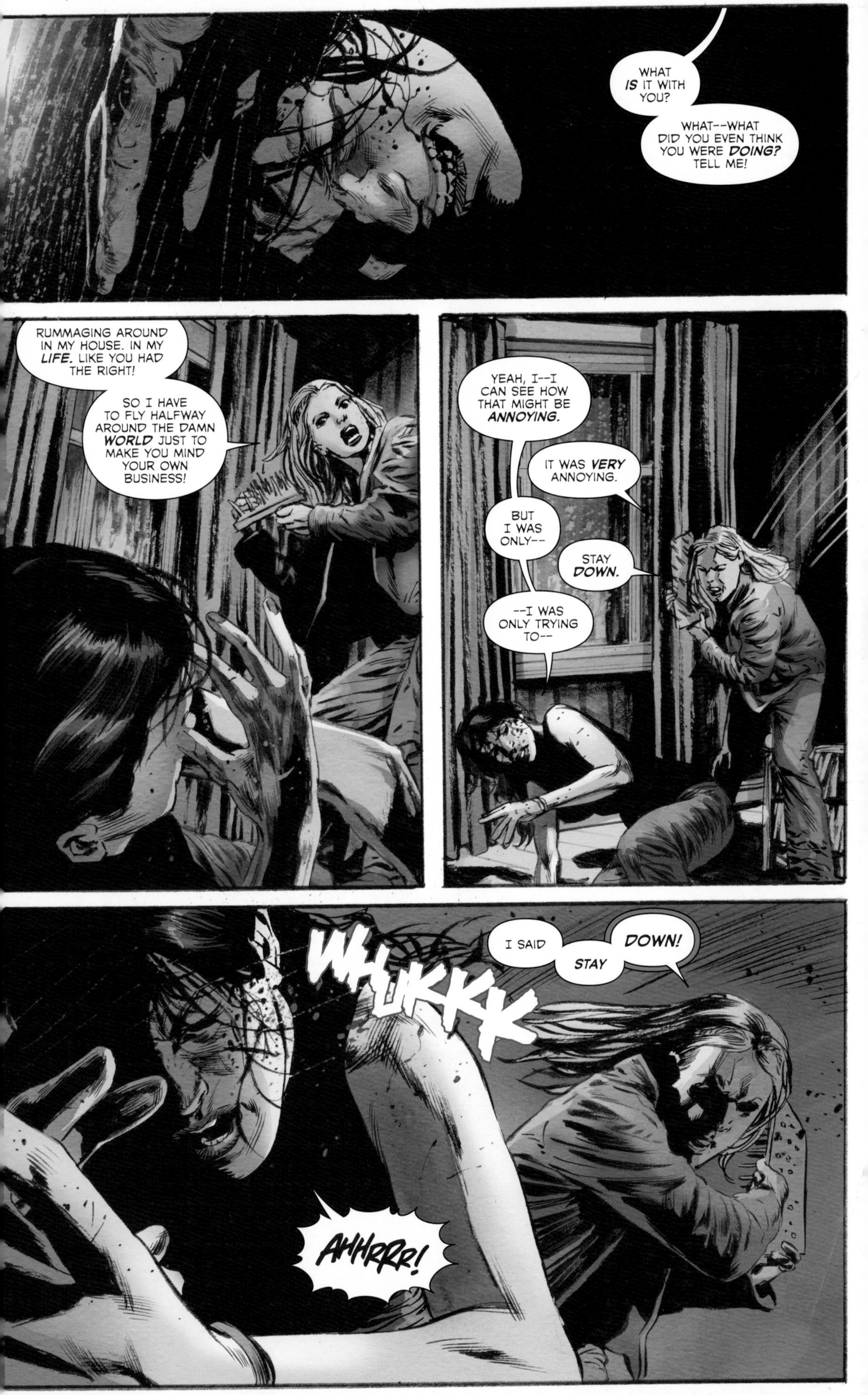

WHAT IS IT WITH YOU?
WHAT--WHAT DID YOU EVEN THINK YOU WERE DOING? TELL ME!
RUMMAGING AROUND IN MY HOUSE. IN MY LIFE. LIKE YOU HAD THE RIGHT!
SO I HAVE TO FLY HALFWAY AROUND THE DAMN WORLD JUST TO MAKE YOU MIND YOUR OWN BUSINESS!
YEAH, I--I CAN SEE HOW THAT MIGHT BE ANNOYING.
IT WAS VERY ANNOYING.
BUT I WAS ONLY--
STAY DOWN.
--I WAS ONLY TRYING TO--
WHUKKK
I SAID STAY DOWN!
AHHRRR!

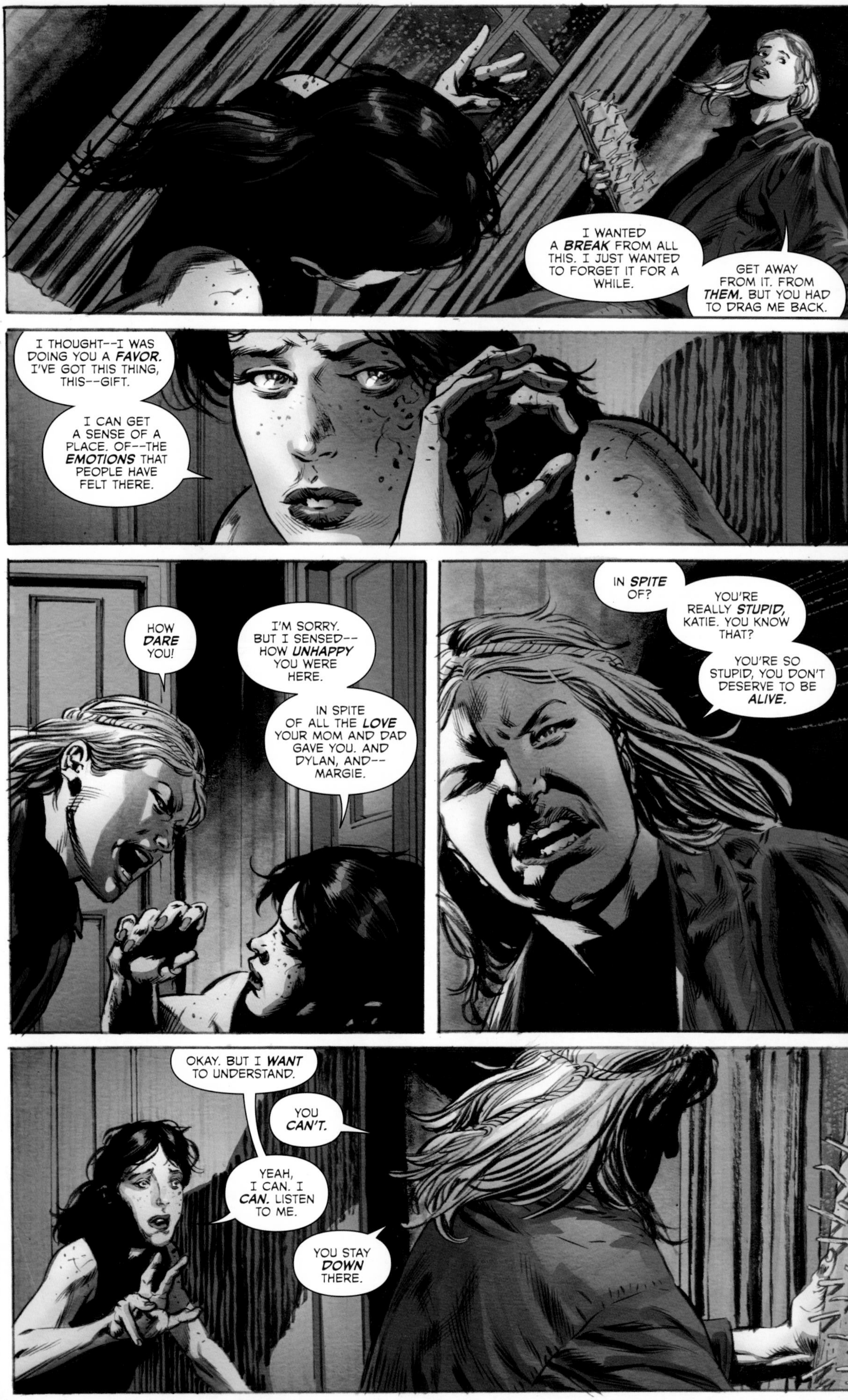
I WANTED A **BREAK** FROM ALL THIS. I JUST WANTED TO FORGET IT FOR A WHILE.
GET AWAY FROM IT. FROM **THEM.** BUT YOU HAD TO DRAG ME BACK.
I THOUGHT--I WAS DOING YOU A **FAVOR.** I'VE GOT THIS THING, THIS--GIFT.
I CAN GET A SENSE OF A PLACE. OF--THE **EMOTIONS** THAT PEOPLE HAVE FELT THERE.
HOW **DARE** YOU!
I'M SORRY. BUT I SENSED--HOW **UNHAPPY** YOU WERE HERE.
IN SPITE OF ALL THE **LOVE** YOUR MOM AND DAD GAVE YOU. AND DYLAN, AND--MARGIE.
IN **SPITE** OF?
YOU'RE REALLY **STUPID,** KATIE. YOU KNOW THAT?
YOU'RE SO STUPID, YOU DON'T DESERVE TO BE **ALIVE.**
OKAY. BUT I **WANT** TO UNDERSTAND.
YOU **CAN'T.**
YEAH, I CAN. I **CAN.** LISTEN TO ME.
YOU STAY **DOWN** THERE.

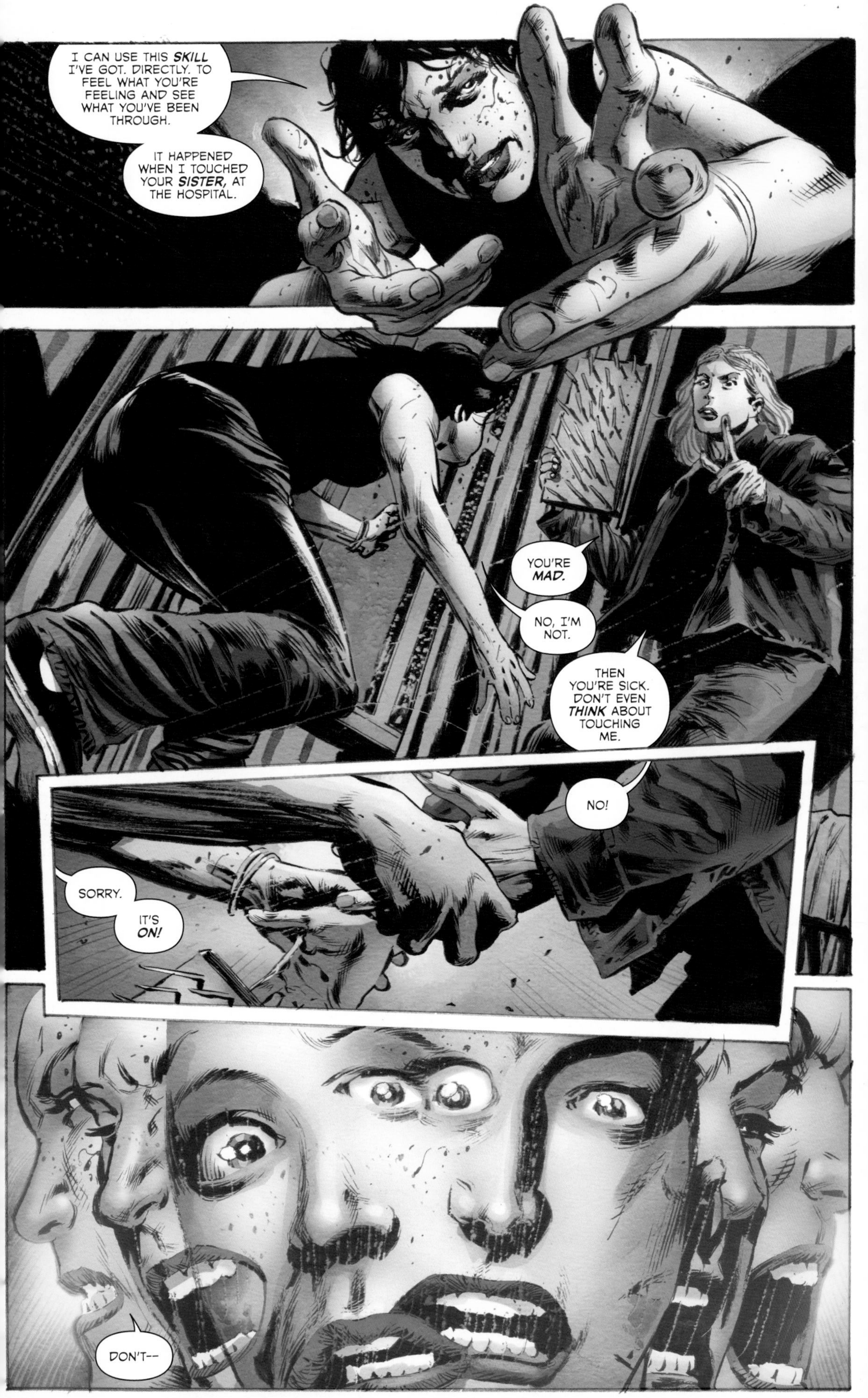
I CAN USE THIS SKILL I'VE GOT. DIRECTLY. TO FEEL WHAT YOU'RE FEELING AND SEE WHAT YOU'VE BEEN THROUGH.
IT HAPPENED WHEN I TOUCHED YOUR SISTER, AT THE HOSPITAL.
YOU'RE MAD.
NO, I'M NOT.
THEN YOU'RE SICK. DON'T EVEN THINK ABOUT TOUCHING ME.
NO!
SORRY.
IT'S ON!
DON'T--

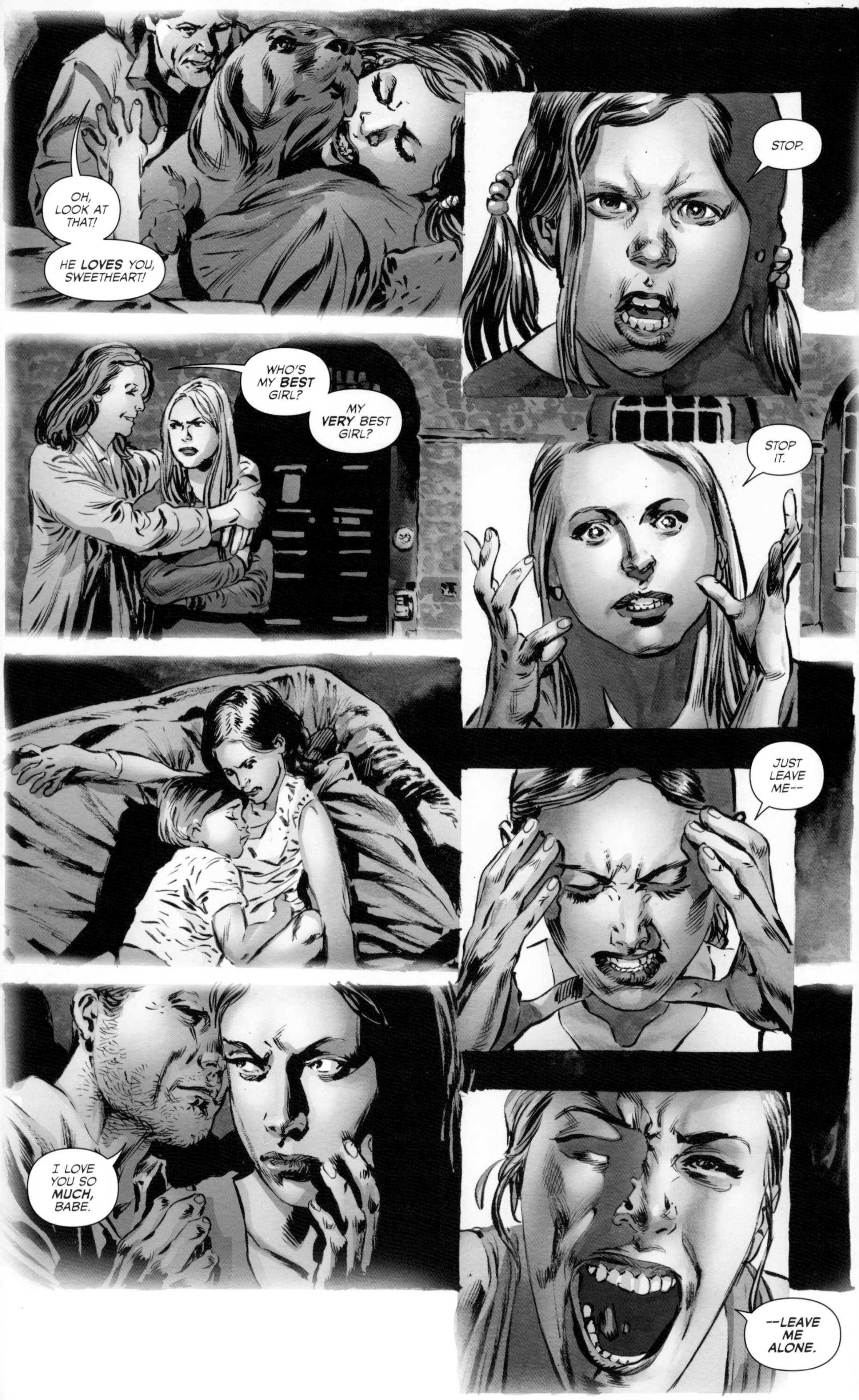

OH, LOOK AT THAT!
HE **LOVES** YOU, SWEETHEART!
STOP.
WHO'S MY **BEST** GIRL?
MY **VERY** BEST GIRL?
STOP IT.
JUST LEAVE ME--
I LOVE YOU SO **MUCH**, BABE.
--LEAVE ME ALONE.

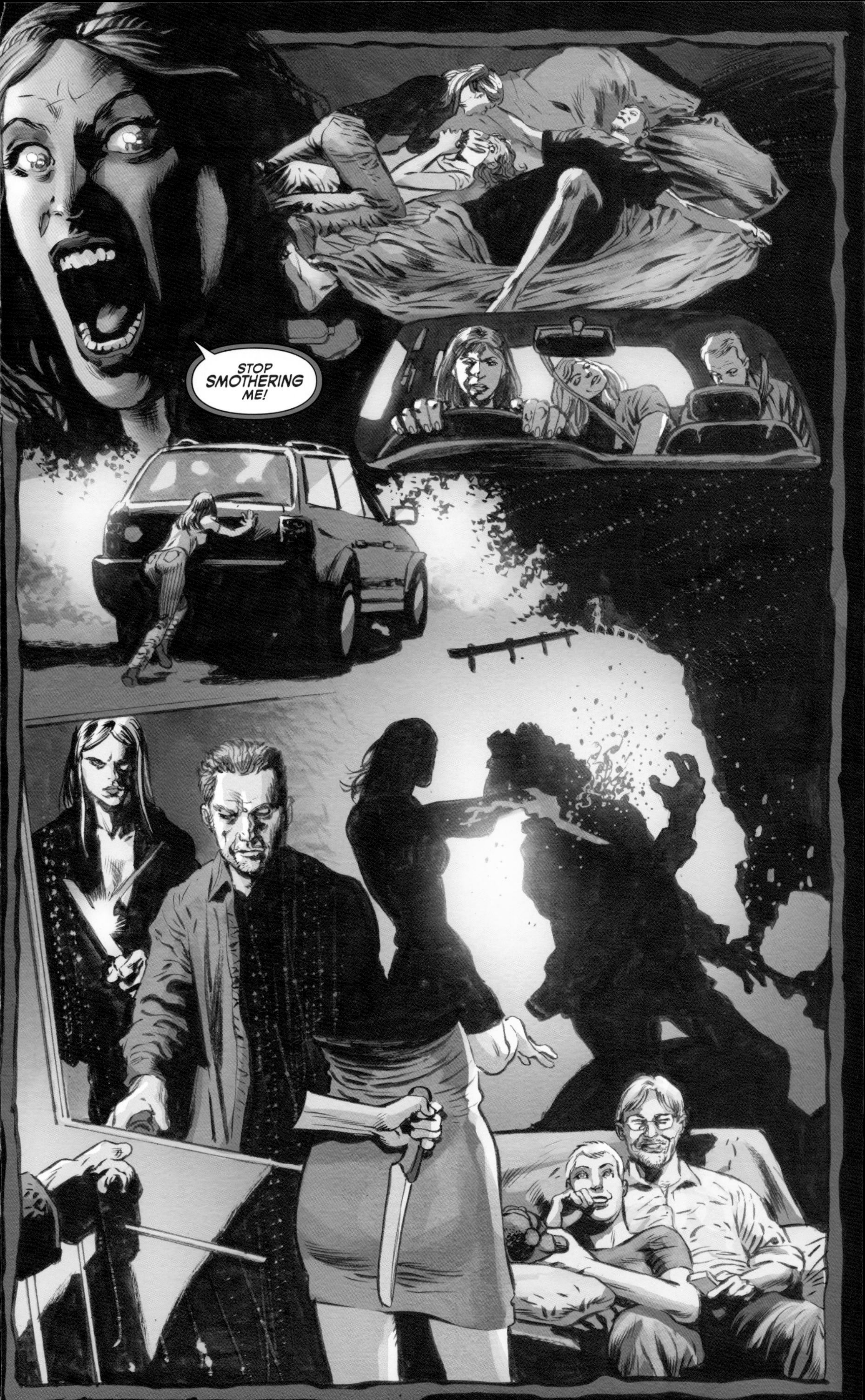
STOP SMOTHERING ME!

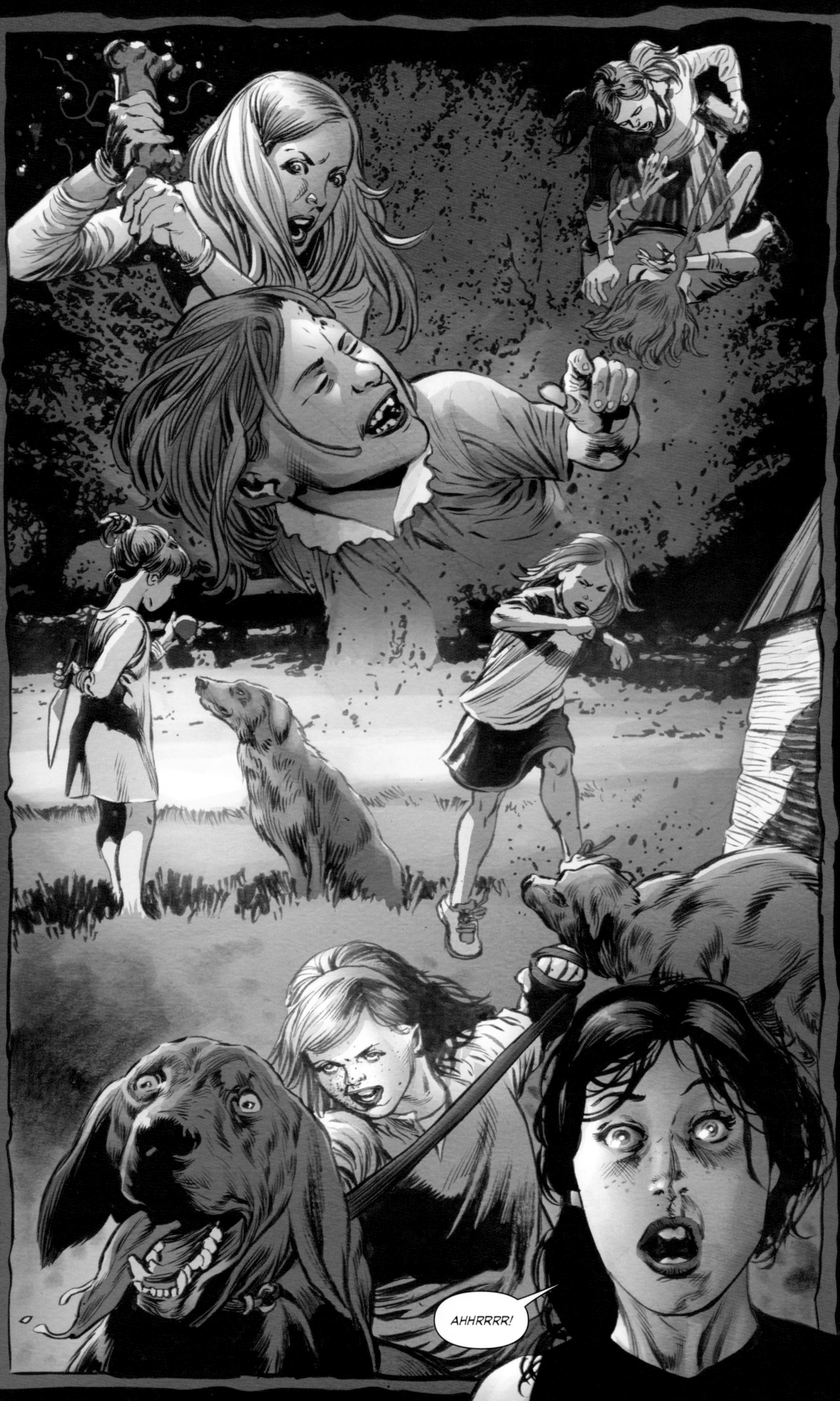
AHHRRRR!

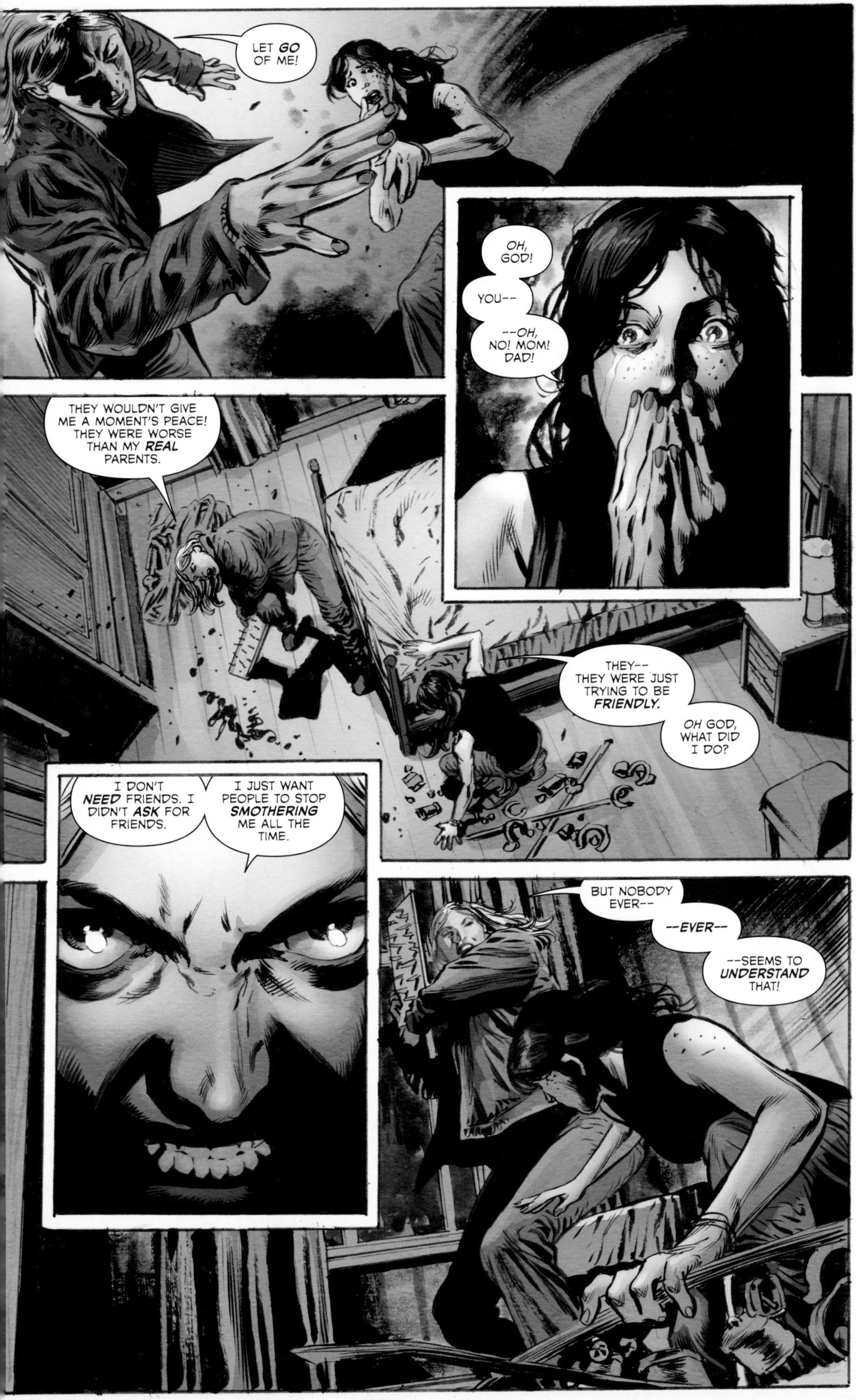

LET GO OF ME!
OH, GOD!
YOU--
--OH, NO! MOM! DAD!
THEY WOULDN'T GIVE ME A MOMENT'S PEACE! THEY WERE WORSE THAN MY REAL PARENTS.
THEY-- THEY WERE JUST TRYING TO BE FRIENDLY.
OH GOD, WHAT DID I DO?
I DON'T NEED FRIENDS. I DIDN'T ASK FOR FRIENDS.
I JUST WANT PEOPLE TO STOP SMOTHERING ME ALL THE TIME.
BUT NOBODY EVER--
--EVER--
--SEEMS TO UNDERSTAND THAT!

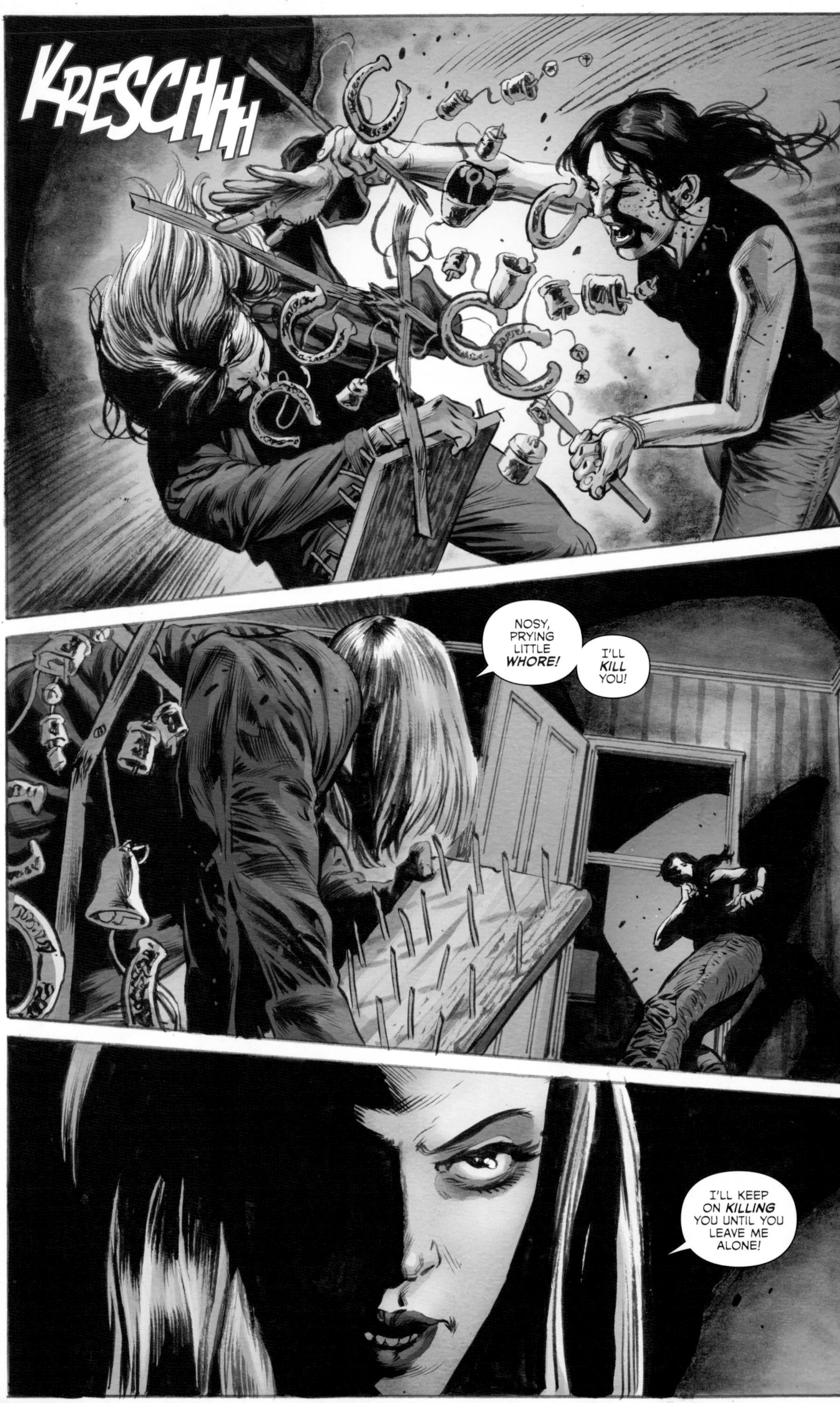
KRESCHHH
NOSY, PRYING LITTLE WHORE!
I'LL KILL YOU!
I'LL KEEP ON KILLING YOU UNTIL YOU LEAVE ME ALONE!

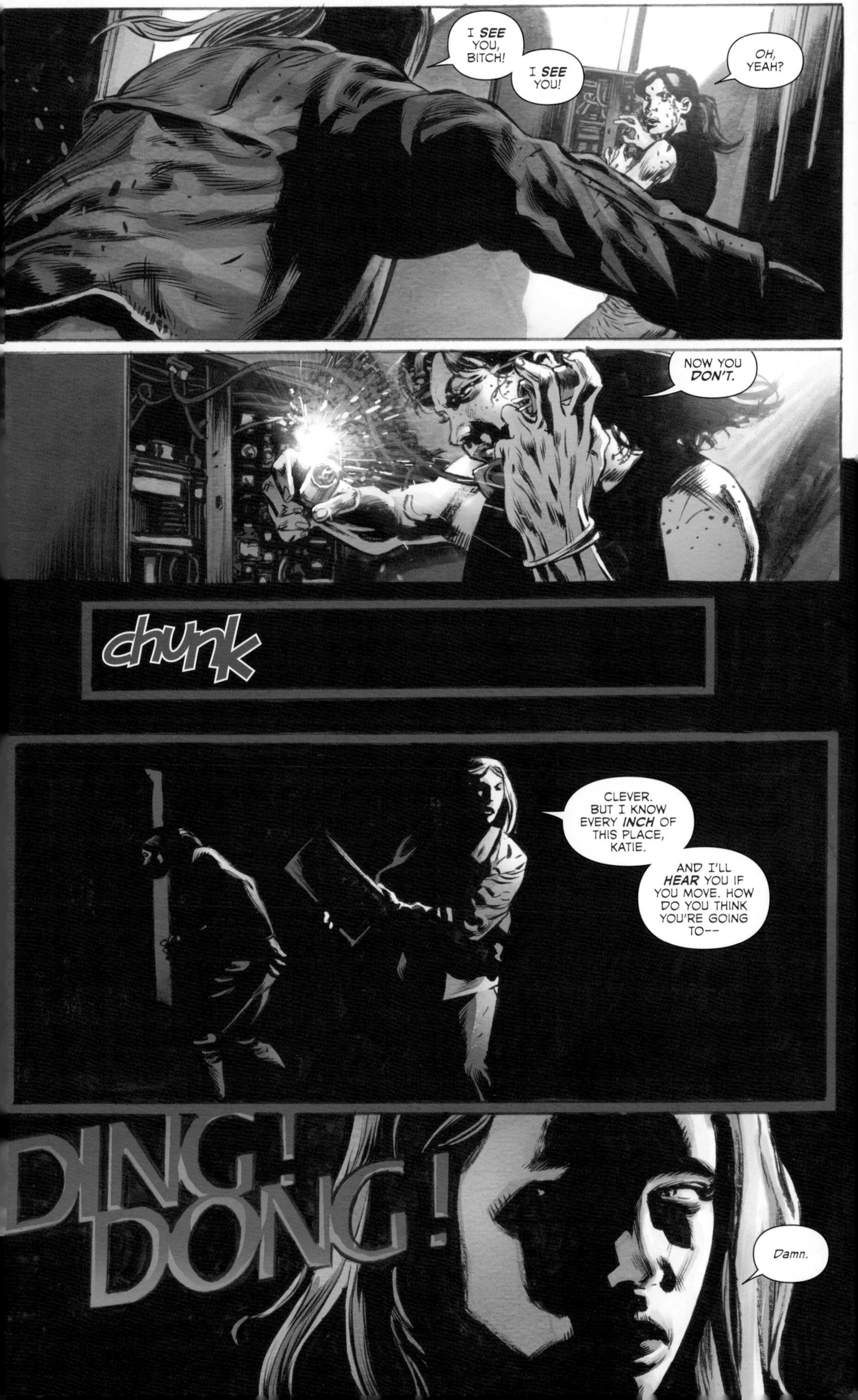
I SEE YOU, BITCH!
I SEE YOU!
OH, YEAH?
NOW YOU DON'T.
chunk
CLEVER. BUT I KNOW EVERY INCH OF THIS PLACE, KATIE.
AND I'LL HEAR YOU IF YOU MOVE. HOW DO YOU THINK YOU'RE GOING TO--
DING! DONG!
Damn.

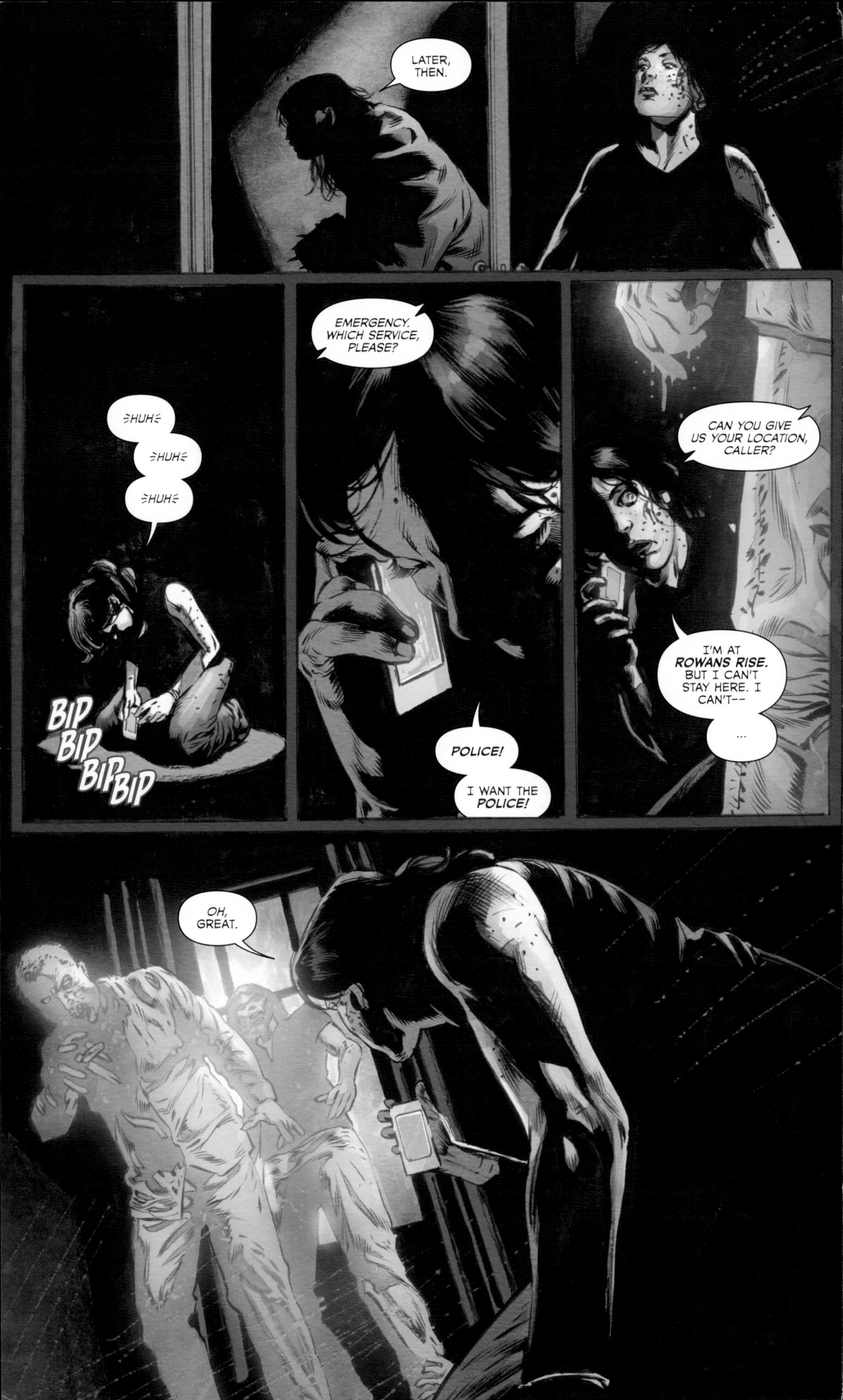

LATER, THEN.
≥HUH≤
≥HUH≤
≥HUH≤
BIP BIP BIP BIP
EMERGENCY. WHICH SERVICE, PLEASE?
POLICE!
I WANT THE POLICE!
CAN YOU GIVE US YOUR LOCATION, CALLER?
I'M AT ROWANS RISE. BUT I CAN'T STAY HERE. I CAN'T--
...
OH, GREAT.

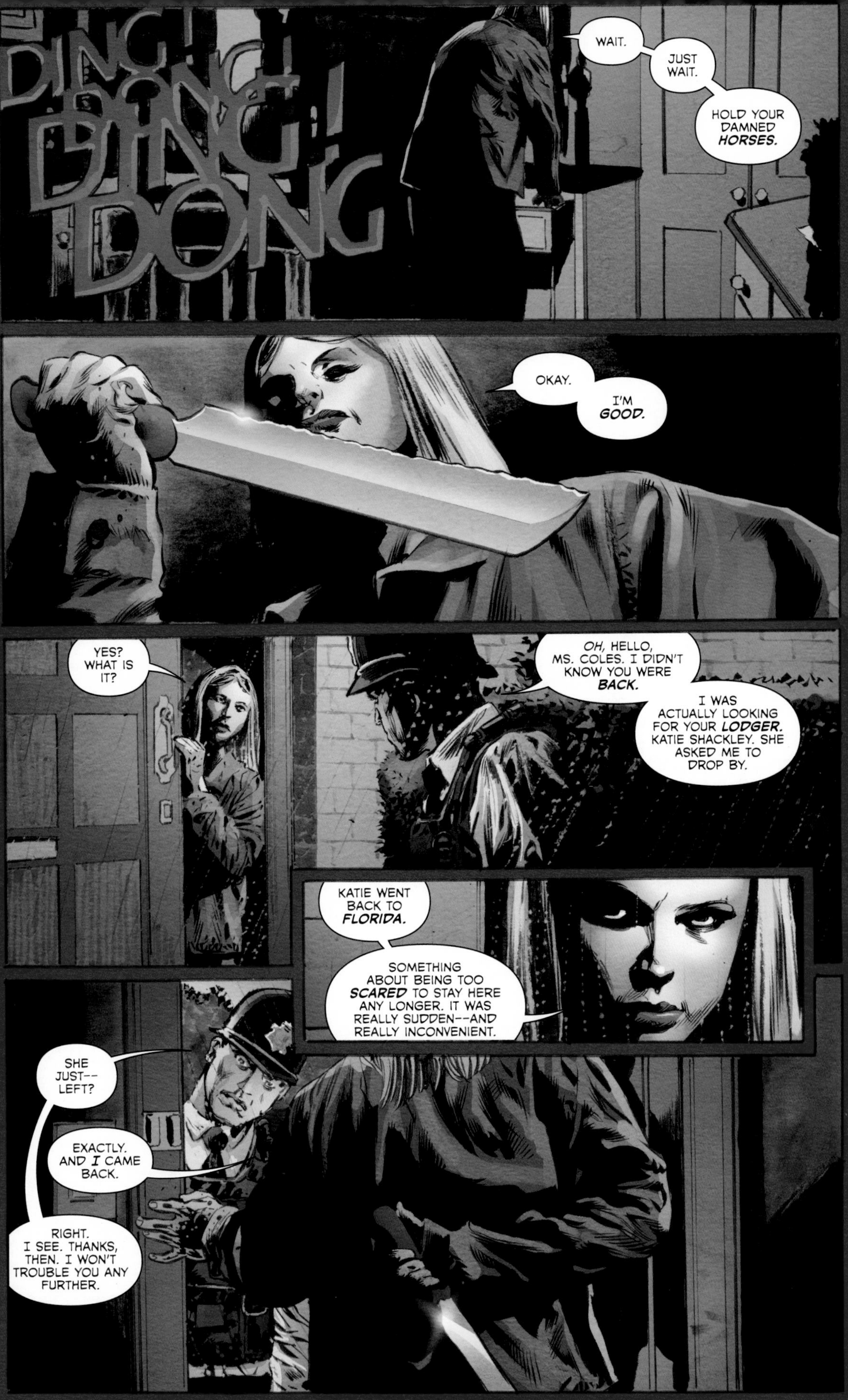
DING! DONG! DING! DONG
WAIT.
JUST WAIT.
HOLD YOUR DAMNED *HORSES.*
OKAY.
I'M *GOOD.*
YES? WHAT IS IT?
OH, HELLO, MS. COLES. I DIDN'T KNOW YOU WERE *BACK.*
I WAS ACTUALLY LOOKING FOR YOUR *LODGER.* KATIE SHACKLEY. SHE ASKED ME TO DROP BY.
KATIE WENT BACK TO *FLORIDA.*
SOMETHING ABOUT BEING TOO *SCARED* TO STAY HERE ANY LONGER. IT WAS REALLY SUDDEN--AND REALLY INCONVENIENT.
SHE JUST--LEFT?
EXACTLY. AND *I* CAME BACK.
RIGHT. I SEE. THANKS, THEN. I WON'T TROUBLE YOU ANY FURTHER.

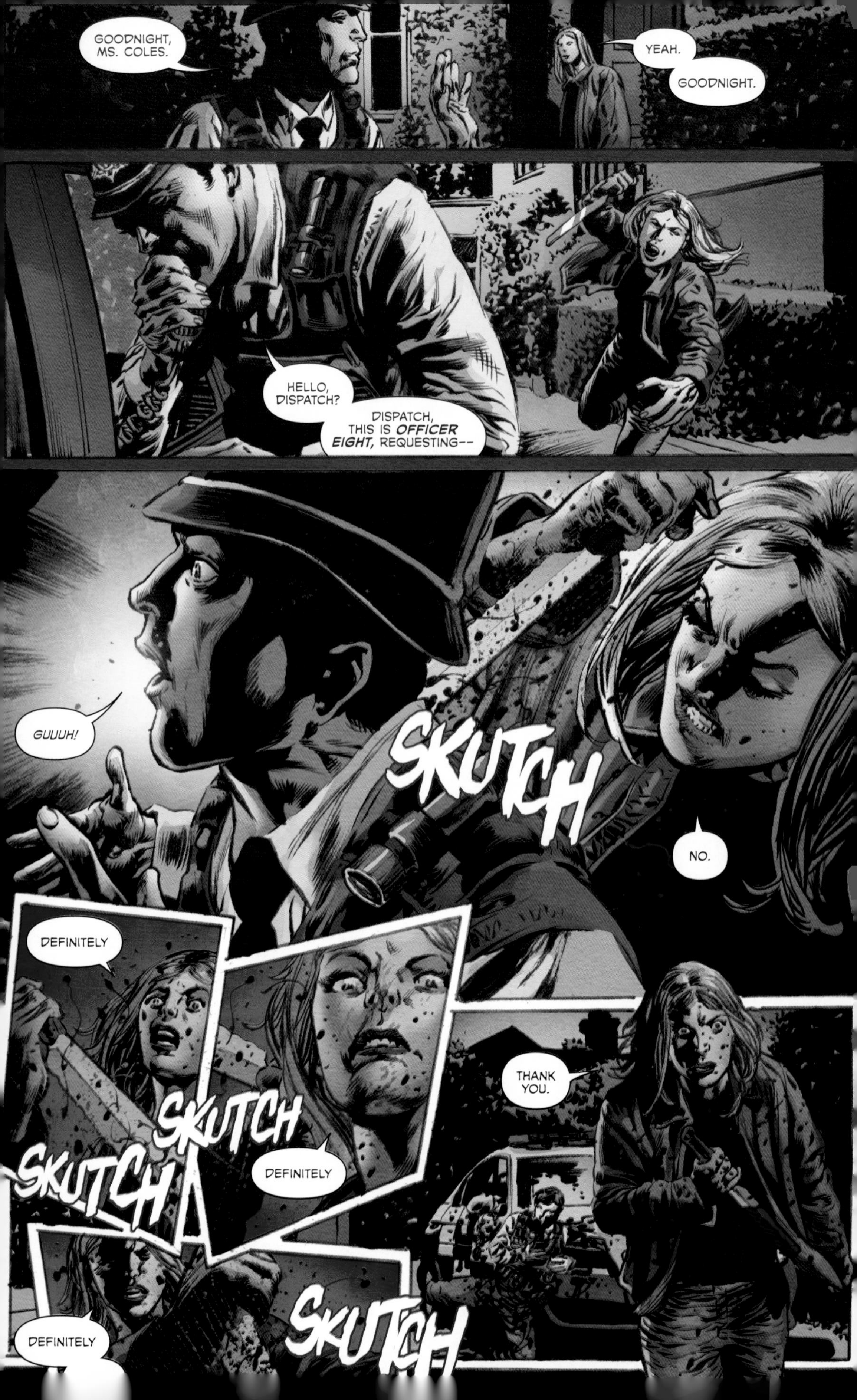
GOODNIGHT, MS. COLES.
YEAH.
GOODNIGHT.
HELLO, DISPATCH?
DISPATCH, THIS IS *OFFICER EIGHT,* REQUESTING--
GUUUH!
SKUTCH
NO.
DEFINITELY
SKUTCH
SKUTCH
DEFINITELY
DEFINITELY
SKUTCH
THANK YOU.

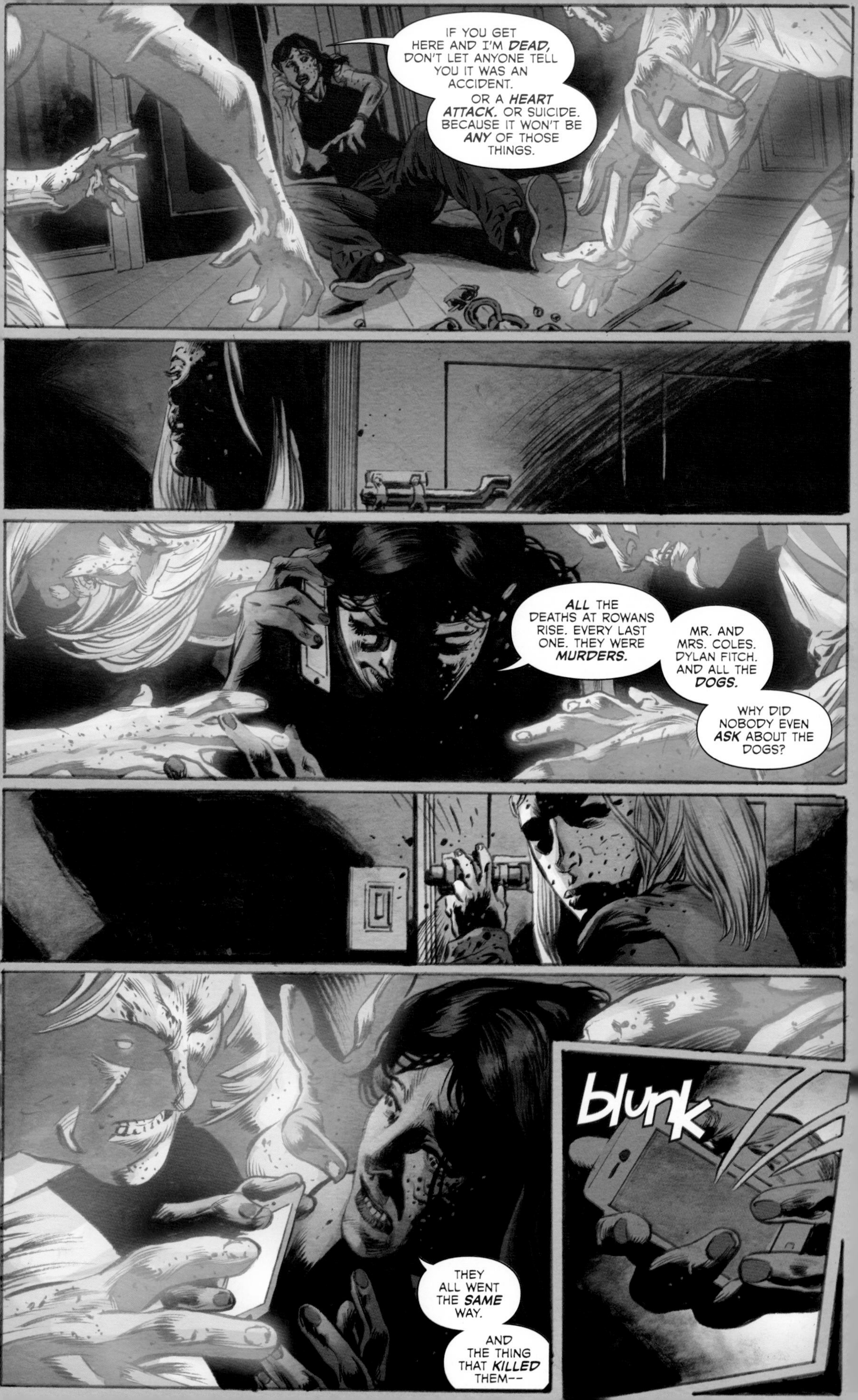
IF YOU GET HERE AND I'M DEAD, DON'T LET ANYONE TELL YOU IT WAS AN ACCIDENT.
OR A HEART ATTACK. OR SUICIDE. BECAUSE IT WON'T BE ANY OF THOSE THINGS.
ALL THE DEATHS AT ROWANS RISE. EVERY LAST ONE. THEY WERE MURDERS.
MR. AND MRS. COLES. DYLAN FITCH. AND ALL THE DOGS.
WHY DID NOBODY EVEN ASK ABOUT THE DOGS?
blunk
THEY ALL WENT THE SAME WAY.
AND THE THING THAT KILLED THEM--

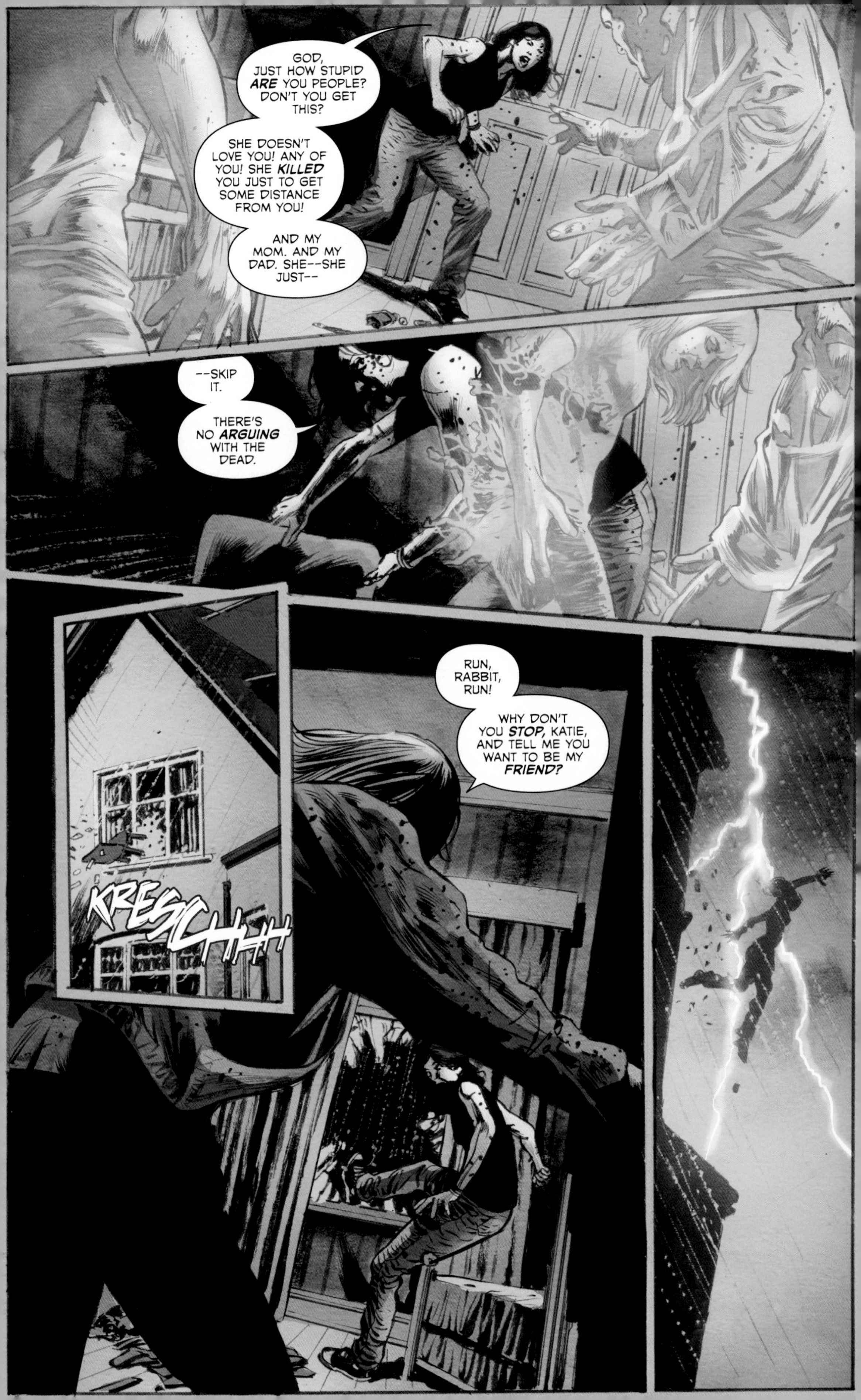
GOD, JUST HOW STUPID ARE YOU PEOPLE? DON'T YOU GET THIS?
SHE DOESN'T LOVE YOU! ANY OF YOU! SHE KILLED YOU JUST TO GET SOME DISTANCE FROM YOU!
AND MY MOM. AND MY DAD. SHE--SHE JUST--
--SKIP IT.
THERE'S NO ARGUING WITH THE DEAD.
KRESCHHH
RUN, RABBIT, RUN!
WHY DON'T YOU STOP, KATIE, AND TELL ME YOU WANT TO BE MY FRIEND?

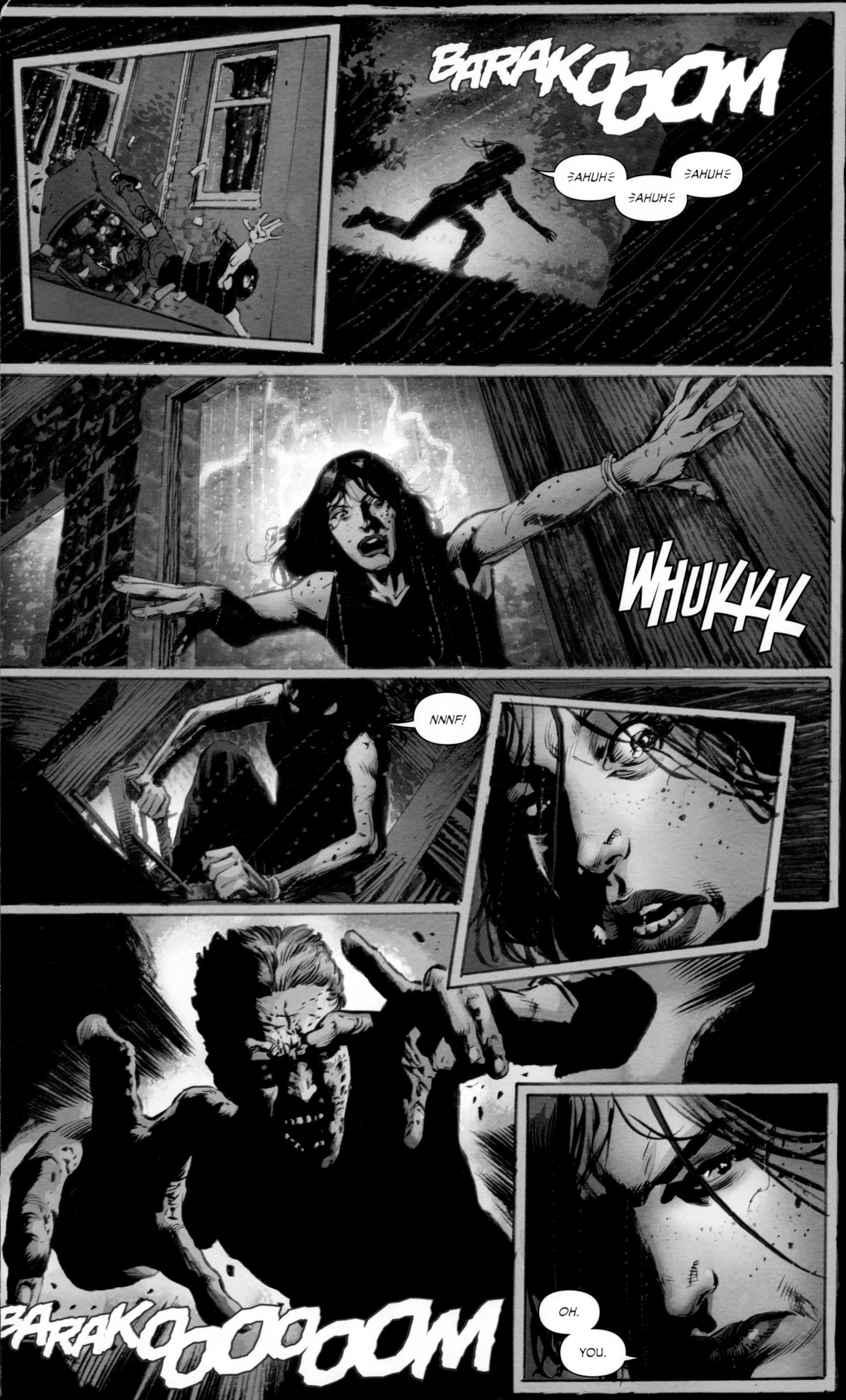
BARAKOOOM
AHUH
AHUH
AHUH
WHUKKK
NNNF!
BARAKOOOOOOM
OH.
YOU.

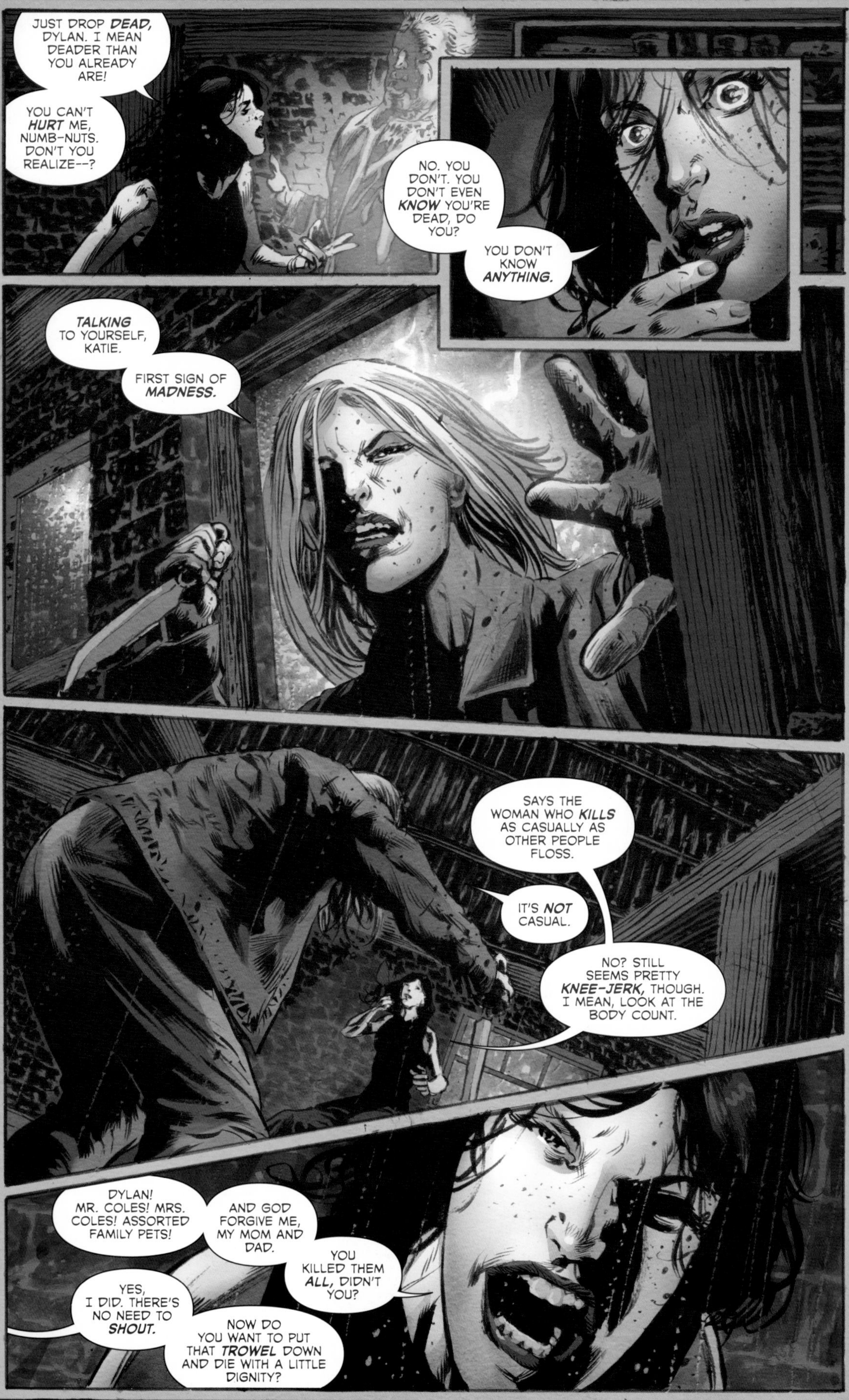

JUST DROP DEAD, DYLAN. I MEAN DEADER THAN YOU ALREADY ARE!
YOU CAN'T HURT ME, NUMB-NUTS. DON'T YOU REALIZE--?
NO. YOU DON'T. YOU DON'T EVEN KNOW YOU'RE DEAD, DO YOU?
YOU DON'T KNOW ANYTHING.
TALKING TO YOURSELF, KATIE.
FIRST SIGN OF MADNESS.
SAYS THE WOMAN WHO KILLS AS CASUALLY AS OTHER PEOPLE FLOSS.
IT'S NOT CASUAL.
NO? STILL SEEMS PRETTY KNEE-JERK, THOUGH. I MEAN, LOOK AT THE BODY COUNT.
DYLAN! MR. COLES! MRS. COLES! ASSORTED FAMILY PETS!
AND GOD FORGIVE ME, MY MOM AND DAD.
YOU KILLED THEM ALL, DIDN'T YOU?
YES, I DID. THERE'S NO NEED TO SHOUT.
NOW DO YOU WANT TO PUT THAT TROWEL DOWN AND DIE WITH A LITTLE DIGNITY?

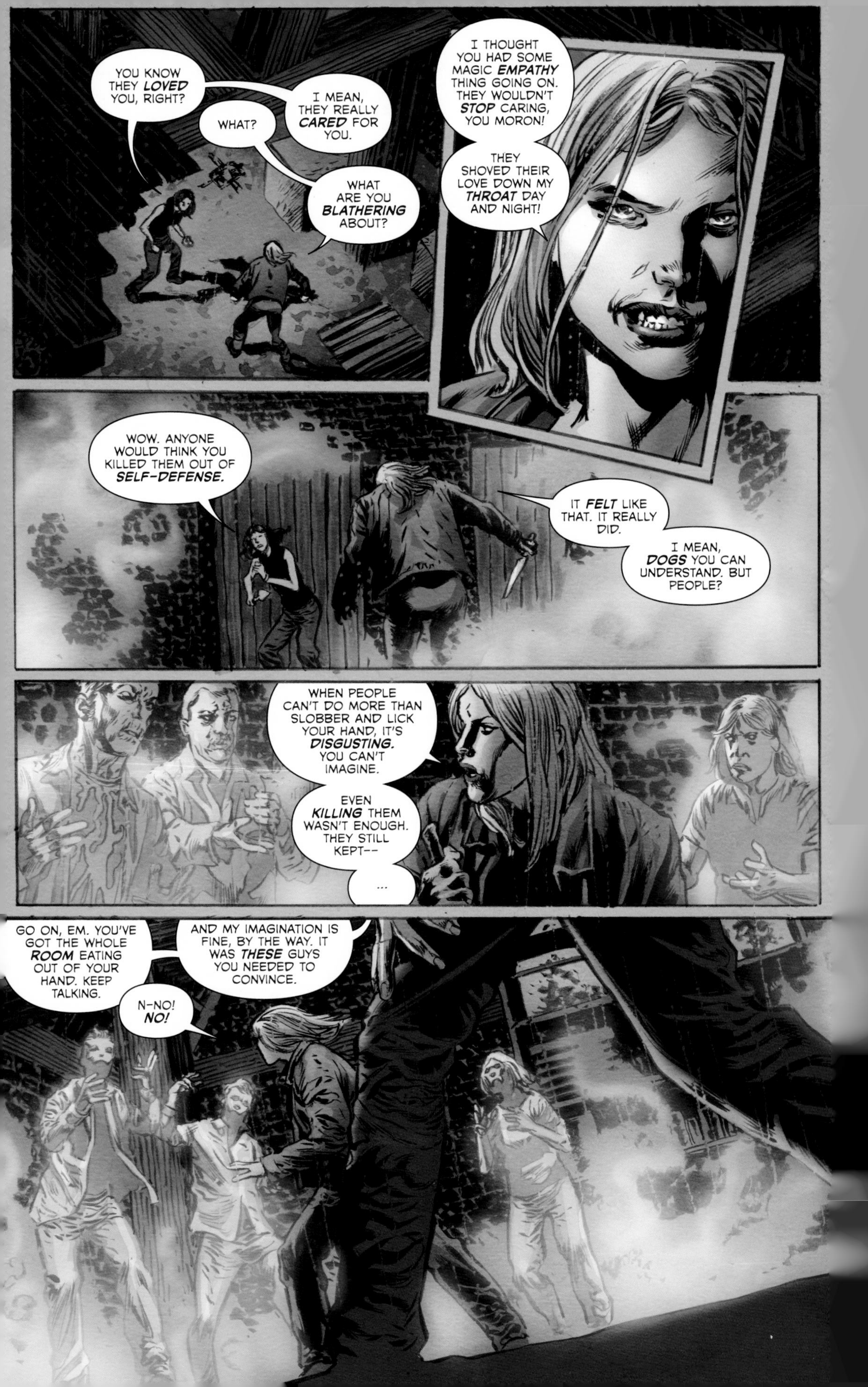
YOU KNOW THEY LOVED YOU, RIGHT?
WHAT?
I MEAN, THEY REALLY CARED FOR YOU.
WHAT ARE YOU BLATHERING ABOUT?
I THOUGHT YOU HAD SOME MAGIC EMPATHY THING GOING ON. THEY WOULDN'T STOP CARING, YOU MORON!
THEY SHOVED THEIR LOVE DOWN MY THROAT DAY AND NIGHT!
WOW. ANYONE WOULD THINK YOU KILLED THEM OUT OF SELF-DEFENSE.
IT FELT LIKE THAT. IT REALLY DID.
I MEAN, DOGS YOU CAN UNDERSTAND. BUT PEOPLE?
WHEN PEOPLE CAN'T DO MORE THAN SLOBBER AND LICK YOUR HAND, IT'S DISGUSTING. YOU CAN'T IMAGINE.
EVEN KILLING THEM WASN'T ENOUGH. THEY STILL KEPT--
...
GO ON, EM. YOU'VE GOT THE WHOLE ROOM EATING OUT OF YOUR HAND. KEEP TALKING.
AND MY IMAGINATION IS FINE, BY THE WAY. IT WAS THESE GUYS YOU NEEDED TO CONVINCE.
N-NO! NO!

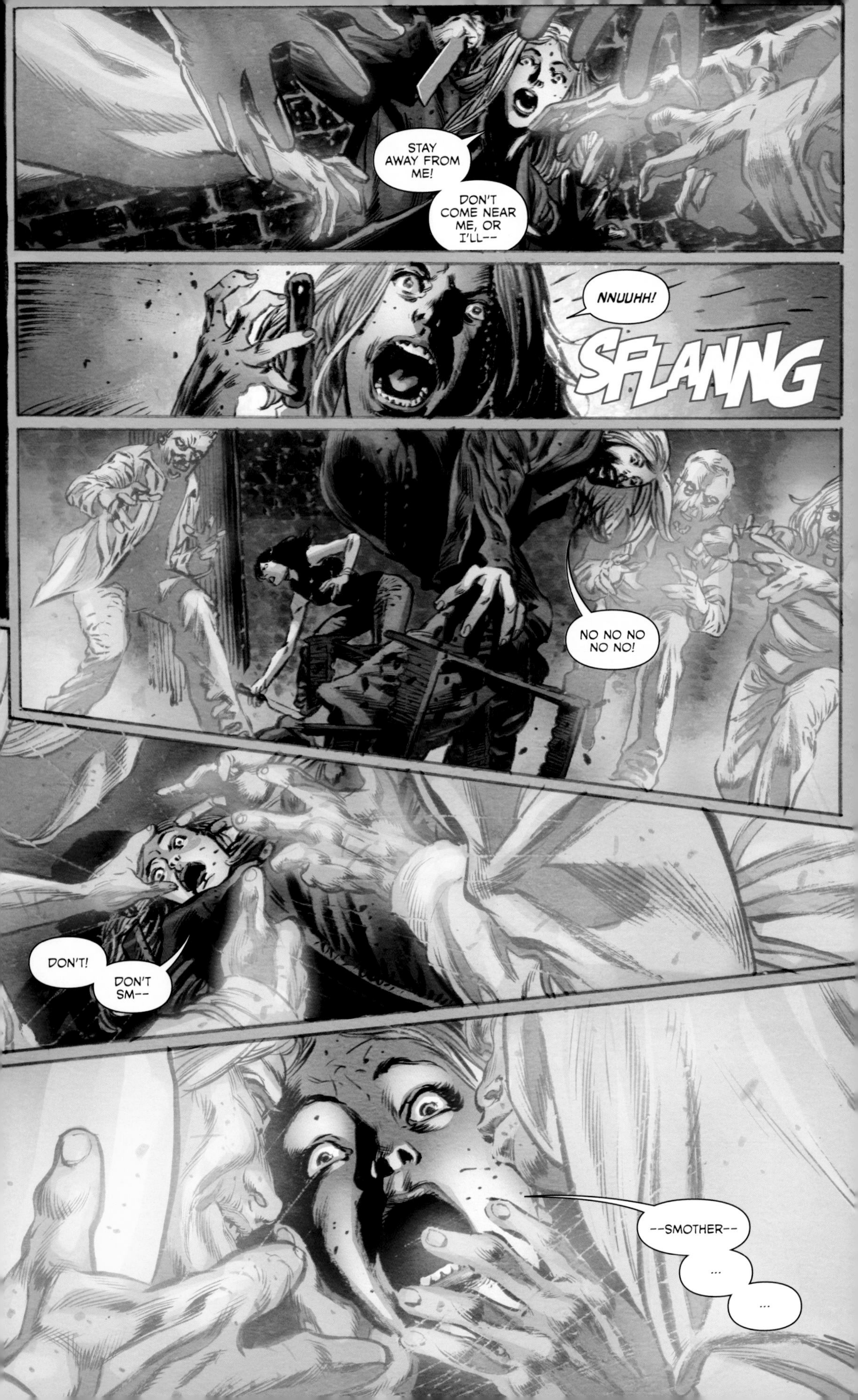
STAY AWAY FROM ME!
DON'T COME NEAR ME, OR I'LL--
NNUUHH!
SFLANNG
NO NO NO NO NO!
DON'T!
DON'T SM--
--SMOTHER--
...
...

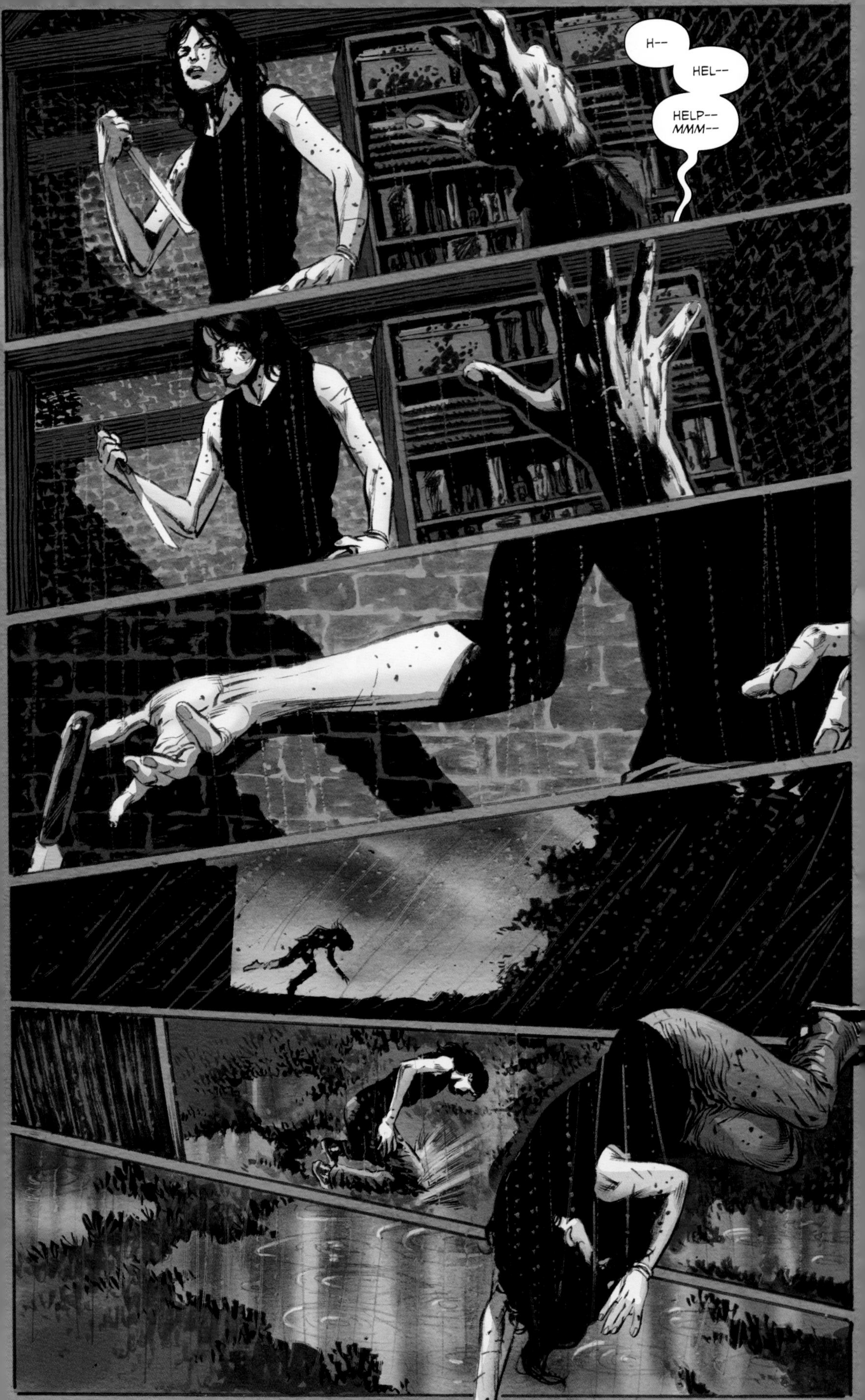
H--
HEL--
HELP--
MMM--

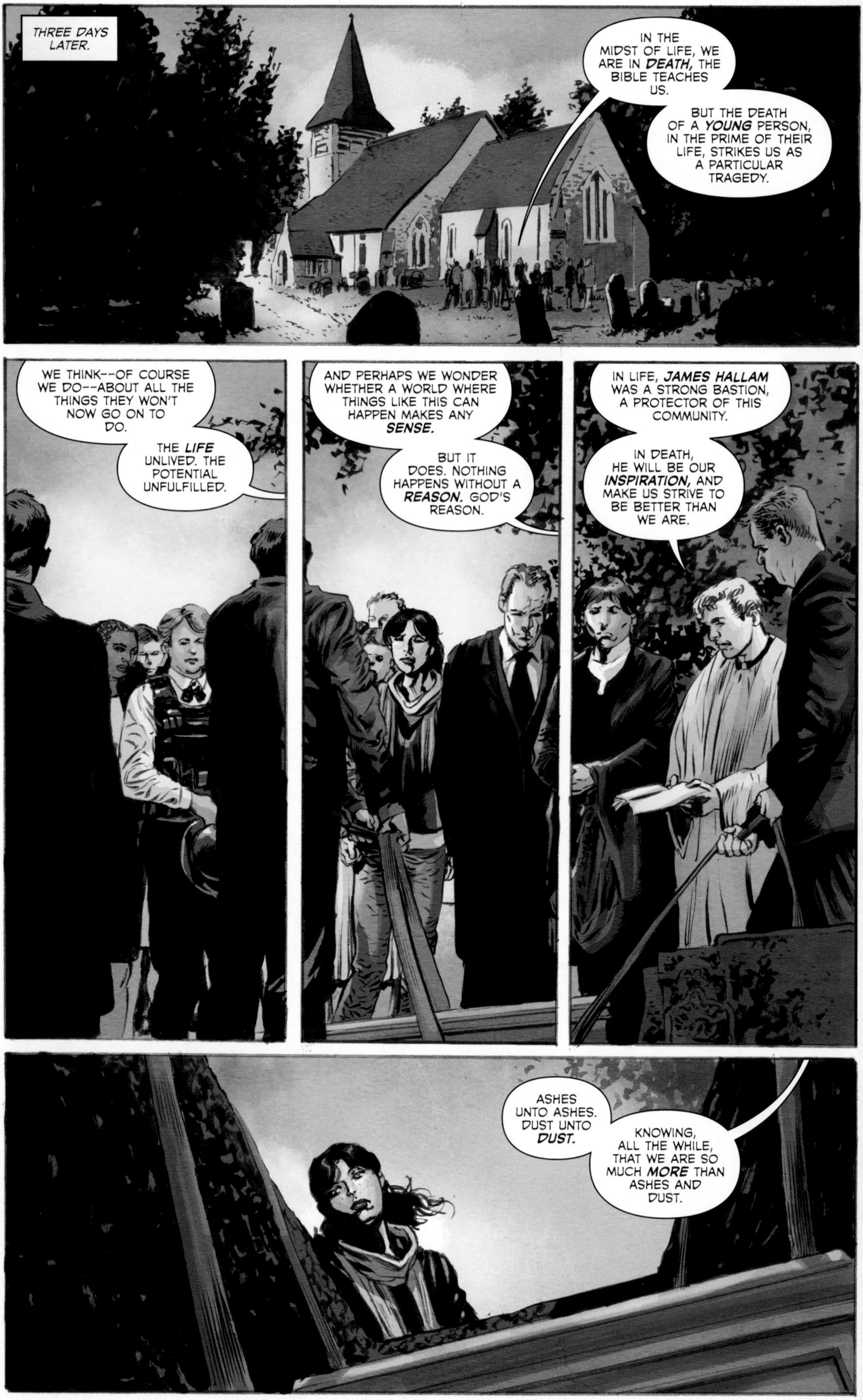
THREE DAYS LATER.
IN THE MIDST OF LIFE, WE ARE IN DEATH, THE BIBLE TEACHES US.
BUT THE DEATH OF A YOUNG PERSON, IN THE PRIME OF THEIR LIFE, STRIKES US AS A PARTICULAR TRAGEDY.
WE THINK--OF COURSE WE DO--ABOUT ALL THE THINGS THEY WON'T NOW GO ON TO DO.
THE LIFE UNLIVED. THE POTENTIAL UNFULFILLED.
AND PERHAPS WE WONDER WHETHER A WORLD WHERE THINGS LIKE THIS CAN HAPPEN MAKES ANY SENSE.
BUT IT DOES. NOTHING HAPPENS WITHOUT A REASON. GOD'S REASON.
IN LIFE, JAMES HALLAM WAS A STRONG BASTION, A PROTECTOR OF THIS COMMUNITY.
IN DEATH, HE WILL BE OUR INSPIRATION, AND MAKE US STRIVE TO BE BETTER THAN WE ARE.
ASHES UNTO ASHES. DUST UNTO DUST.
KNOWING, ALL THE WHILE, THAT WE ARE SO MUCH MORE THAN ASHES AND DUST.

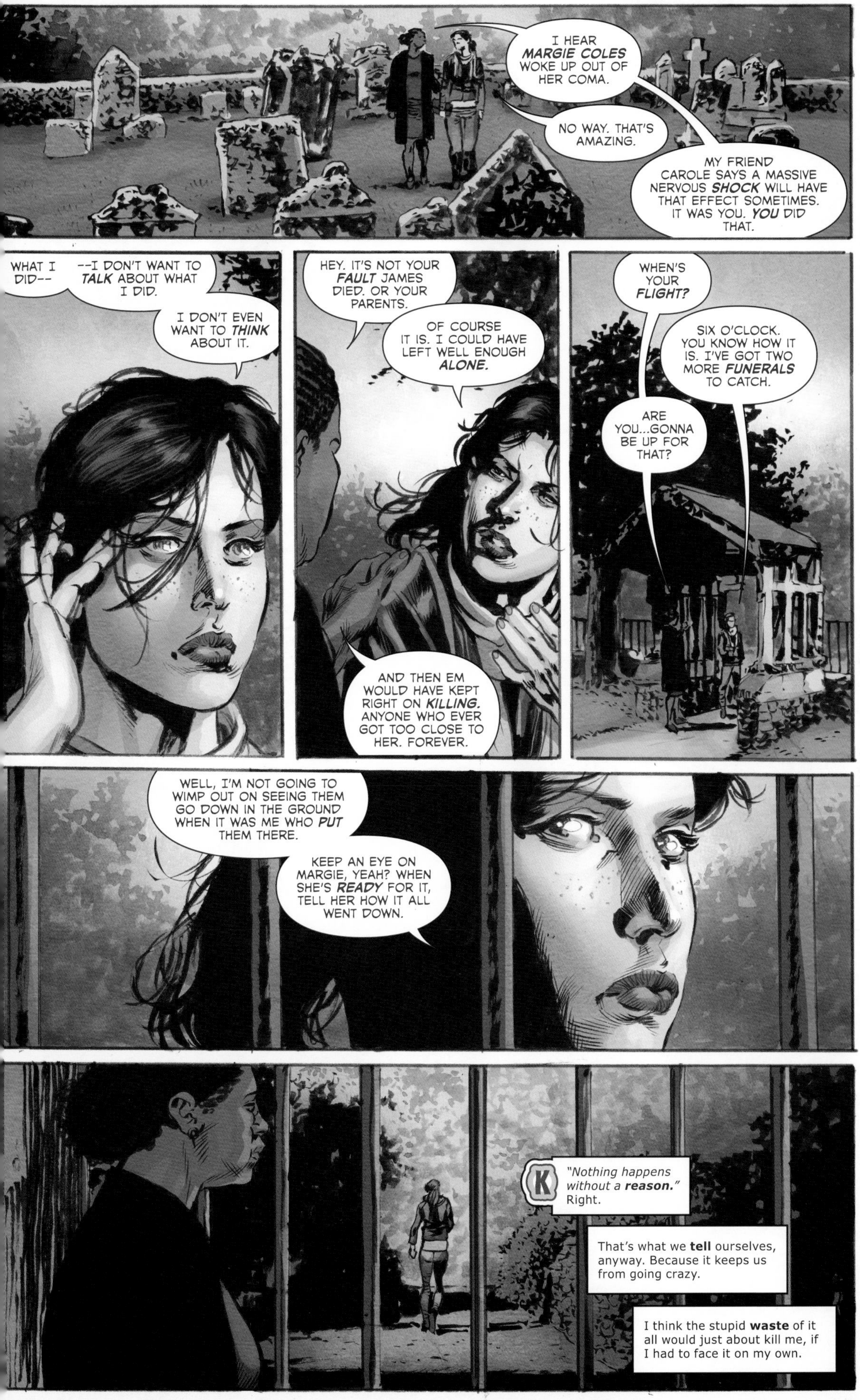

I HEAR *MARGIE COLES* WOKE UP OUT OF HER COMA.
NO WAY. THAT'S AMAZING.
MY FRIEND CAROLE SAYS A MASSIVE NERVOUS *SHOCK* WILL HAVE THAT EFFECT SOMETIMES. IT WAS YOU. *YOU* DID THAT.
WHAT I DID--
--I DON'T WANT TO *TALK* ABOUT WHAT I DID.
I DON'T EVEN WANT TO *THINK* ABOUT IT.
HEY. IT'S NOT YOUR *FAULT* JAMES DIED. OR YOUR PARENTS.
OF COURSE IT IS. I COULD HAVE LEFT WELL ENOUGH *ALONE.*
AND THEN EM WOULD HAVE KEPT RIGHT ON *KILLING.* ANYONE WHO EVER GOT TOO CLOSE TO HER. FOREVER.
WHEN'S YOUR *FLIGHT?*
SIX O'CLOCK. YOU KNOW HOW IT IS. I'VE GOT TWO MORE *FUNERALS* TO CATCH.
ARE YOU...GONNA BE UP FOR THAT?
WELL, I'M NOT GOING TO WIMP OUT ON SEEING THEM GO DOWN IN THE GROUND WHEN IT WAS ME WHO *PUT* THEM THERE.
KEEP AN EYE ON MARGIE, YEAH? WHEN SHE'S *READY* FOR IT, TELL HER HOW IT ALL WENT DOWN.
K
*"Nothing happens without a **reason.**"* Right.
That's what we **tell** ourselves, anyway. Because it keeps us from going crazy.
I think the stupid **waste** of it all would just about kill me, if I had to face it on my own.

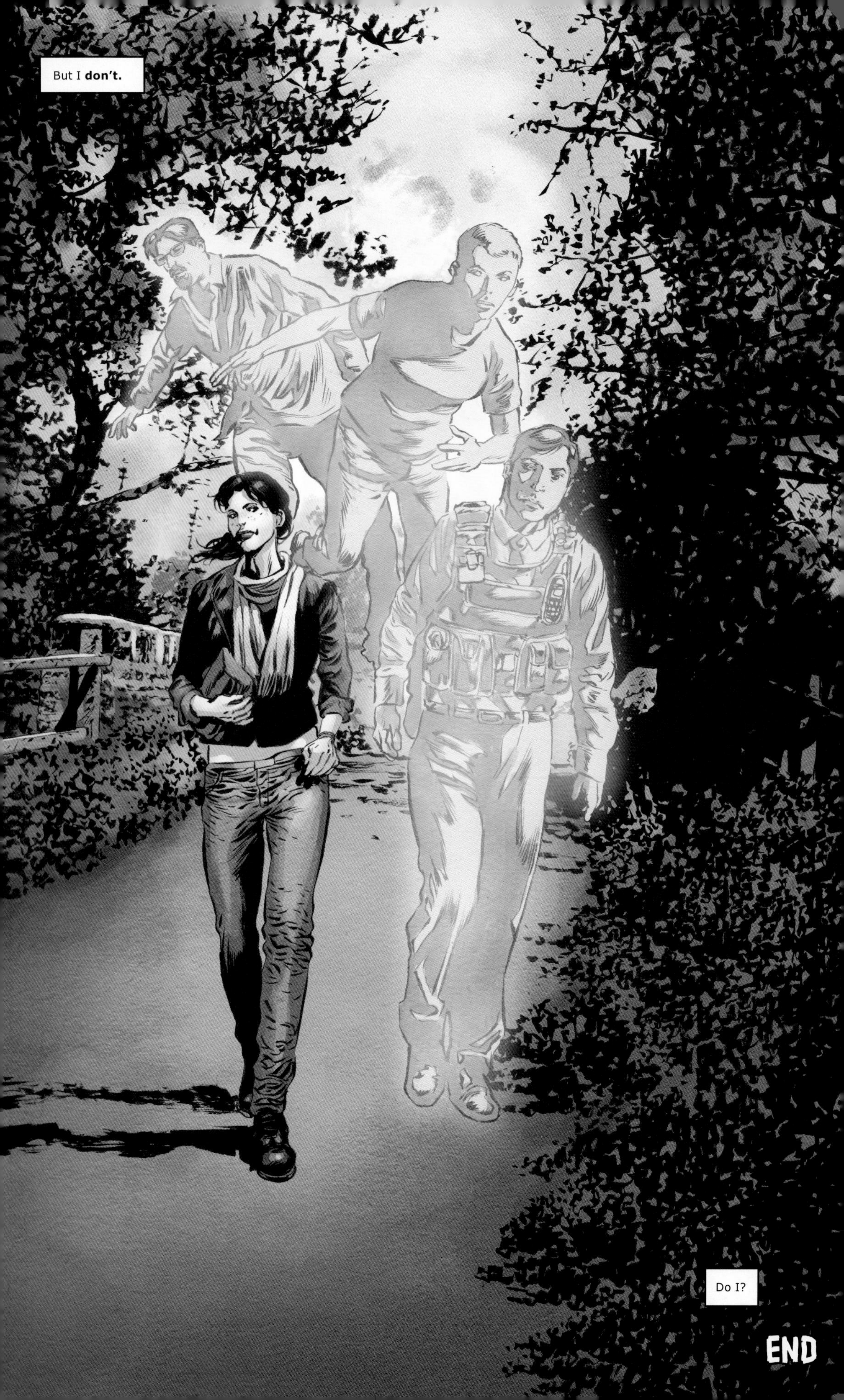
But I **don't.**
Do I?
END

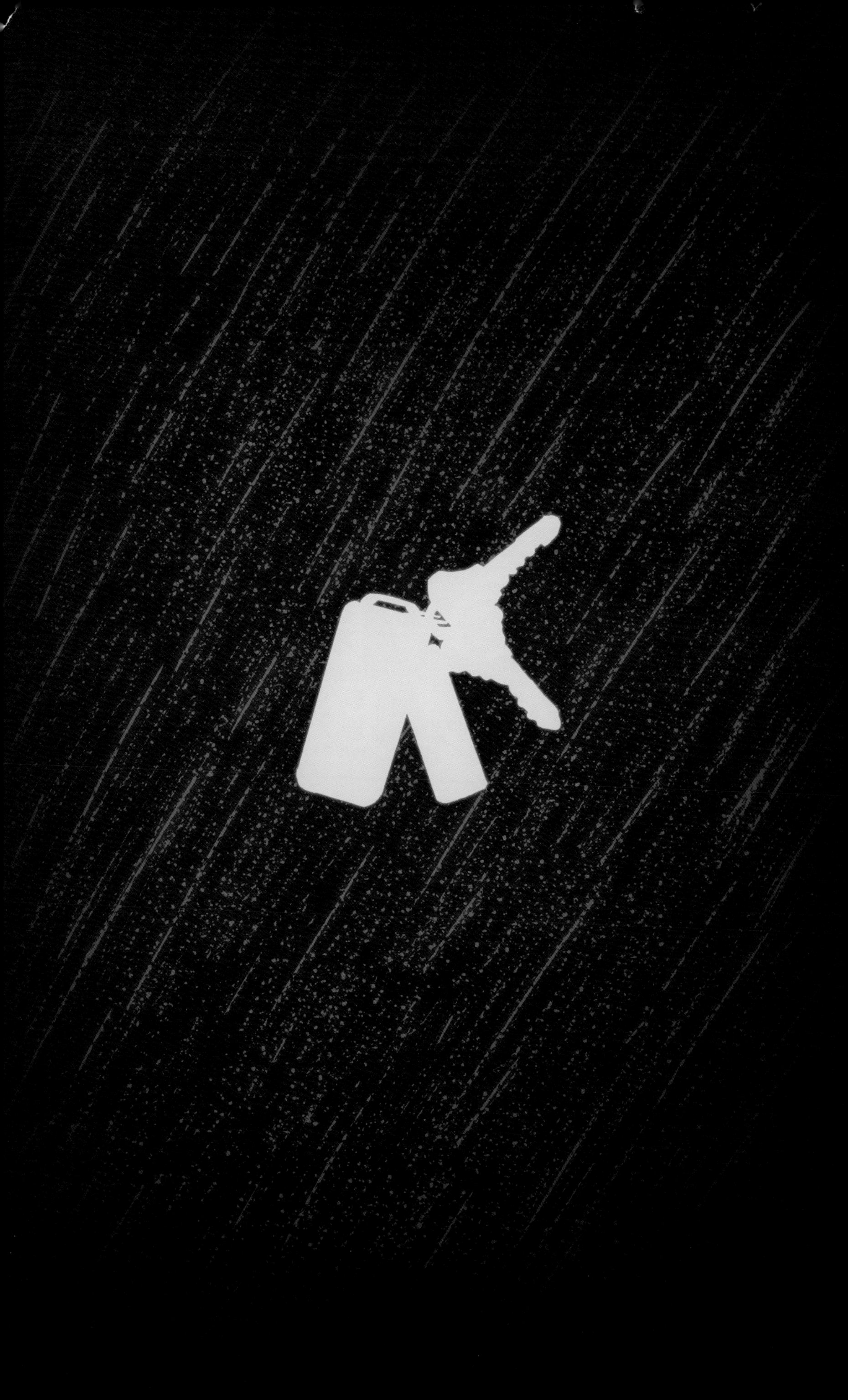

COVER
GALLERY

Issue One Cover
Mike Perkins
colors by **Andy Troy**

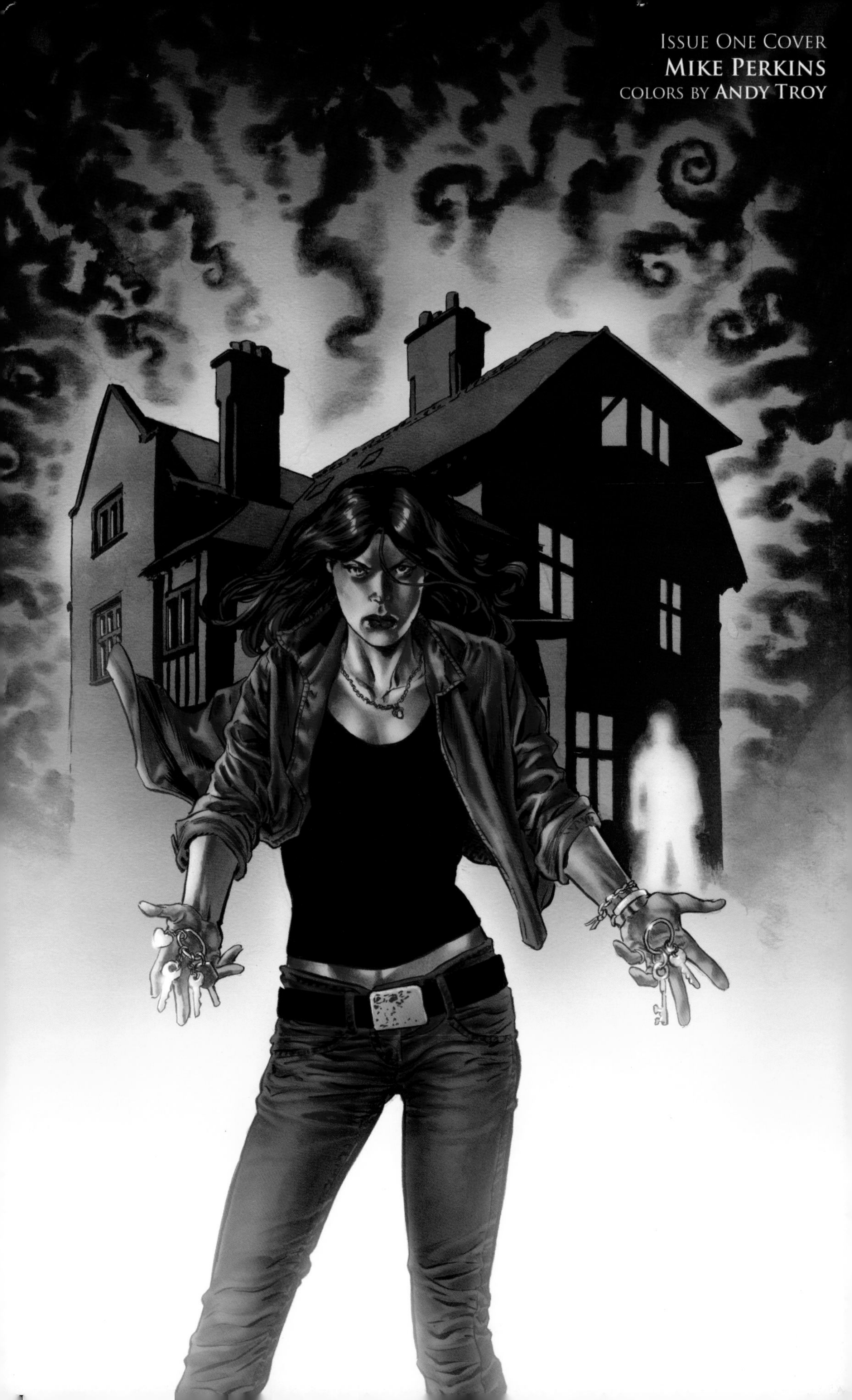

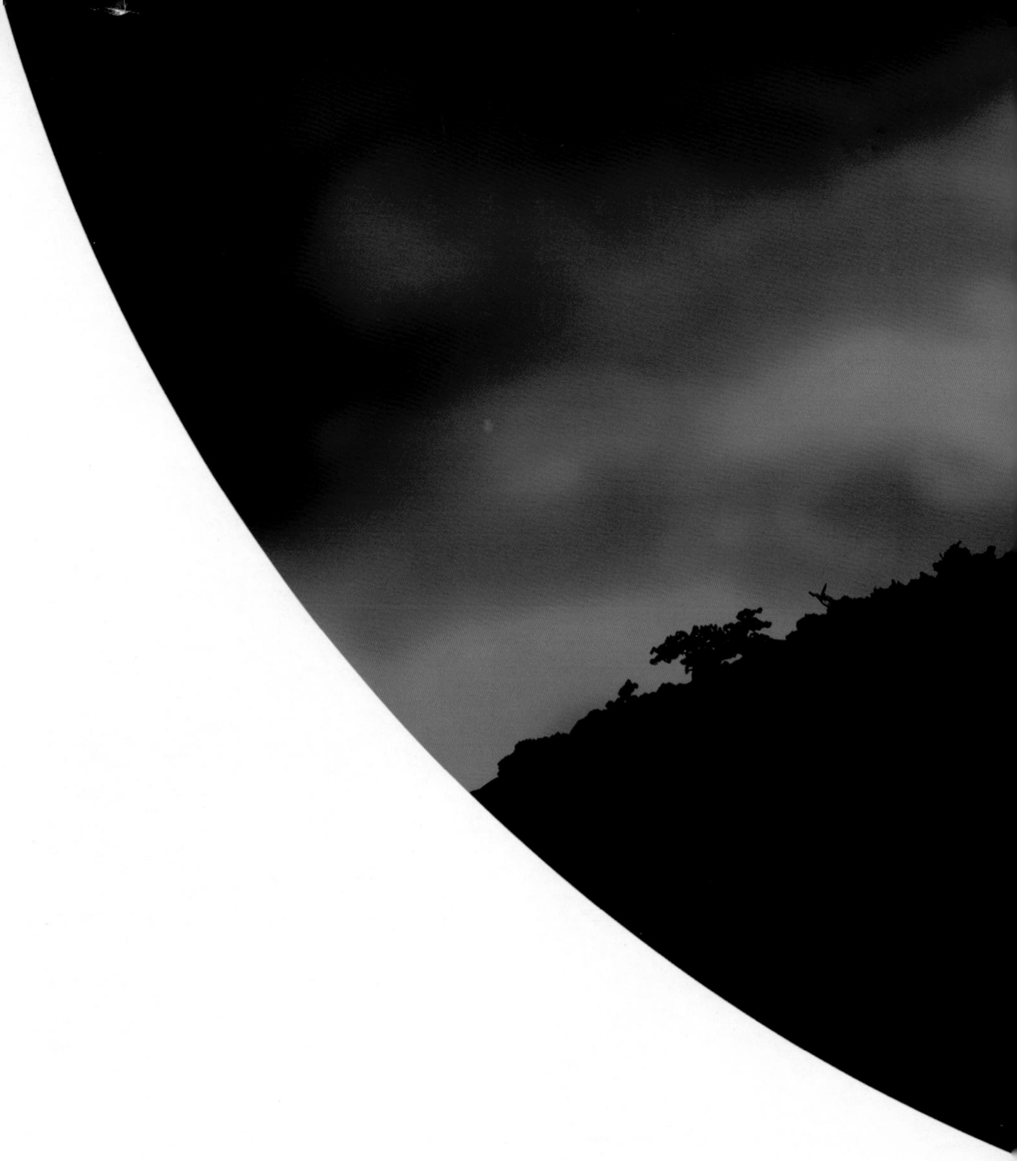

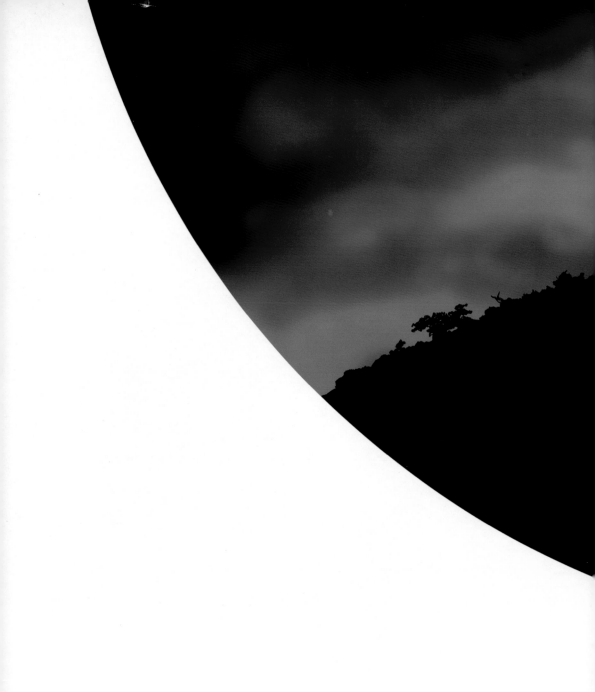

Issue One BOOM! Ten Years Variant Cover
Felipe Smith

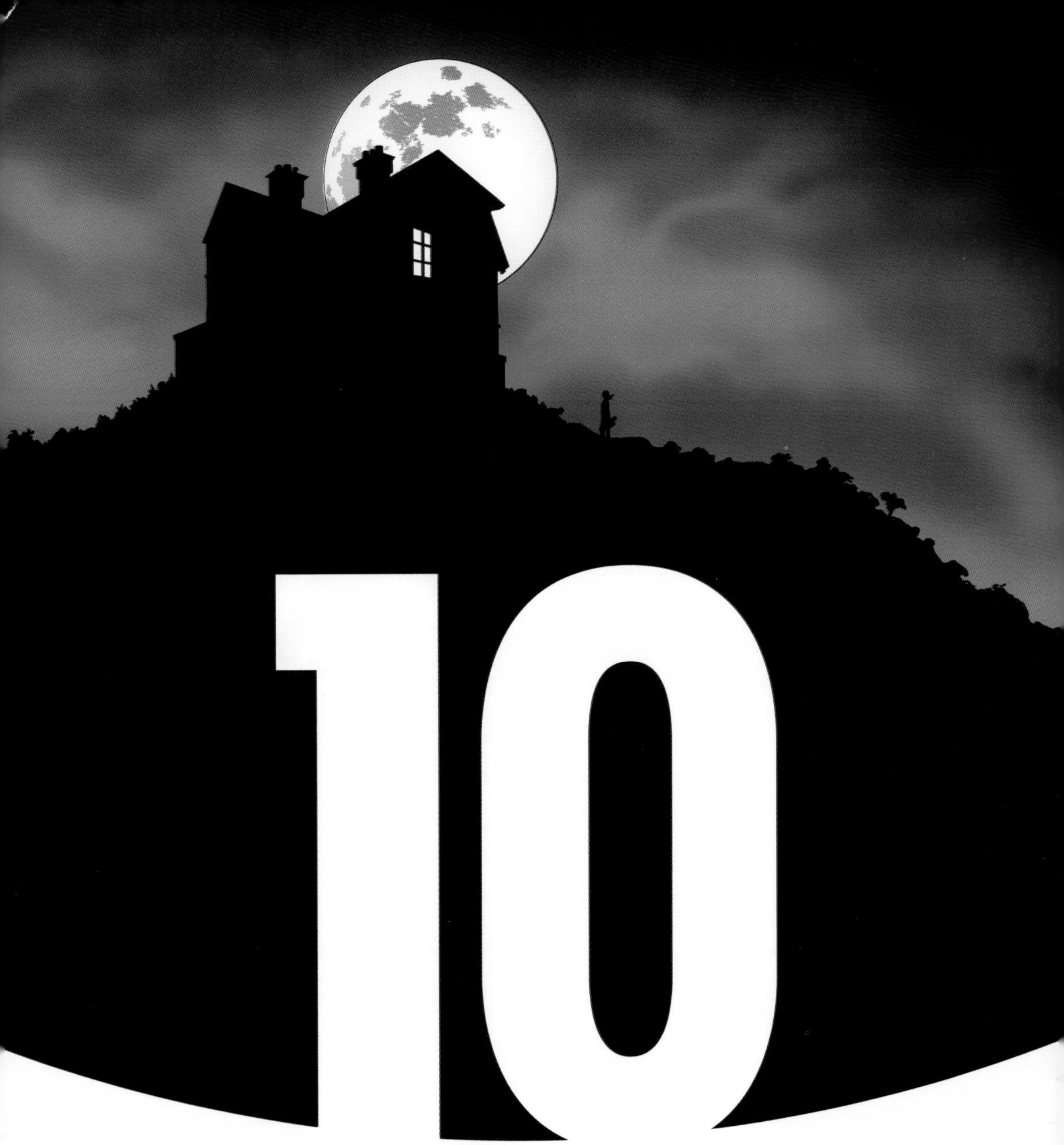
10

Jackpot Variant Cover

Mike Perkins

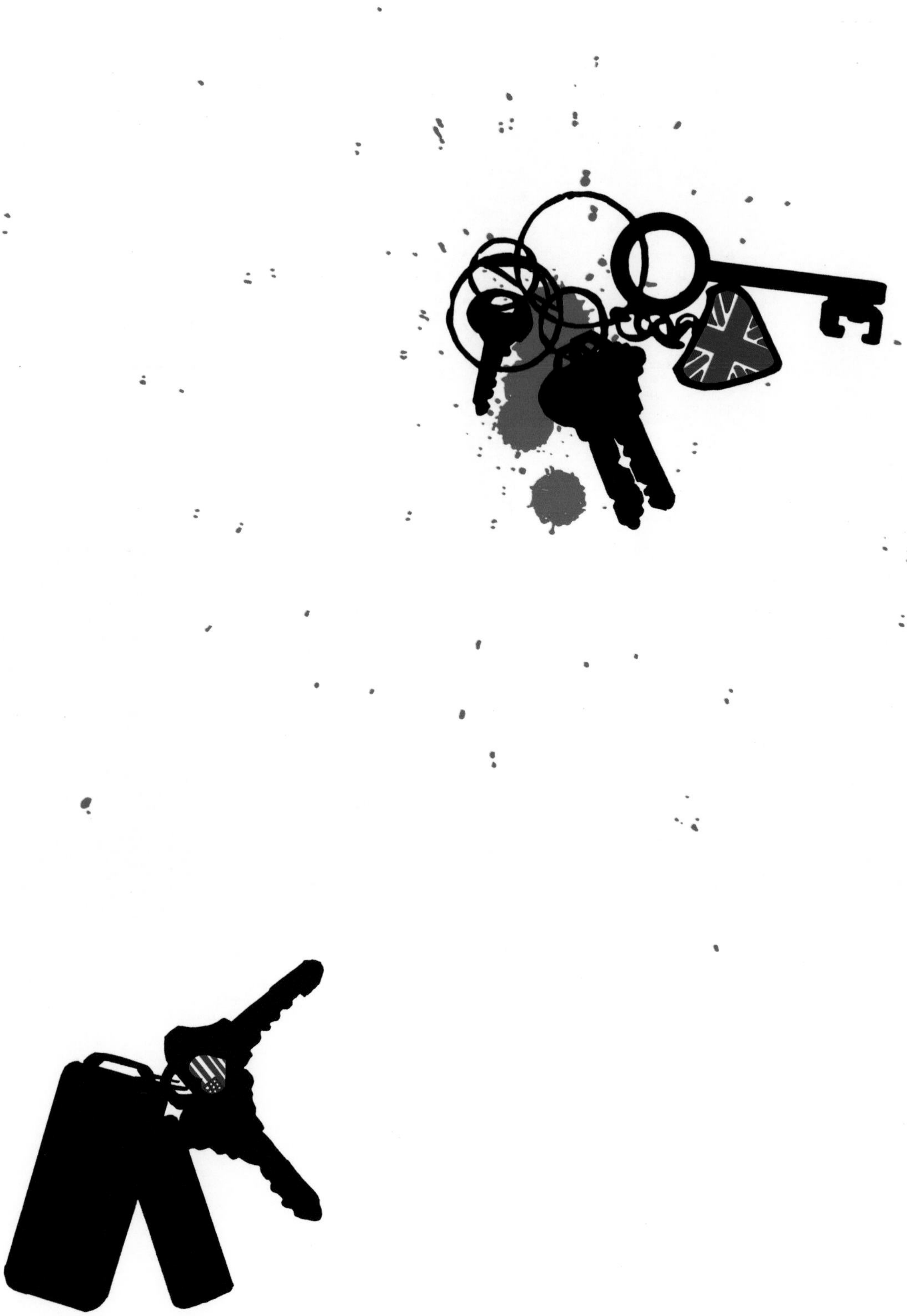

Issue One Variant Cover
Andre de Freitas

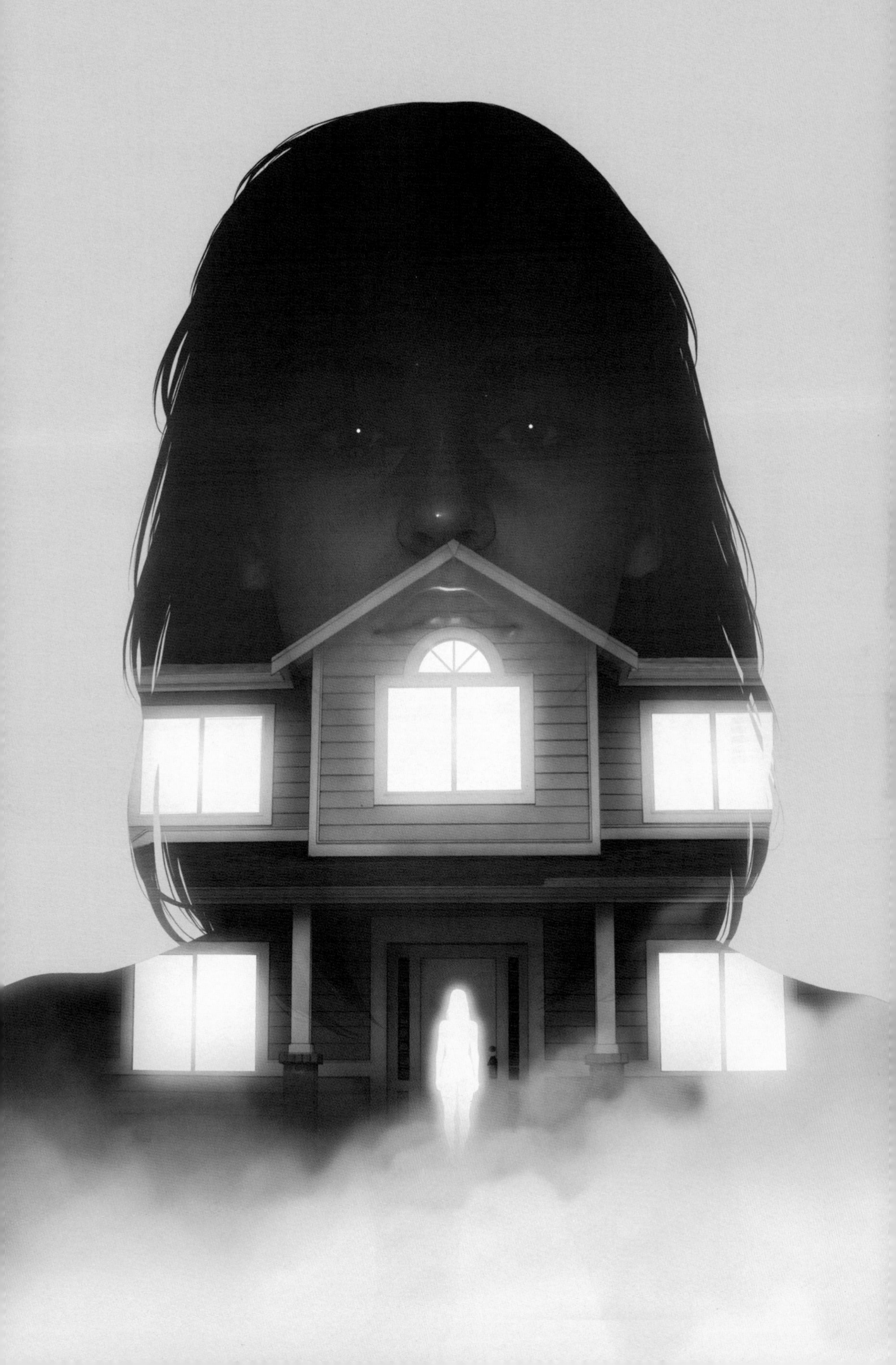

Issue One Second Print Cover
Mike Perkins
colors by **Andy Troy**
design by **Kelsey Dieterich**

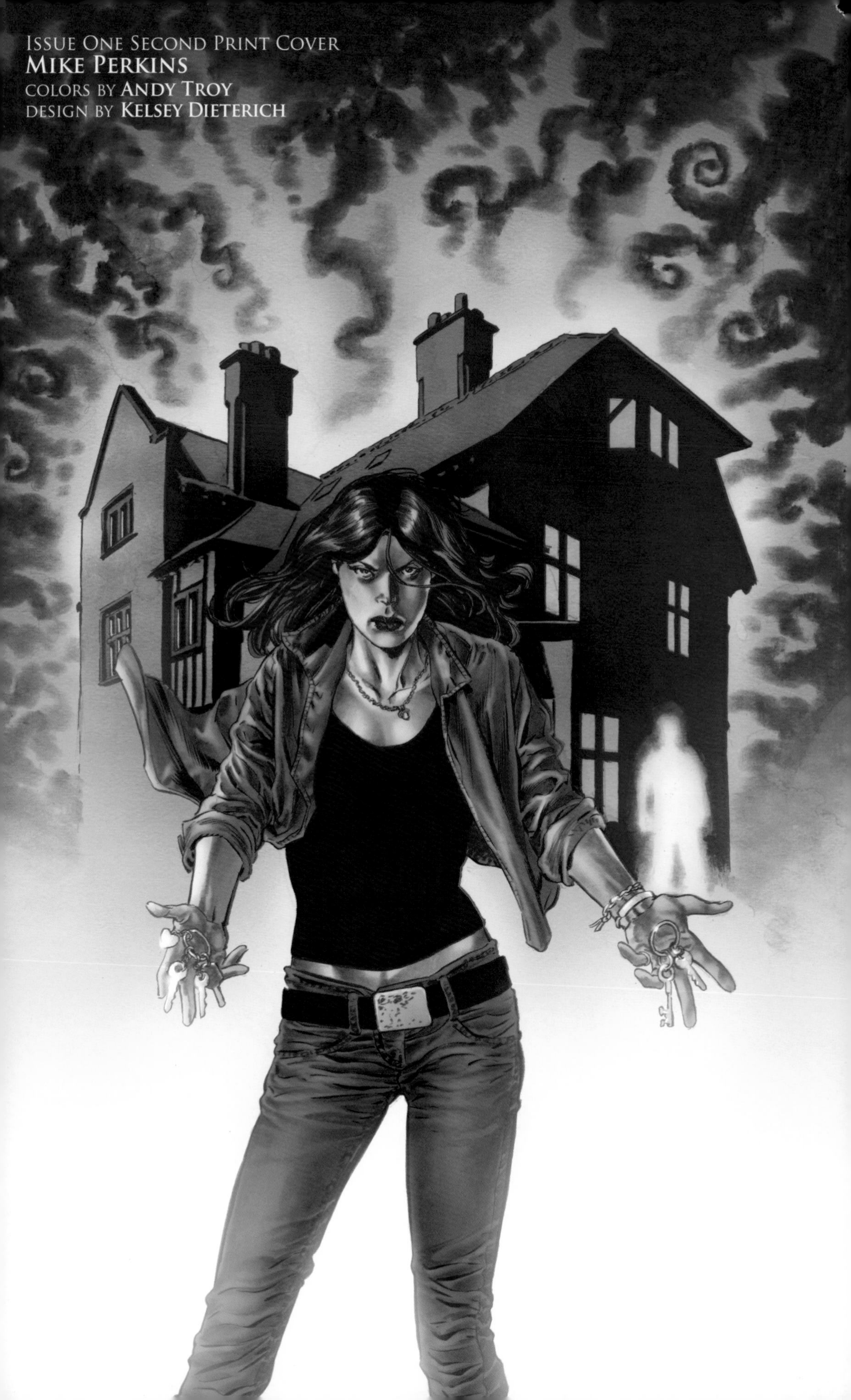

Issue two Cover
Mike Perkins
colors by **Andy Troy**

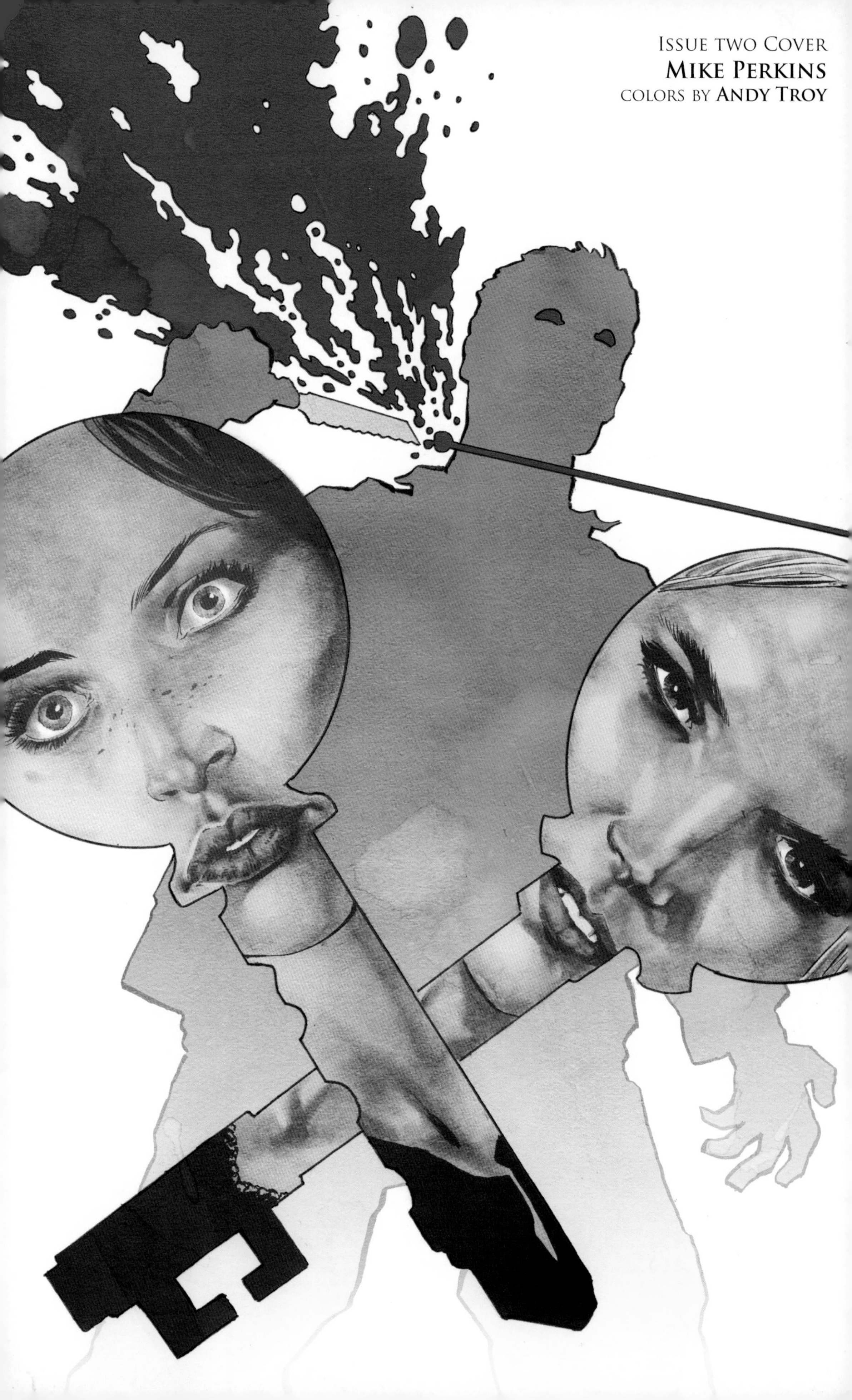

Issue three Cover
Mike Perkins
colors by Andy Troy

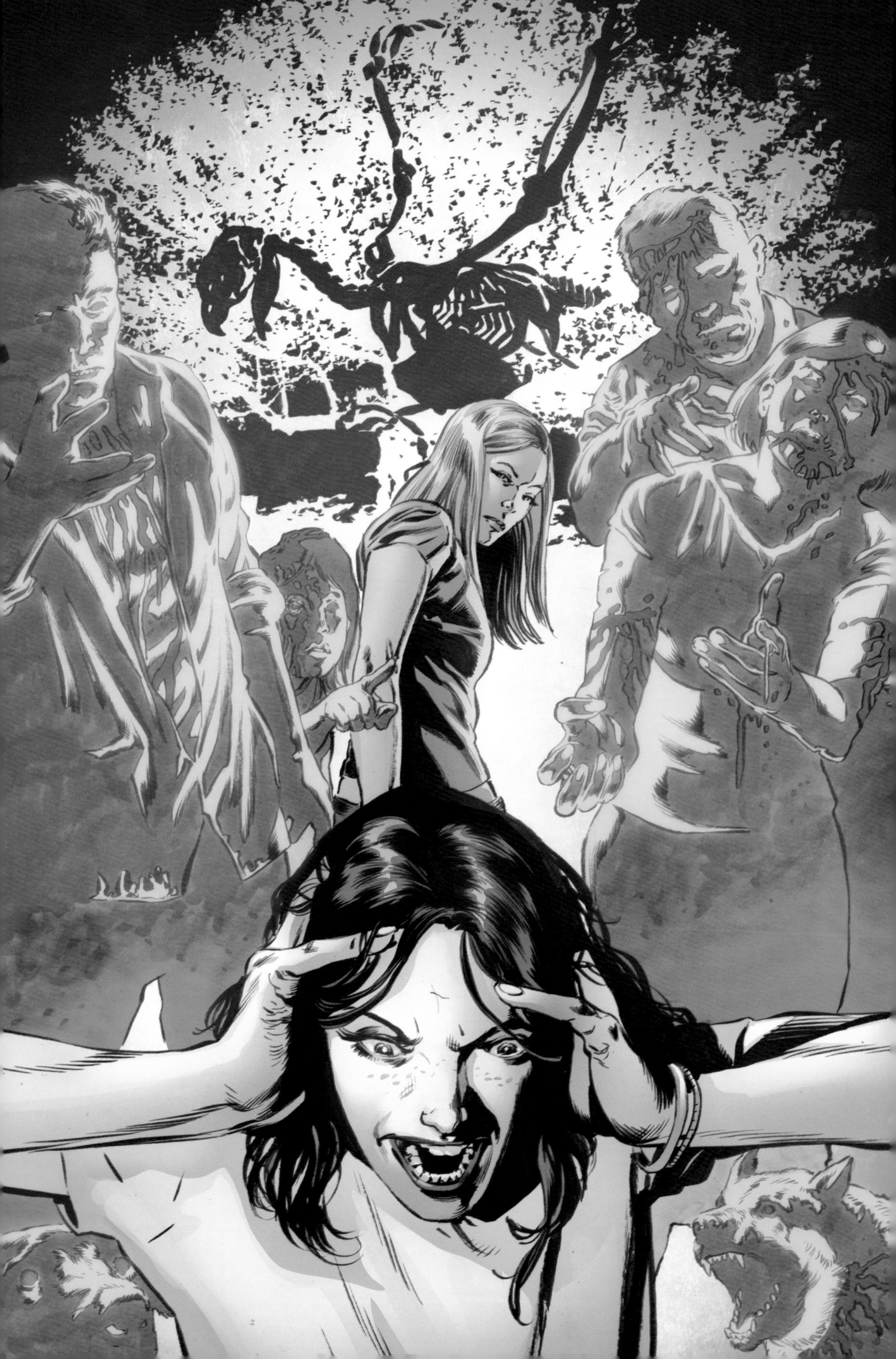